THE MORAL PROJECT OF CHILDHOOD

The Moral Project of Childhood

*Motherhood, Material Life, and Early
Children's Consumer Culture*

Daniel Thomas Cook

NEW YORK UNIVERSITY PRESS
New York

NEW YORK UNIVERSITY PRESS

New York

www.nyupress.org

References to Internet websites (URLs) were accurate at the time of writing. Neither the author nor New York University Press is responsible for URLs that may have expired or changed since the manuscript was prepared.

Library of Congress Cataloging-in-Publication Data
Names: Cook, Daniel Thomas, 1961–   author.
Title: The moral project of childhood : motherhood, material life, and early children's consumer culture / Daniel Cook.
Description: New York : NYU Press, [2020] | Includes bibliographical references and index.
Identifiers: LCCN 2019004713 | ISBN 9781479810260 (paperback) | ISBN 9781479899203 (cloth)
Subjects: LCSH: Motherhood. | Child consumers. | Consumers.
Classification: LCC HQ759 .C727 2020 | DDC 306.874/3—dc23
LC record available at https://lccn.loc.gov/2019004713

New York University Press books are printed on acid-free paper, and their binding materials are chosen for strength and durability. We strive to use environmentally responsible suppliers and materials to the greatest extent possible in publishing our books.

Manufactured in the United States of America

10 9 8 7 6 5 4 3 2 1

Also available as an ebook

For Jessica: I can do nothing of worth and can be nothing of worth without you. Period.

CONTENTS

LIST OF FIGURES

Introduction

Before it can imitate an articulate sound, it can understand the looks, the tones, and the actions of others, and according to the nature of these influences, will be the character of the impression produced. The first moral impression a child receives is its first lesson on religion; and this first idea is the foundation on which we are to base the superstructure of all future moral training.

—*The Mother's Magazine*, June 1837.[1]

Childhood confronts one inescapably as a moral problem. To contemplate childhood necessitates engagement in and with moral discourses. One cannot speak of, speak to, gaze upon, consider, or analyze any particular child, or various childhoods, without entering into and becoming entangled with morally infused vocabularies concerning the rightness and wrongness, appropriateness or inappropriateness of one's actions and, indeed, one's thoughts. Every decision made on behalf of a child favors some aspects of the world over others. No word or deed directed at a child, no object intended for a child's possession or space crafted for children's use, no image fabricated for their eyes or sound made resonant for their ears, no amount of attention or inattention paid their activities, voices, or perspectives—in none of these can neutrality reside. Childhood, in this way, abhors and disallows moral agnosticism. It poses problems that must be handled and negotiated in some manner—be it by institutions and structures or by people.

Children and childhood demand a ceaseless attention, a perpetual monitoring, largely due to the uncertainties they are said to imply and embody. Children, left to their own, threaten a disorder upon ongoing relations. Infants and young children do not initially speak the language of their adult hosts, walk on their own, or sanitize themselves. They often appear indifferent to the usual uses and functions of things—throwing objects that best remain stationary, putting indigestible things in their mouths and, at times, treating food as if it were anything but edible. In some socio-historical contexts, like that of some Protestants of seventeenth-century Europe, the professed corporeal inchoateness of the child presented a moral hazard of such profound dimension that typical social practice demanded the manual molding of the infant's body (e.g., tight swaddling) and the use of devices like cradles and walking stools to urge adult physical uprightness onto the child, who then would become eligible for salvation.[2]

Extreme and particular, perhaps, these seventeenth-century responses to a felt sense of infant formlessness nevertheless speak to a general dynamic. The regular and never-ending stream of new children into social life represents a source of perpetual uncertainty regarding the reproduction of social structures and practices.[3] Childhood can be understood as functioning like other social institutions (e.g., marriage, the family) in the ways it works toward transforming the indeterminate and incipient into something knowable, thereby making children into cultural objects thought to be able to be shaped, guided, and steered.[4] Notions of good and bad children—and right and wrong childhoods—no doubt exist so defined in some form across swaths of social life, both cross-culturally and trans-historically. Accordingly, the impetus and necessity to identify, name, and distinguish correct from incorrect ways of exhibiting child-ness—and to enforce or cajole the same—represent a fundamental and definitional feature of childhood, more so perhaps than do age or generational considerations in and of themselves. Childhood, in this way, manifests unavoidably and primarily as a moral project.

Historically, politically, and practically, mothers and conceptions of motherhood reside squarely at the crux of this ceaselessly ambiguous, morally saturated cultural space of childhood. Indeed, it is one of many labors of motherhood to participate in the superintendence of meaning in children's lives by arranging, policing, and manipulating various semantic and material elements of the child's world to assist in producing some sort of order. In so doing, mothers commit profoundly moral acts on a daily basis to the extent that their actions necessarily draw on sets of beliefs with which they attempt to parse the appropriate from the inappropriate, the good from the bad, and the sacred from the profane. The definitional work in which mothers engage both employs and responds to notions about children and childhood that may be dominant or active in their social worlds. Working conceptions of children's inherent propensities—for instance, to lean toward good or evil, or perhaps to waver in indifference[5]—set the conditions for the kinds, intensities, and timing of interventions, the forms of supervision, and the modes of discipline thought necessary for suitable guidance. Situated at the confluence of children's nature and childhood's nurture, mothers are those most often held personally responsible for navigating the dense undergrowth of competing and confusing narratives and expectations, and they thereby regularly assume the liability for a failed or diminished child subjecthood.[6] Regardless of whether such "failure" materializes, it is the consequent fear—the overarching sense of peril—that children may not turn out "right" that structures the essential contours of contemporary motherhoods.[7]

The incessant, felt necessity to expend effort (semantic, political, cultural) in shaping the childhoods at hand makes for the moral project of childhood—something acutely, but not exclusively, located in the province of motherhood. At the point of juncture between childhood malleability and maternal responsibility stands the emergent, historical assertion of children's subjectivity, agency, and personhood. These three elements—childhood's pliability, maternal accountability for children, and children's subjecthood—entangle and tussle with one another in a variety of ways to make what I call a "moral architecture." The moral architecture of childhood, as I deploy it herein, is composed of sets of tensions and dynamics that structure the terms of assessment for proper and improper ways of considering children's being and becoming. That is to say, childhood in this view manifests as an interlocking nexus of efforts—rather than simply as an age-related stage in the life course—that attempt to affix moral value and to ascertain the dimensions of personhood of the youngest members of social life.

The Moral Project of Childhood sets out to theorize and historicize key ideological and epistemological underpinnings of a moral architecture of childhood in the nineteenth century, making the case that the figure of the child consumer—emergent in its own right in early twentieth-century Anglo-American contexts—represents an embodied problem through which questions of value and personhood find enduring, albeit changing, cultural purchase and resonance. At once held responsible for and ensnared by children's being and subjectivity, mothers and the space of motherhood prove to be politically and philosophically inseparable from the struggles that enable the "child" to congeal both economic and sentimental value—a combination some consider logically, morally, and perhaps also historically problematic.[8] Drawing on materials published in periodicals intended for women and mothers beginning in the 1830s, I locate some of the ghostly cultural antecedents and ingredients that form the consuming child.

Throughout this discussion, I inspect an array of discourses about Christian motherhood, the elements of cultural taste, the discipline and punishment of children, and questions of children's property rights and of the uses of money by and for children. I do so in the attempt to trace some outlines of a not-quite existent, but ascendant, social fact— the child consumer. Fundamental problems stemming from a growing acceptance of children's spiritual, intellectual, and behavioral pliability drive the assembly of a moral architecture—one that is built from an extensively elaborate ideology of maternal responsibility coupled with the increasingly hegemonic presence of child subjectivity. This dynamic— rather than a specific persona or trait—provides the key mechanism, the generative core, that ultimately establishes the constellation of tensions and problems often recognized as the "child" and forms the basis of latter-day children's consumer culture.

In the following chapters I consider the Protestant origins of the child consumer—a somewhat unlikely pairing—not as a simple product of a new configuration of domesticity in the nineteenth century, but as informative of understandings of contemporary, normative middle-class notions of childhood. This "child," I contend, rose out of some of the same kinds of tensions and relations that sociologist Max Weber famously demonstrated were productive of modern capitalism and, in this way, must be understood not only as a manifestation of economic dynamics but also as a site of and generative forum for them.[9] The analysis herein seeks to link, in a direct and continuous way, the central and irrevocable place of the "mother" and motherhood with the emerging predominance of a particular kind of child subject and subjectivity prevalent in late twentieth and early twenty-first centuries in wealthy, Anglo-American, Global North contexts. The implication here centers on how the ideological strains deposited onto mothers and infused into constructions of motherhood produced conditions favorable to the appearance of what was to become identified as the child consumer, a figure perhaps only one cultural DNA marker separated from the "child," conceived generically.

A Conception of Childhood: A Pursuit

The "child consumer," as understood herein, does not simply indicate a young person who owns things, purchases things, or has things purchased on her behalf. It is not about only those moments or slices of childhood where commercial objects are clearly present and apparently relevant. Indeed, a good part of this text will not address children's shopping or mothers' shopping for children, or advertisements aimed at children or marketing efforts with children in mind (but see chapter 5). There is no discussion of brands or branding. Scholarship clearly demonstrates that these sorts of commercial efforts, language, and modes of thinking did not reach a critical point until at least the late 1890s in the US and UK.[10] Rather, the thrust of the persuasive effort undertaken on the pages to come concentrates on making visible and relevant the prefigurative elements and rhetorics from which the child consumer emerges as a possible and viable cultural persona—one that stands as model and ancestor for strong strains of contemporary, normative childhoods.

In making my case, I entertain the notion that the child consumer contains origins, and thus trajectories, beyond those often assigned to it in scholarship. Writers regularly proffer the germ of this figure as arising within the private, domestic sphere of the (American and British) Victorian home, which was overseen by (largely) non-wage-laboring, native-born white women who were living in relative abundance and who could devote a measure of material and emotional resources to children.[11] It is a context characterized as a place where some combination of Enlightenment and Romantic views of childhood held sway over evidently religious Protestant notions.[12] Indeed, one finds in literature[13] and children's periodicals,[14] in tracts offering child-rearing advice,[15] in treatises on domestic labor and virtue,[16] and in the rising educational theories and movements of the nineteenth century,[17] the growing assertion of an educable, malleable child often coupled with a presumption of innate innocence. It was a child decreasingly subjected to the retribution of damnation, as hell itself declines in its presence and force for an important swath of Christian life and faith by century's end.[18] This "child"—this construct—also decidedly references a white, non-slave, middle-class persona that, as historian Robin Bernstein demonstrates so well, comes to stand for the very embodiment of an innocence that itself is never innocent and is always racialized.[19]

The general tenor of this historical narrative presents a triumphalist tone whereby Calvinist/Puritan conceptions of the child—with their undertones of harsh discipline and suspicion of many things resembling play and amusement—were overrun and swept away by the sentimental, compassionate, not-so-intensely religious family of the middle class.[20] The child and its emergent material-commercial life and surrounds appear to some as an efflux of the sentimental Victorian home and economic conditions—as something of a straightforward product of these circumstances, like affluence,[21] sentiment,[22] or nostalgia.[23] In these accounts, generally speaking, economic interests began to "target" the child as a market with toys, amusements, and publications, while the parents occupying these white, middle-class homes of England and the US Northeast exercised their distance from an old order that had been generally allergic to anything associated with popular, commercial life. The new toys and celebrations for children, like Christmas[24] and birthdays,[25] were said to invoke and infuse a sentimental aura around the family and childhood, paving the way for subsequent iterations of children's consumer culture. In this general narrative, the new child emerging from the mid-nineteenth-century Anglo-American bourgeois household often appears as victor of sorts—a break with the past—even as, in the same breath, many note that the victorious version of the child also enabled childhood to become a site for consumer commercial attention, interests and, ultimately, expansion.[26] Indeed, this middle class expressed itself as new and modern, in part, through its nouveaux ideas about child development, nurture, and training and its consequent disposition toward material life which, in themselves, served as something of a rebuff of previous notions and practices.[27]

My task here is not so much to challenge outright the general view regarding the social locational origins of something resembling the contemporary child consumer, for it most assuredly has significant roots in the Anglo-European middle-class feminine sphere of the private home of the eighteenth and nineteenth centuries. Rather, I aim to reframe and reconceptualize them by reimagining childhood and motherhood as historically entwined moral projects that form the basis—not the outcome—of the child consumer and, crucially, of a consequential version of subjecthood and desire. The implication here is that consumption and the child consumer manifest not as outputs, but as ingredients. In this work, I seek to pursue a conception of childhood—and related notions of the child and child consumer—as dwelling in and emerging out of a set of ongoing moral tensions involved in grappling with the problem of personhood and the locus of self and responsibility.

The idea of childhood at issue—clearly culturally constructed and historically contingent, as many have noted and demonstrated so well[28]—does not simply represent a time period of the life course or a group of beliefs about young persons. Rather, in the perspective put forth here, childhood arises as a dynamic perplexity that never quite resolves itself but that, as an ongoing problematic, enables—indeed, demands—assertions regarding human nature. The "child," as figure and trope, regularly congeals a number of presumptions and contentions about human origins, about the locus of agency and control, about rights, and about the veracity of morality, and is thereby situated as a site of perpetual contestation for these fundamental dimensions of being and knowing. A child, in this view, manifests discursively as a node—a meeting point—of a kind of incomprehension or puzzle about the breadth, reach, and exigencies of subjecthood.

In the context of the present inquiry, the legacy of modern childhood resides less in which view of the child has become dominant in any particular context or era than it does in how a particular configuration of childhood coalesces endless, and endlessly emergent, definitional struggles regarding the constitution of moral personhood. Put another way, childhood stands not just as some kind of self-apparent tabula rasa where differing systems of belief and power imprint themselves in competition for ideological prominence. Nor is it only a cultural site where economic interests inscribe themselves onto supple minds and docile bodies. Childhood also comprises a dynamic admixture made of and made by these contestations and struggles, existing in them, blending with them, arising from them and, importantly, generative of them. Construed in this manner, childhood unfolds not transparently as the subject of this or that moral concern or this or that definition and struggle—i.e., not narrowly the locus of panics about, for instance, overwrought materialism or "too much" media—but as the very ingredients of the concerns and struggles themselves. Childhood, here, is neither side of the struggle, but the struggle itself. What I hope to offer is another vantage point—one made possible by the works that have preceded—of a way to begin to think about the child in one's midst as something other than a refugee from economy.

A Pre-Capitalist Child? Discontinuities between Production and Consumption

The Moral Project of Childhood sets out to reconceive of children, childhood, and the "child" as inseparable from market considerations and logics, rather than as necessarily and inherently oppositional to or derivative from them. From the approach outlined here and elaborated below, I understand the ongoing changing tensions between children and the marketplace not as positions arising from outside the moral problem of children's consumption, but as themselves integral to the efforts and practices that make and remake the child consumer as cultural figure and social fact. Once one entertains the proposition that there is no Archimedean point outside the child–market (or value) dynamic—no place to stand that is beyond the cover of the moral frame of childhood or of economic life—then one is in a position to see them in terms of each other, of the light they shed and the shadows they cast. Every effort to avoid, deny, resist, repel, redefine, or re-categorize child consumption as something other than constitutive of childhoods—be it from concerned parents, bloviating public ideologues, or market actors like promoters, retailers, and marketers—itself recasts, reinforces, and reproduces the interwoven, interdependent structure of childhood and commercial value. When, for instance, a mother, speaking of her efforts to feed her children, remarks that she doesn't approve of "commercialism" and only buys organic products for her infant,[29] she is redrawing and thereby reinterpreting a place where a "market" ends and her child begins, but she is not removing her child or her actions from considerations of market value.

The necessary interconnectedness here espoused between child and market forms not the endpoint of investigation and theorizing, but its point of departure. The strong thesis I put forward in this work asserts that children have not only been born *into* a consumer culture, but that modern childhood, in a sense, continues to be born *of* it. Child and consumption do not simply inform or mutually reference each other in some straightforward, tit-for-tat, transactional manner. Rather, more fundamentally, children and what has come to be known as "consumer culture"[30]—and hence "economy" more generally—do not exist and have not existed apart from one another when approached from the perspective of materiality and material culture. Mothers, advice-givers, and observers in the mid- to late-nineteenth and early twentieth centuries wrote comparatively little of a direct threat of commercialism and commercial goods to their children, instead concerning themselves with how character and the "self" would be built up from children's engagements with things and goods, including money. Rather, questions of taste—in its many forms—informed the configuration of a bourgeois childhood, which quickly became a normative ideal (see chapter 2). Indeed, the narrative of the outright toxic nature of children's consumption and commercial-media life per se did not take hold strongly until about the 1980s in both the scholarship and public culture of the Global North.[31] A good deal of scholarship and virtually all casual observation, however, remains enmeshed in habits of thought whereby the child is understood or presumed to have *become* a consumer in some manner—i.e., the accepted notion that children have moved from being initially detached from consumer–commercial life to having significant involvement in it, both historically over time and ontogenetically, that is, over the life course. The former view represents what comparatively little there is on the history of children's consumption[32]; the latter, the basis for the field of consumer socialization.[33]

The idea that there exists, or must have existed, some place historically or experientially prior to commercial exchange where children dwelled untouched remains entrenched. In this book, I refer to the structure of thought that presumes an initial separation of children from economy as invoking a "pre-capitalist child"—a notion underlying the conceptualization of both the commodification of childhood and of childhood innocence. Innocence and commodification rely upon the idea of a pre-capitalist child and do so in two familiar senses: *historically*, prior to the onset of capitalism; and *ontogenetically*—from birth—as a time in the life course antecedent to the sullying effects of commerce in which the child is imagined and deployed as having a cosmological or spiritual existence prior or exterior to pecuniary relations and meanings.

Both forms of the pre-capitalist child haunt the descriptions, prescriptions, and proscriptions related to contemporary childhoods, serving as background imagery against which to view and comprehend the present formations. Through these constructions, in different ways, ideas of the pure, the sacred, the profane, and the polluted creep into and animate everyday conversations, public discourse, and academic theorizing. Positing a historically pre-capitalist child enables critique of contemporary adulthoods through, for instance, the projection of an earlier time when play and children's imaginations were free from structured curricula, play dates, over-scheduled lives, an ambient media environment, and the loss of "nature."[34] In naming the figure and construction of the "pre-capitalist child," I call into question the presumption that commodification represents an infiltration from the "outside" of the social relations that configure childhoods, a notion that implicates the abiding cultural notion of childhood innocence

Otherwise insightful and incisive sociologies, social histories, and theories stumble and come up short precisely because the authors tend to presume the existence of an earlier uncommodified childhood and family life that have then been overtaken by the exigencies of capital.

Sociologist Sharon Hays's seminal work on the ideology of intensive mothering, for instance, sets up something of a "separate spheres" landscape whereby the worlds of mothers and children are put in opposition to the demands of capital (here in the form of mothers' desire or need to work for wages).[35] This tension fuels a set of impossible-to-satisfy demands and expectations on mothers that become manifest in "intensive mothering," which, Hays argues, conflicts with the "ideology of the workplace and ethos of modern society."[36] Mainly a post–World War II phenomenon, intensive mothering, for Hays, arises out of the demands of market culture, which are in opposition to domestic, maternal values and which, in turn, make hegemonic demands on mothers to be child-centered, primary caregivers who are guided by experts and expected to be emotionally absorbed in a labor-intensive, never-stop parenting. For

Hays, the main culprit is the market economy: "The more powerful and all-encompassing the rationalized market becomes, the more powerful becomes its ideological position in the logic of intensive mothering."[37] As she explains, "the more widely the rationalized market has spread its net, the more the child, the child's innocence, the child's needs, and the child's life have become a central focus of family life. This is far too systematic to be treated as mere coincidence."[38]

Undoubtedly, intensive mothering represents a real, structuring set of expectations and demands on contemporary mothers in ways outlined by Hays. Yet the nearly one-to-one correspondence asserted between the "rationalized market" and the centrality of the child obscures the ways in which moral and cultural factors in line with commercial dynamics could combine to produce the seedbed for the ideology of intensive mothering she details so well. Hays's presumption takes an economic mechanism as structuring the place and position of the child, rather than also considering ways in which cultural notions of the "child" could form and inform market relations. As will be seen below, strong intimations of "intensive mothering" are evident in the nineteenth century in the discourses about Protestant concerns for children's salvation, about bourgeois Victorian mothers' preoccupations about taste, about questions of the discipline and punishment of children, and about children's relations to property and money. These, I argue, contribute to setting a template for what would become known as the child consumer—the child Hays sees as central to the ideology she names and critiques.

Along similar lines, sociologist Arlie Hochschild's notion of the "commodity frontier" in many ways repeats and reproduces received oppositions between sentimental and market worlds.[39] This idea of a commodity frontier, sometimes also referred to as a "market frontier,"[40] encodes tensions and differences between "commodity" and "gift." Concerned about the "outsourcing" to the marketplace of what had previously been domestic, mainly female, labor, Hochschild invokes the imagery of a "wall" between market and non-market life that requires people to "jump over," "borrow across," or "listen through" it so as to negotiate appropriate feelings in the context of commercialized arrangements.[41] Clearly, it is important to investigate changing dynamics between types of exchange, to examine whether market transactions alter the terms of social relations, and to question how it is that people think about and handle the emotional and practical differences that may arise. At the same time, the imagery deployed here reaffirms the divisions and boundaries under scrutiny to the extent that they continue to demarcate the very divides that require reconceptualization. In her approach, "home" and "sentimental life"—and, by implication, children and childhood—remain outside of and categorically antagonistic to "the market," thereby making it an onerous task to consider how "child" and "family" can live in, derive from, and participate in generating commercially inflected relations.

The presumptively innocent, pre-capitalist child, whose worth resides beyond all economic-market value, marks the default moral position for practice, policy, and philosophy—even if not consistently put *into* practice, policy, and philosophy. This child remains implied in invocations of "family" and, certainly, of motherhood.[42] In many ways, a core element of this childhood derives from the insistence that it does *not* indicate or imply economic, commercial, or pecuniary values. Viviana Zelizer's noted work theorizing the revaluation of children in the 1880–1930 period both captures and elides the emergent dynamics of children's consumption at this juncture.[43] She documents a cultural shift in the value of children from being considered economically useful and valued in monetary terms toward a sentimental view that holds children as economically worthless but emotionally priceless. This transformation, according to Zelizer, ultimately rendered the child "extra commercium"—i.e., outside of market valuation[44]—to the extent that economic and sentimental value were thought exclusive of one another.

It is clear, however, that children in no way departed the market sector altogether, but came to participate in it mainly as consumers, rather than as laborers. The question opened and left unaddressed here centers on how the priceless, "sacred" child of sentimental, non-monetary value has thrived and co-existed alongside and, I would say, within a churning children's commercial culture that has expanded in scope to reach global proportions over the ensuing decades. What is missed in Zelizer's conceptualization relates to how new valuations—economic and otherwise—arose and took hold *through* the child, not in spite of it, by implicating childhood as a site to explicate and engage with particular kinds of moral-commercial value (see also the conclusion).

For Zelizer, the debates over child labor, black-market babies, and child insurance evinced some demarcations between "market" and "sentiment," whereby the child moved from one side to the other of a dividing line. To be sure, all of these practices drew on and responded to something like a market logic of a capitalist economic system and, in that way, might be considered similarly as forms of "commodification"—i.e., of being turned into exchange value—and thus decidedly inconsistent with an emotionally priceless child. The absence of child labor or work—or the diminished possibility of it—provides an important boundary condition in the moral valuation of children, but it does not exhaust the ways in which monetary and market value can and do mix together. The kinds of economic valuation Zelizer addresses in these instances reside and move about in a register qualitatively different from that of consumption and consumer practice. The concerns voiced by child labor reformers, advocates, and others, documented by Zelizer, spoke to actions thought to have been done *to* children—many of whom were more or less coerced into labor (by parents or circumstances), sold on the black market by adults, or assigned a monetary value through life insurance—whereas children's consumption appears largely as something said to be done *for* them or done *by* them.

Here a crucial conceptual matter comes to light. Consumption, commercial culture, and the "child consumer" do not represent a straightforward reversal of, underside to, or complement to production and the laboring child. The history and imagery of child laborers in Western industrial capitalism—from Dickensian narratives[45] to Friedrich Engels's descriptions of horrendous conditions in England[46] to the images from photographer Lewis Hine[47]—bear out a largely shared understanding that industrial work for many of these children was hard, often coerced, ignoble, and exploitative. Consumption, on the other hand, in many ways involves an ethos and consideration of desire, subjectivity, wish fulfillment, and agency significantly distinct from an ethos of labor.[48] The rise, expansion, and elaboration of a children's consumer culture in the early twentieth century in this way does not so much signify a transformation of "the child" from laborer to consumer as it indicates and implicates the cultural arrival and presence of a new configuration of person or social personage—one where pleasure and desire, subjectivity and choice step to the forefront of consideration, even as these battle with ongoing strictures, arising notions of development, and the fraught, politically charged position of mothers. It is in this sense and from this view that one can entertain the idea that characteristics associated with the "child consumer" antedate the onslaught of large-scale children's consumption and its culture and serve as a common fund of qualities providing for a "modern" childhood.

The effort put forth here in the following pages, then, strives to reorient narratives about the trajectory and shaping of a normative—perhaps "generic"[49]—conception of childhood. It is a conception that has become dominant since the mid-twentieth century as a white, middle-class, Global North ideal and, putatively, as a model for psychological science,[50] for law and public policy,[51] and for international bodies and actions,[52] and stands as the measure of a "correct" parenting and upbringing.[53] To maintain that "child" and "child consumer" need to be considered as variations on a theme also serves to urge a stepping aside from accounts that intimate a pre-capitalist child having been overcome by commercialism, or a Protestant childhood overtaken by sentimental-Romantic notions, or an economically useful child pulled asunder by an emotionally priceless one. In so doing, I anticipate that reframing the shape, character, and momentum of childhood as a social institution and as a moral project will provide opportunities for rethinking the rhetorics governing thought and action regarding what sorts of beings children are, what kinds of childhoods they should have and, ultimately, what shapes motherhood.

Periodicals, an Imagined Community of Motherhood and Children's Interiorities

The Moral Project of Childhood deploys a historically inflected approach and draws on historical research, but is not itself a proper history of childhood or consumption. Although akin to historical sociology, it nevertheless secures little affinity in those quarters. I concur with sociologist Philip Abrams, who several decades ago found no analytic or practical purchase in separating sociology from history.[54] Rather than beginning with specific problems in mind to be answered or solved, he urged investigators to assemble questions and concerns into a "problematic," a "rudimentary organization of a field of phenomena which yields problems for investigation."[55] In a sense, the "problem"—the structure of the problem—becomes the thing pursued in the course of an inquiry as that which is to be encountered, unpacked, and examined for the insights that may ensue.

In approach and temperament, this work stubbornly follows a thread of concern through a rather narrow and specific dimension of social expression with the idea of laying bare a kind of epistemological genealogy—clearly indebted to Michel Foucault[56]—of a particular, but ultimately universalizable, conception of the "child" and childhood. In addition to asking "What is a child?"—a question that has rightly animated the field of childhood studies for over three decades[57]—I also ask "When is a child?" That is, under what conditions does a "child" become something recognized, pointed to, and treated as a "child"—practically, discursively, institutionally—and how do those conditions respond to and structure how and where this "child" becomes manifest in social practice? The quotation mark key on one's keyboard could easily be worn down in the effort to demonstrate the extent to which one is aware of the tentative, problematic nature of one's terms and concepts. Nevertheless, periodic, reflexive indication of the conditionality of the categories of child and childhood assists in reminding both reader and author of the denseness of the ideological underbrush and epistemological thicket to be traversed.

As discussed, motherhood and the positionality of mothers reside squarely and inextricably at the core of the moral project of childhood and of the child consumer, particularly in the ways they become inflected in the handling of the uncertainties posed by children's malleability. The substance of this study draws on texts written mainly by women and mothers for women and mothers regarding the nature of the child, as found in published advice literature in a variety of women's periodical magazines, among others, in the US from the 1830s to the 1930s.[58] I considered it important to examine these publications because of their public nature to the extent that they offer statements and interpretations to audiences that extend beyond an immediate, face-to-face world. In articles, editorials, letters, and responses, presentations of what, who, and "when" a child is or should be arrive in tandem with who, and what a "mother" is, should be, and should do. In this way, I see them functioning as something akin to an "imagined community" or communities in Benedict Anderson's sense, whereby construals of mothers and motherhood, and of children and childhood, are fabricated, negotiated, and exchanged through media with the effect of creating a sense of commonality, of shared conception and concern.[59] A good deal of the texts over this time and across these publications consist of women writing to women, mothers to mothers, and would-be mothers to would-be mothers, as well as contributions by men who often appeared as credentialed experts like medical doctors and, later, psychologists. As Anderson notes, the concern of inquiry does not rest on some strict truth or falsity of these communities but is distinguished "by the style in which they are imagined."[60]

In this sense, the effort undertaken in this book pursues styles of imaginative motherhoods and childhoods. From the outset, I have incorporated the selective nature of these discourses into my interpretations, understanding that advice given does not equal advice followed,[61] and that the "child" in question remains unmarked and unremarked upon as white, free, and of a particular class formation in the US Northeast. Indeed, I bypass the question of the direct, causal relationship between advice literature and maternal child-rearing practice not because such connections are irrelevant or unimportant; rather, I find such a question something of a distraction from this project to the extent that it tends to divert attention from the set of practices of the writing and reading of childhoods and motherhoods. The practices of writing childhoods and motherhoods—in expert and non-expert realms alike—organize robust arenas unto themselves, even as they represent selective, incomplete universes of discourse. For, as Margaret Beetham asserts, the nineteenth-century periodical in particular constitutes a "feminine form" beyond the simple facts of its content or presumed readership, but also because of the weekly and monthly cadence of publication that was often read within the home as part of, not separate from, domestic activity.[62] The heterogeneity of content of women's periodicals, for Beetham, "refused a single authorial voice," thereby enabling multiple readings, both sympathetic and resistive.[63] At the same time, I wish to highlight how different invocations and demonstrations of authority stand as the central, driving thrust of the genre—be it represented by those who are mothers and speak for motherhood, by those who speak for church teaching, by those who write as women and men of letters, or by those who enjoin conversations through editorials and letters to the editor.

"Advice" implies judgment, a moralizing or exhortation aimed, at once, in favor of some view or program and against others. Even if they do not take the advice given word-for-word, readerships coalesce periodicals into communities of discourse over time and participate in the voicing of and by women and mothers. As a feminized space, the imagined communities of nineteenth-century women's periodicals enabled participation in and experience of quasi-public gatherings of women, something often not allowed or not practiced in public, geographical space outside the home.[64] Here, some may gather to behave and enjoin each other as folk experts of a sort on the nature and intricacies and children and child-rearing. Indeed, as Beetham points out, the often anonymous nature of the readership, and oftentimes of the authorship,[65] in these magazines "positioned readers as members of a reading/writing community rather than simply as consumers."[66] Contradictory in their advice and underlying philosophies about women and gender, the discourses in such magazines nevertheless regularly reinforced traditional, oppressive roles and attitudes for and toward women. At the same time, Beetham argues, "across the plurality of voices there was a shared assumption that the project of the magazine was both to address 'the lady' and to define who she was."[67]

A strong, emergent kind of periodical and readership began to address *mothers* as an audience throughout the middle of the nineteenth century, thereby facilitating the possibility of sharing this identity and these practices outside of one's immediate circles. Compared to advice books and treatises on housekeeping, periodicals offered a regularity of contact, current information, and the promise of entering and re-entering an ongoing conversation. Here, the connective thread materializes in the form of the child—as object, subject, and discourse—around and through which mothers and writers could imagine and explicate childhoods into spaces beyond present contexts and circumstances in the process of referencing their concerns as mothers. In this way, maternal advice in the mother's periodical, particularly in the nineteenth century, may be understood as a consequential forum for the construction of a particular, and ultimately prevailing, version of childhood.

As will be elaborated on in the chapters to follow, "advice" in these periodicals demanded that mother-readers construe the perspective of their children and these publications did so—as exemplified in the epigraph at the head of this chapter—with increasing intensity and regularity over the nineteenth century and into the next. In prayerful moments and concerns about morality, in questions of taste as well as in terms of punishment, reward, property, rights, and money—in all of these, the maternal audience was prevailed on to imagine the world through their children's eyes. Practicing appropriate motherhood and facilitating a good and correct childhood could not come about absent a theorizing of what Carolyn Steedman refers to as "interiority."[68] For Steedman, from the late eighteenth century onward, conceptions of childhood and the presence of child-figures in literature, science, psychology, philosophy, and stage performance provided materials to express notions of time and historicity. The child, she argues, came to operate as a "component of the adult self"[69]—i.e., as means to imagine one's past as well as related notions of history, development, and narrative.

The point I make through the interrogations below proposes that motherhood and mothers themselves served as particular and particularly crucial vehicles and sites for envisaging the "interiority" of the child. Indeed, I go so far as to posit that an indispensable component of an arising bourgeois motherhood turned on a woman's ability to construe, theorize, and act on the interiorities of her children. Examining these occasions in this way thereby offers a different and significant entrée into considering the ideological trajectory of modern selfhood and subjecthood alongside Steedman's suggestions. That is to say, the "community" that imagined particular kinds of motherhood into public being did so strongly by considering and striving to know the interiority of an imagined, consequential "child." The posture toward the child—toward striving to know the child in this way—I contend, found resonance with an emerging psychological science toward the end of the nineteenth century and with an arising commercial culture in the first decades of the twentieth and beyond. It is this attitude—this impetus to see as the child sees and know as the child knows—that becomes a lasting, definitional legacy in the form of of a contemporary, dominant, normative conceptualization of childhood.

Discussion of Chapters

A key test of any inquiry, as I see it, centers on considering how one might learn something from one's inquisition that was not implied, encoded, or predetermined by the structure of the problem—the shape of the question—in the first place. That is, have I learned anything from this project that I did not teach it? The most straightforward response is in the affirmative. In the initial phase of the project, I expected to write a quick background chapter on nineteenth-century childhoods as an indication of some early precursors to the child consumer and then spend most of the remaining effort concentrating on the post-1900 period. However, when I began to look into early women's and mothers' periodicals, I was struck by the ways in which the child and mother came under intense, relentless definition and redefinition, particularly in Christian periodicals aimed at maternal education. In these homilies about proper Christian motherhoods, I recognized an emergent, core dynamic that could be found active and formative in "modern" working conceptions of the child and thus of the child consumer, leading me to question the received account of the triumph of the innocent, bourgeois Romantic child over that of strict Protestant conceptions, and thus the categorical opposition of this child to commercial culture.

As I looked further into these discourses and constructions of motherhood and childhood in these realms over the nineteenth century, I realized quickly that I was on well-trodden ground. Over a sustained period of time, scholars of all stripes have examined early Christian motherhood, Republican motherhood, and the Victorian middle-class family, child, and domesticity from historical, literary, women's studies, and childhood studies perspectives, to name a few (see chapters below for discussion, citation, and elaboration). I wondered how I was going to see or say something not already well digested, like the importance of the belief in childhood malleability or the preoccupation with materiality in Victorian domesticity. How was I going to avoid restating well-documented and known aspects of these worlds and this period? To be sure, there are many points in this text where the wheels of my wagon follow the exact grooves of those who have come before; it would be folly to ignore the insights and signposts of others.

At the same time, *The Moral Project of Childhood* offers contributions in a number of ways. For one, many of the histories and studies examining nineteenth-century childhoods may address the female domestic "sphere" but do not spend much effort considering the place and practice of *mothers* particularly, thereby leaving children and motherhoods as implied, side considerations. This absence mostly likely stems from an assumption that nineteenth-century middle-class women's lives and experience necessarily included their practices as mothers and also, perhaps, from a concern that focusing on motherhood would once again make women merely derivative of their maternal role and position. By speaking directly to the identities of women as mothers—and drawing from these—the following discussion allows a consideration of how a version of motherhood has formed and, as well, enables a concentrated effort to interrogate the place of the child and childhood in this process.

In a similar vein, others pay a great deal of attention to "parenting" practice, again sidestepping the mothers and the specific political and ideological situation of motherhood. Still others look at goods or market sites specifically implicating children, but tend to slide into the notion of a pre-capitalist child, discussed above. The present work takes as its core the co-construction of motherhood and childhood, demonstrating how the emergence of the idea that the child's moral, social, and psychological character as malleable directly informed the practical politics of motherhood, and has done so in different ways from at least the 1830s onward.

Secondly, the analysis trains itself on the ways in which writers and actors construe the child's subjectivity and follows how imputations of agency, knowledge, reflexivity, and memory come to be deployed both as inroads to children's experiences—their ways of knowing and seeing—and as bludgeons to enforce particular, circumscribed roles for mothers. Mothers generally come under increased ideological pressure due to the growing acceptance and legitimacy of children's perspectives, which compound the moral responsibilities they are to bear. That is, not only does the malleable child require perpetual attention and direction, but the child's wishes, desires, and viewpoints must likewise be taken into account and perhaps treated as having a primacy over mothers' views and wishes. Thirdly, these tussles between children's subject positions and subjectivities and mothers' liability and responsibility find expression through the material ties of the home and marketplace, and not despite the market. Fourthly, the project seeks to demonstrate how the pursuit of the child's interiority manifests as ongoing maternal duty and comes to inform commercial practice, thereby providing the foundation for a particularly definitional sort of child subjectivity.

The Moral Project of Childhood is best read front to back, as each chapter builds on the insights and concepts of the preceding one. Chapter 1 takes up Max Weber's problem of the Protestant ethic, arguing that the concerns he traced regarding salvation are one-dimensional to the extent that he ignored women, mothers, and children in relation to doctrine. The arising problematic in early nineteenth-century Protestantism of how *children* were to be saved—or, at least, be eligible for salvation—is foundational to what I identify as an emergent moral architecture of childhood and informs subsequent constructions and configurations of childhood, motherhood, and the child consumer. Here, I demonstrate, construals of child subjectivity and salvation in Evangelical mothering periodicals map out a moral dynamic between child interiority and maternal responsibility. Chapter 2 engages directly with Victorian senses of taste with regard to the arrangement of children's—mainly girls'—moral biographies and how this child was thought to be made through, not despite, engagement with the material world of goods and things.

In chapter 3, I discuss how concerns expressed about the discipline and punishment of children took children's perspectives and subjectivities into account—i.e., with mothers and advice-givers increasingly seeking to parse the extent to which children understand punishment and know right from wrong, and what "kind of child" is produced when rewarded for complying with parental wishes (rather than punished for disobedience). In chapter 4, concerns of taste and the dynamics of reward come together in discussions about simplicity in children's worlds (clothing, toys, play), about money (allowances), and about the ownership of their own things. In each of these arenas, things and materialities are presented as vehicles for producing proper childhoods, not as oppositions to them. Here, writers began to situate material life at the crux of children's rights by implicating children's pleasures, desires, and knowledge as central to the realization of a true sense of personhood, of an authentic self.

Chapter 5 interrogates some ways in which "child" and "consumer" came to be put into cultural conversation with one another in the 1900–1930 period. Emerging discourses of psychological science and of the child consumer converge in rendering children's subject positions, desires, and experiences of pleasure as legitimate and authoritative. Indeed, it is clear that one significant dimension of children's rights—which would emerge as a central element of twentieth-century childhoods—took hold as rights to possess things and rights to desire things. Consumerism provided a new layer of support and legitimacy for centering and prioritizing children's subjectivities—often manifesting in the form of wants and desires—which came to gain the status of a child's right, undergirded by developmentalism. Mothers, store clerks, copywriters, advertisers, and others were encouraged to locate something of a true sense of child interiority by consulting the child's perspective and reactions and, in so doing, bring the moral project of the child consumer full circle into the context of commercial enterprise. In the concluding chapter, I discuss how contemporary marketing practice, the valorization of the "creative child," and the practices of maternal provision derive from, speak to, and extend the dynamics of malleability, maternal responsibility, and child subjectivity.

1

A Moral Architecture

Protestant Salvation and the Mother-Child Nexus

If the mother is their oracle in all matters of right and wrong; if she is their umpire in all their differences; if she is their comforter in all their trials, and their chosen confidant, into whose ear they may whisper all their secret griefs, she possesses every desirable advantage for doing them good. She may almost entirely counteract the influence of every other person, and thus secure her children from the debasing influence of immorality with which they must necessarily come in contact.
—"Maternal Authority," *The Mother's Magazine*, March 1844[1]

Questions regarding the moral constitution of children pressed on many Americans living in the Northeastern US during the late eighteenth and early nineteenth centuries. Long-held, albeit changing, doctrines of Protestant Calvinism and Evangelical Christianity were encountering emergent Enlightenment and Romantic ideas of childhood education and of the primacy of grace and innocence.[2] At the crux of these encounters was the problem of the nature of children's moral character—i.e., the extent to which it was fixed or malleable, innate or learned, divinely formed or a product of human intervention. At base, the tensions at issue can be represented, on one hand, by a strict view— held in various intensities of belief and practice—whereby children were thought depraved, perhaps evil, at birth and their fate in terms of ultimate salvation was both divinely predetermined and unknown by anyone except the Creator. Over and against this view arose the didactic perspective expressed by John Locke (1632–1704) in his *Some Thoughts Concerning Education* (1693), where he put forward a conception that young children could be directed or molded by early impressions and thereby guided, though in limited means, by education.[3]

Ruminations about the degree of children's spiritual elasticity had inched toward the center of theological-philosophical concern among Protestant theologians over the decades prior to the nineteenth century. Historians Moran and Vinovskis note the extent to which parents ignored or understated the seventeenth-century Puritan ideology of infant damnation,[4] gradually accepting the idea of infant regeneration (i.e., early conversion to Christianity). As well, the Lockean notion of the intellectually malleable child encouraged faith in the ability of education to affect attitudes and practices. The English middle class of the eighteenth century seemed to embrace schooling as a form of class mobility,[5] while in seventeenth- and eighteenth-century New England, the Puritan avoidance of early childhood schooling, coupled with their aversion to fiction, poetry, and other forms of reading that were not "factual" and not directed toward knowing the teachings of the Bible, speaks to a different view of the child.[6] Didacticism in children's books and in the newly minted children's periodicals[7] increasingly resembled forms of play and amusement[8] and helped instantiate the educable child in and for the rising middle classes on both sides of the Atlantic before the onset of widespread, common schooling.[9]

Awash in a sea of (pre–psychological science) developmental practices, materials, and forms of knowledge,[10] Evangelical Protestantism found itself, in a way, philosophically cornered—caught between its own determinism of fate for the child's soul and the relative open-endedness of the impact of early childhood influence.[11] An intellectually malleable child also intimates a morally pliable one and thus poses a problem of existential proportions for the faith. If children moved toward or away from God differently than had been suggested by and since John Calvin's (1509–1564) influential theology, then significant swaths of teachings would be called into question, in particular the notions of predestination, depravity, and election.

The Evangelical Protestant response in the first half of the nineteenth century centered on theorizing the subjectivity of the young, preliterate child in relation to an already overdetermined, "extensive" conception of domestic motherhood. This response represented a shift from a dominant patriarchal mode whereby the spiritual life of a child, on arrival at the "age of reason," was often left to the male head of household, male preacher, and theologian.[12] Into a mother's lap landed the providence of the faith and indeed the reproduction and survival of the faith community itself in the person of an infant. As the "child" came to be seen as something that *can* be saved—or, at least, guided toward salvation—and yet unable to save itself, the burden of interlocution with the divine increasingly fell into maternal hands in the domestic sphere, rather than on clergy in the space of the church.[13] It was up to women, particularly mothers, to "curb the will" of the child before the onset of reason so as to effect a long-lasting redemption.[14] Hence, problems concerning who the child is, what it thinks, how it knows and, how it changes—issues of epistemology, ontology, and ontogeny—also became enfolded into the Protestant mother's charge.

In this chapter, I trace interminglings of Lockean with Protestant conceptions of child malleability and innateness and their implications for the mother-child nexus in the nineteenth century. I do so by revisiting the key questions of predestination—famously theorized by Max Weber as generative of a capitalist spirit—and of changing notions of innate depravity through the lens of Christian motherhood as discussed in an early Evangelical magazine directed toward and often written by women, many of whom were mothers. Unconsidered by Weber, the experiences and concerns of mothers and the incessant problem of child malleability combined to undergird a new kind of understanding of the child—one which ponders, and perhaps enables, the privileging of the child's subjecthood as consequential for this-worldly action in the form of mothering practices and ideologies.

The rise to prominence of a particular bourgeois, modern child subject and subjectivity, I argue, came about by and through the actions of mothers, who increasingly incurred the charge to contemplate and theorize the child's "interiority," as Carolyn Steedman has put it.[15] The duty of knowing, intuiting, and imputing the actions, motivations, and responses of her children devolved to white, Christian mothers, largely taking the form of measures to counteract the uncertainties posed by ambiguities regarding depravity, sin, and election. The "Liberal Protestantism," exemplified and brought forth in the writings of Horace Bushnell[16] in mid-century, enacted something beyond a "feminization" of religion through sentiment and affect, as Ann Douglas[17] has argued; it also indispensably assisted in ushering the "child" to the forefront of consideration in ways consequential to the subsequent rise and cultural predominance of a "modern," consumerist child subjectivity.

I argue that these dynamics blended to form the basis for a moral architecture that made the twentieth-century "child consumer" a possible, permissible, and viable cultural persona and subject, one that preceded and underlay large-scale early child psychological science. Like all architecture, it is an architecture of relations, not things—of stress points, balances, and structural pressures—the result of which is an apparent stability made possible by an often unseen dynamism. The dynamism here resides at the interface of children's subjectivity and mothers' interlocutions. In the main, the legacy of the struggle of late Calvinism and Evangelicalism with the world of their time is neither a pious child nor an irreverent one, neither depraved nor innocent, but rather it is the very tensions forming their interrelations and co-constructions. The opposing terms remain locked to each other, informing each other of possible re-formations—angel or devil, exploited or empowered—which neither side completely "wins." This child represents, in other words, an active, ongoing compromise formed about the problem posed by a presumed underlying pliability of character and being.

The Protestant Ethic and the Problem of Consumption

Sociologist Max Weber theorized how a capitalist "spirit," which favors and indeed celebrates material accumulation, somewhat paradoxically arose out of central aspects of Protestantism that denounced this-worldly preoccupation with possessions and self-adornment.[18] He argued that the response to the contradictions posed by the doctrine of predestination (see below) channeled energy and effort into the sphere of economic production as a "calling," thereby making capitalist pursuit something of a blessed endeavor. Weber, however, could not quite put his finger on how the Calvinist-inspired dynamics he analyzed made for a rising culture of *consumption* at the time of his writing in 1905. Asceticism may have underpinned the motivation of the entrepreneur in diverting excess money away from personal use and into productive operations, thereby enabling a key dynamic of capital creation. But the turn toward self-indulgence and socially sanctioned pleasure-seeking, evident in the late nineteenth and early twentieth centuries, is not in accord with Weber's analysis. At the conclusion of his text, he sounds an ominous note:

Material goods have gained an increasing and finally an inexorable power over the lives of men as at no previous period in history . . . In Baxter's view the care for external goods should only lie on the shoulders of the 'saint like a light cloak, which can be thrown aside at any moment.' But fate decreed that the cloak should become an iron cage.[19]

Weber invokes the metaphor of an "iron cage" to refer not to overweening bureaucratic rationality, as is often supposed, but to describe what he saw as a "fateful" new relationship between people and material things.

Sociologist Colin Campbell endeavored to rethink the Weberian thesis in light of consumer culture whereby a Romantic ethic, which emphasized and allowed hedonistic self-pleasure, arose as an alternative to the Calvinist ethic of self-denial and came to exist alongside it in modified form.[20] Campbell pointed to changes in the relationship between "belief and emotion"[21] whereby the experience of grace became an important emotional element in Protestant practice, a development that ultimately linked well with a rising Romanticism in literature, art, and philosophy.[22] Campbell, like Weber, largely ignored the place of women, and specifically mothers and motherhood, in the unfolding of this complex historical dynamic, and he made no substantive mention of children or childhood. He acknowledged, quite late in his argument, that women had been the audience for romantic, sentimental fiction for at least two centuries, offering a stereotypical gender division between male instrumentalism (puritanism) and female sentimentalism to account for the co-presence of both of these "ethics" in the same social class.[23]

Other scholars also have sought accommodation and interconnection between high, Evangelical Protestantism and a growing culture of sentiment and consumption in the nineteenth century—rather than a wholesale conquering of one over the other—although not necessarily in direct response to Weber. Historian Peter Slater discusses how the often-ignored emotional component of Protestant faith and practice figured into understandings of disciplining children. He notes that New England writers, from the notorious Cotton Mather (see below) and John Witherspoon in the eighteenth century to authors Louisa May Alcott and Lydia Maria Child in the nineteenth, advocated for mixing love with authority so as to effect a gentle sort of coercion with children.[24]

Feminist historian Ann Douglas famously wrote of the connection between nineteenth-century middle-class American women of the Northeast and the sentimentalization of religion and, ultimately, of mass culture overall.[25] Many of these women, argues Douglas, wrested a measure of cultural influence from men, especially the clergy, by exalting "feminine" qualities of taste, manners, and domesticity over traditional male values of rationality and instrumentality and did so largely through consuming and producing sentimental literature.[26] As economic production continued its move from home to factory over the early part of the nineteenth century, a sentimental culture adopted by white, Northeastern US, middle-class Protestant women infused religious education with a softer "persuasive" ethos—more akin to the address of literary writing or perhaps, later, of advertising than that of the authoritative Word of God—thereby transforming religious practice in the process.[27]

Historian Lori Merish, in turn, locates the origins of nineteenth-century female-dominated consumer culture by way of Scottish Enlightenment ideas that connected virtue with civility and that, when combined with a growing sense that taste was "innate" to women, worked to produce a new female subjectivity that legitimized their participation in the marketplace as consumers.[28] Importantly, she argues that a form of "pious consumption" arose out of the tensions between Protestantism and a rising material world of goods wherein luxury and good taste, both situated in the female domestic sphere, were seen as exerting a civilizing influence on the family.[29] Merish helps bring Campbell's idea of the intermixing of Romanticism and Protestantism into the female world of domesticity, giving some direction to understanding how consumption can arise out of the latter world, which stressed personal denial. Like Campbell and Douglas, however, she spends little time or space discussing the ways in which mothers and children/childhood figured into the formation and deployment of new subjectivities and new forms of consumption, their roles often implied in the terms "domestic," "household" and "family." Together, along with Weber, they neglect to consider or theorize, to any significant extent if at all, the generative core of cultural practice and reproduction—the mother-child nexus—in their contemplations of the rise of capitalism and consumption in the context of Protestantism. As a consequence, the social worlds they describe sometimes appear rather dimensionless, generationally speaking, with little offered in the way of engaging with problems crucial to the everyday consideration of what was to become known as parenting.

What is missing, and what will be attempted here, is an examination—an informed conjecture—that uses the "child" as a lens to link changes in dominant iterations of Protestantism with the rise of domestic consumption in the mid-nineteenth century and beyond, taking Evangelical (and other) discourses of mothering as points of departure. The crucial switch point centers on how the Lockean rumblings concerning the educable, malleable child, noted above, spread tremors across foundational conceptions of human nature generally *through* a rethinking of child predestination and depravity by way of theorizing both materiality and interiority—of both the child and the mother. Some scholarship tends to highlight the dissipation of the notion of child depravity at this time as consequential for a new conception of childhood to emerge and take hold[30]; it is important, however, also to recognize and incorporate depravity's twin—i.e., predestination—into the theorization of the transformation of this version of childhood. Concerns about and reformulations of children and children's salvation form a pivot point in a key change in Protestantism—and, moreover, in childhood generally—one which inextricably implicates mothers and motherhood.

The Child Dilemma in Calvinist Conception

For a narrow but virulent and influential swath of American Protestantism, the problem of child "education," in a broad sense, arose from the contradiction posed by the idea of predestination—and related notions of depravity and atonement—inherited from the teachings of sixteenth-century theologian John Calvin. Described and analyzed in useful detail by Weber, predestination derived from the notion that all things, including one's ultimate salvation or damnation, had been determined from the beginning of creation and that only the Supreme Being held knowledge of any particular person's outcome.[31] In Weber's analysis, the impact of this doctrine in many ways rendered action in the everyday world impotent in terms of salvation because those who were among the Elect—i.e., those few who were to be saved—knew no more of their lot than those many who were damned. Furthermore, neither damned nor saved could affect an outcome about which no one had knowledge.[32] For Weber, the spurious connection between this-worldly action and other-worldly salvation ultimately rendered the idea of predestination untenable in everyday life because the "psychological sanctions" arising from this doctrine in its strict form could not serve as a useful guide to practical action.[33] The solution to the predicament of predestination, propounded by Calvin's successors like Baxter, was to instruct that people behave *as if* they were among the Elect, i.e., to act righteously with a belief they have been chosen and will obtain salvation. Indeed, holding this *certitudo salutis*, this certainty of one's salvation, became an absolute duty of followers in combating the temptations of the Devil.[34] For many, according to Weber, laboring in a vocation, a calling, charted a wise path of such action—a pathway which, combined with commercial efforts, made for a fortuitous blend of asceticism and material productivity characteristic of a modern capitalist ethos.

The deep dynamic at work in the various aspects of this doctrine—as Weber demonstrates so eloquently—resides in the very incompatibilities, the very contradictions, that are revealed in the unfolding of their worldly implications, i.e., in practice. In the early 1800s, American Protestantism—especially among the hardline Evangelicals—grappled with the complications of child-rearing in an atmosphere where the increasing recognition of the malleability of young children for training and education continued to encounter the waning, but extant, strictures of predestination and depravity.[35] At the heart of this tension dwelled questions of responsibility, culpability, knowledge, and ability. Young children could not labor in a calling to exalt the glory of God on earth as Calvin had instructed; not yet able to read, they could not grasp the Word on their own without assistance; their actions furthermore increasingly became understood as imperfect measures of deep motivation.

For sixteenth- and seventeenth-century American Puritans—an especially stalwart strain of Protestantism located in New England (the ones who, for a time, outlawed Christmas celebrations)[36]—the response to the inability to read signs of predetermined election was to err on the side of caution, assuming that the Devil was in all things, including especially children, according to social historian David Stannard.

Stannard quotes Cotton Mather, a highly influential minister and key player in the infamous Salem, Massachusetts, witch trials of 1682, discussing children in 1689:

> They are no sooner wean'd but they are to be taught . . . They go astray as soon as they are born. They no sooner step than they stray, they no sooner lisp than they ly. Satan gets them to be proud, profane, reviling and revengeful as young as they are.[37]

Children, especially infants, in this view existed in a state of depravity, wallowed in the Original Sin of Adam and Eve, and required conversion.[38]

Peter Slater points to the growing discomfort on the part of Calvinists regarding Original Sin, total depravity, eternal hell, and purifying grace, which "locked together to make an imposing imperative" on parents, children, and the faith community.[39] In the decades leading up to the nineteenth century, the notion of moral education—of the ability and responsibility to "train up" the child toward God—acquired a growing legitimacy as theologians found ways to make the this-worldly effort of education compatible with lingering strictures regarding divine election or conversion.[40] One way through the theological thicket was to frame infant moral education as something of a civic duty and responsibility, necessary for the day-to-day life of the community.[41] Such responses appeared to have been useful and acceptable so long as there was no hint that moral education—undertaken by finite mortals on this earthly plane—would somehow supplant adult conversion or the workings of grace.[42]

The "child"—the educable, malleable child—was becoming a problem. The moral ontology of these doctrines, having become desynchronized from the social ontogeny of childhood, made the strong, early program of Calvinism virtually untenable. The survival of the faith and the faith community required intercession—an intercession to help situate the child at the center. That is, if children were no longer thought to be depraved from the start, and perhaps not damned from the beginning time and the beginning of life, and if the soul now "presents itself like wax to seal"[43]—a reference to Locke's view of the child's mind—then the locus of salvation moves from the unknown, unseen, and divine to the known, seen, and mortal, materializing in the figure of the mother in the sphere of the home.[44] Early moral education would occur in and through domestic space and, in many ways, on domestic terms as a form of moral regulation. The shift from the pulpit to the parlor entailed shifts in tone, affect, and mode whereby the rationality of doctrine and the linearity of the written word require a translation into everyday, mundane practice around the house[45] and put in terms that young children could grasp. Nora Doyle, in her history of motherhood in early America, understands the increasing domestic responsibility of mothers at this time as a transfer of duty toward ensuring civic action for those occupying the generation after the American Revolution, as women's reproductive functions began to exist side by side with sentimental, domestic, and socially productive and reproductive practices.[46] For those concerned with the reproduction of faith in Evangelical Christian communities in the US Northeast, women—and mothers in particular—came to occupy a crucial site as, increasingly, men left the household to labor in the new capitalist economic spatial arrangements that helped create new boundaries between the domestic world and the world of work.[47]

Mothers of Impression: *The Mother's Magazine*, Child Salvation, and Affective Persuasion

In New England and elsewhere in the US Northeast, numerous local maternal organizations opened during this time, serving several functions. According to historian Julia Grant, these organizations sought to combat isolation and validate mothers' roles in a patriarchal familial system[48] while disseminating child-rearing advice locally as well as through publications like *The Mother's Magazine* (1833–1848).[49] Arising out of the religiously viscous environment of Utica, New York, the magazine sought to reach beyond a local and sectarian audience to provide a forum for spiritual training and discussion about Christian motherhood among Christian mothers—rather than among clergy—and, ultimately as Meckel argues,[50] as a tool for Christian reform.[51] Schertz offers that *The Mother's Magazine* "supplied the first widespread material in the USA specifically written for mothers" and served as an integrated media for a "curriculum for motherhood,"[52] which helped weave together the lessons and ethos whereby mothers were to move to the center of Christian life and education. Periodical founder Abigail Whittelsey made it clear from the outset that she conceived of Christian motherhood as a kind of calling[53] and the magazine as a kind of "moral media"[54] that would "create an educated ministry of Christian mothers."[55] As Margaret Beetham observes, the periodical "concerned itself exclusively with the moral and spiritual aspects of mothering; there was nothing on cookery, needlework, or the practicalities of sickbed nursing."[56]

On the pages of *The Mother's Magazine* writers sketched out and often implored the white, free, pious child into social being by implicating mothers deeply, directly, and inescapably as authors of their own children's character and ultimate salvation, as well as the salvation of the entire "race." Written for those involved with maternal organizations, the core tension centered on the problems of handling young children's presumed susceptibility to influence (itself in tension with notions of innate depravity) and the consequent difficulties of preparing them to receive scripture and formal religious instruction when they become literate and knowledgeable. In specific, the timing, shape, and parameters of children's knowledge, their ability to comprehend religious teaching, and the locus and emergence of reflexive volition—i.e., to knowingly act upon the world—served as the focal points for the enactment of an emergent, imagined community of motherhood.

The character of children, one writer reminds the readership in 1844 in a clearly Lockean reference, is "entrusted to mothers" who bear the "importance of rightly training youthful minds, while, like wax, they are capable of receiving any impression, either of evil or good."[57] An impression-able child posed perhaps as much danger, and certainly as much challenge, as the innately sinful one. The moral bearings of a child thought originally sinful and depraved brings a sense of certainty, of known possible problems, the tendencies of which can be anticipated and countered, much like the furniture and swaddling studied by Calvert.[58] An impressionable child, on the other hand, can be imprinted by most anything and brings with it a multiplicity of burdens cascading upon mothers, whose vigilance and diligence carry significant consequence. The same writer urged mothers to attend to the choice of children's playthings, as tastes "are often acquired, and habits formed, which exist through life, that may be distinctly traced to the apparently trivial toys of childhood."[59] Her case in point is Napoleon Bonaparte, whose first toy, supposedly, was a miniature cannon:

> Who will say that the little brass cannon was not the indirect cause of the butchery of millions of our fellow-creatures; of the groans and tears of widows and orphans . . . But for that toy, and instead of a Hero wading through the blood of his countrymen . . . we might have seen, for aught we know, a powerful minister of Christ, a second Paul; one who, by the superiority of his mind, in the hands of God, might have created a new era in the civil and religious history of the world.[60]

Hyperbolically but perhaps no less sincerely enjoined, the future of Christian civilization rests, as it were, in the laps of mothers whose every decision and action "impresses," it seems, indelibly. One senses in these tracts scripted for mothers' eyes a kind of urgency, perhaps desperation, of purpose. It was as if they and the larger faith community were being squeezed on one side by the ever-present specter of uncontrolled and unwanted influences on the malleable child and, on another, by a growing secular, or at least inadequately pious, world. Children were constantly growing into and encountering this world made up of heathens, Catholics, greed, indulgence, and distractions of all sorts promising to divert child and adult alike from the path toward salvation[61] and which necessarily stand in the way of building nation and empire.[62] Add the ever-present fear of early mortality of young, unconverted children and one is faced with a concentrated, pressurized, and highly surveilled social location where concerns about a kind of "faith suicide" may have animated fears about social and biological reproduction in ways similar to the "race suicide syndrome" decades later.[63]

With child, family, community, and history at stake, the work of training children up for early conversion required understanding—or attempts to understand—of how young people learn, the content and focus of their motivations and attitudes, and possible sources of diversion (i.e., the wrong toy). The need to assess and theorize the young child's learning process in order to affect one's parenting and pedagogy sat squarely in the crux of the definition of mothering for these Christians—in a sense, making them forerunners of latter-century child study practitioners and experts.[64] The unformed mind of the infant—the great threat to and greatest hope for a future based on Christian values and moral posture—offered a space for pre–psychological science theorization of infant interiority, as is brought to bear for instance by this contributor to *The Mother's Magazine* in 1833:

> It comes to us as ignorant as the clay in which it dwells; is helpless and dependent. It literally knows not anything of itself, of the world in which it lives, or that for which it is a candidate. Necessity and observation will soon lead it to the use of its limbs, and the exercise of its animal powers, and it may acquire a considerable amount of useful knowledge without our instruction. Its intellectual powers will also be laid under contribution to its wants, and without any particular attention effort on our part, it will make considerable advances in the onward march of mind. But its moral culture must be the result of mind acting upon mind; and as soon as it becomes the subject of this operation, its religion instruction has begun.[65]

The part of the child that is made, not born, is most significant—its moral bearing or "culture"—and lies at the feet of motherhood. Not a transparent practice with clear, immediate outcomes, the education of preliterate young children toward Christ and scripture required minute attention to the details of everyday life, thereby making the home, in essence, a nursery catechism. In this vein, as Schertz notes, *The Mother's Magazine* offered a "colourful tapestry of moral tales, discipline, guidelines, impassioned speech [and] calls to faith" as part of an attempt to provide "moral regulation" for mothers.[66]

A Calvinist writer, noting the growing importance of the idea of education due to the popularity of Locke's ideas, reminds the maternal readership that education does not stop once the child crosses the threshold of the home into the larger world:

> Education includes in it a long-continued training of a child; and a regular and steady course of exertions on the part of a parent to form those habits and feelings, which will most conduce to his[67] well-being, in a temporal and spiritual point of view. Children should not only be instructed in learning . . . but as soon as practicable, in the knowledge of

the character of God, as revealed in the Scriptures—in their accountable-ness to him—in their state in his sight,—and should be early led to the Savior, as able and willing to save them from the dangers to which they are exposed.[68]

The kind of child encrafted here, among other things, remains a child attendant to example and practice rather than guided by precept.

The basis of religious strength—and hence its greatest vulnerability—lay in the pre-literate, pre-rational child, the child of Rousseau rather than the rational-able child of Locke. Yet a simulacrum of Locke's im-pressionable mind can be found in in the child's soul or character.[69] It is by the associative element and property—according to these hardline, though transforming, Evangelical Protestants—that children will form favorable impressions and feelings toward God and thereby be disposed toward early conversion. It is by example, in the end, that the soil is pre-pared to receive the Word of scripture, particularly when children are to leave the home and engage with the world in schools and with peers, where the dangers of pollution become evident.

Mothers, above all, writes another in the second issue of *The Mother's Magazine* in 1833, must behave consistently, as they are under constant surveillance by their children, who "research" them in pursuit of exam-ples of proper behavior: "Nothing is lost or overlooked . . . all [actions] are watched and remembered, every scrap is treasured up, and . . . made to pass in careful review [by the child]. . . . Now imagine the child, while engaged in this research, to have discovered in his mother's conduct, or instructions, some inconsistency or contradiction." The incongruity between a mother's words and her actions puts the child in a "state of painful incertitude."[70] This anonymous author instructs the maternal readership that children notice "little things" and that they spy on her, admonishing: "Mother, watch yourself. Your child watches you; his eye watches every motion; his ear bent to catch every sound from your lips. In his little bosom is treasured up every careless word and motion, and no effort of yours can ever avail to unlock or plunder his storehouse."[71] The threat posed by insufficiently self-monitoring mothers appears as great as or greater than innate depravity. Auto-surveillance necessitates presuming or theorizing some aspect of the child's interiority on the part of the mother and adjusting accordingly.

When examined from the vantage point of eternity, the haunting presence of the depraved, predestined child is positively counter-indicative to education, training or "influence" of any ultimate consequence. Maternal organizations and their publications, however, insinuate otherwise—that maternal and parental intercession can indeed affect not just the appearance or behavior of redemption, but perhaps also ultimate salvation itself.[72] Yet, underlying such unstated promises dwells a regimen of discipline whereby the presumed readership and local organizational participants display to themselves and to each other the acts of faith and belief through the rearing of their children. One piece, written by "A Mother" in 1836, rhetorically poses the question, "Is it not a melancholy truth, that the children of Christian parents, who have been dedicated to God, are too much like the children of unholy parents, in their feelings and conduct?"[73] She continues on to exhort mothers to "train up" their children in God's law until "he" can read the Bible for himself, scolding that "O Christian parent, you possess the privilege of taking the hand of your beloved child, and leading him to God morning and evening, and supplicating for him the influences of the Spirit. If you have neglected to fulfil this obligation, do not complain that your child is prayer-less."[74] A mother or parent may or may not affect the will of the Almighty, but she cannot blame others for the lack of piety of her own children.

The notion that enacting motherhood constitutes a "privilege" for women was echoed often during the first decade of *The Mother's Magazine*. Mothers were privileged because they alone held the power to mold a good Christian person from the outset, to steer her or him away from untoward influences and bad early habits toward a righteous path: "How sweet to a mother is the task—no, I cannot call it a task—the *privilege* of directing the opening affections of the infant soul to the great object of love and trust." When children "are thrown into an inquisitive state," the habits formed early by the vigilant mother will direct the child "to its Father in heaven."[75] Motherhood, here, serves not simply the education of the child but the salvation of the world by enabling the salvation of the child, particularly during a historical period when fervent religiosity was on the rise during the Second Great Awakening. One letter writer, "A." (who could very well be the editor, Abigail Whittelsey), explains to the reader that "we have the privilege of living in a time when

Christians begin to believe that the world is to be converted and to act as though it might be done through their agency. This fact increases our responsibility."[76]

The schizoid character of these discourses—the demand to act where the effect of such action remains unclear—and of the positionality of mothers becomes stark at times and gives indication of the unsettled nature of the child-doctrine-mother relationship. Lest there be any doubt about the cosmic impotence of one's actions, of the sheer conceit of personal impact on the plan of God, the readership is reminded of their place in the order of things by the Maternal Organization of the Calvinistic Church in Worcester, Massachusetts in 1836:

> God has placed in our hands means for operating on the human mind in its most susceptible stage, with power to make impressions which the finger of time can never efface . . . Never, never may we for a moment forget, that the power of renovation rests not with us. We may bend the sapling, and give to it a direction which it shall never be able to overcome, but we cannot ensure blossoms and fruit.[77]

In the same year, the readership is warned that

> it is impossible for their [children's] parents to remove that depravity, or to renew their [children's] hearts, or to discharge them from the penalty of that curse, by any thing that is in their power to do. . . . A great point, therefore, is gained, when a mother is convinced that it is utterly out of her power, by the most faithful and un-remitting efforts to remove this depravity, or to renew the hearts of her children . . . She must feel that this is the work and office of the Holy Spirit. But a mother has it in her power to *restrain this depravity*, and to prevent its breaking out in overt acts of transgression . . . To this end, let a mother seriously and conscientiously improve every opportunity which may be afforded, to express her decided approbation of the right conduct of her child, and in the same way her disapprobation and displeasure in witnessing that which is vicious.[78]

The child here exhibits just enough mutability of character to cast suspicion upon any mother who does not produce a holy, pious Christian or at least a child who performs Christian-ness. Yet, the ultimate contours of the final product rest not in her hands. Her power extends only so far as restraint—restraint of a prior, extant depravity.

The haunting presence of some sort of original depravity notwithstanding, mothers—and parents and ministers generally—were seen as embodied pedagogical instruments, whose every act was deemed consequential for child salvation. Everyday practice in the form of mundane maternal example could render the need for discipline unnecessary. "The daily example of a mother, whose actions are all guided by the benign influence of religion in her heart, is, it is believed, more powerful in its effects on her children, than all the force of severe discipline, or of a rigid course of direction, in what is considered the part of maternal duty," wrote one mother in 1836.[79] Another, in a section on "Practical Hints," assured the readership in November of that year that training and obedience can be woven into everyday life:

> This work requires no set lessons nor long prayers; nothing to take you from your accustomed employment. With one infant in your arms, your eye can follow the others; your ear can listen to their conversation; and never should a mother's ear be more attentive, than when her children are at play, to watch the first rising of selfishness or passion, and meet it with a word from the Bible. Let their play ground be always near you, if possible, and let eye and ear be on the alert, for the adversary of their souls is near, and he will flee at the sound of the word of God.[80]

On everlasting guard for the slightest deviance from the righteous path, mothers cannot simply instruct children in the sacred word. They themselves set the example of piety in their actions: "You, above all others, should present a living example of all that is 'pure, lovely, and of good report.' There must be consistency between your example and instructions, or you labor in vain. If the Bible with its holy sanctions is to govern your child, it must pre-eminently govern your life."[81] The mother, hence, functions as the fount of sanctity in the eyes of the child and as such exists in perpetual surveillance by both the Almighty above her and by the little one at her bosom: "Every duty which the Bible enjoins, they will expect to see fulfilled by you. Your children will look with a searching eye on your life and deportment. Oh hinder them not by an unchristian example."[82] In so doing, as Slater explains, parents sought to ensure that the aura of the afterlife remain perpetually at the edge of their consciousness, as aspiration and as threat.[83]

Parental example extends to the affect imparted to specific activities such as prayers, the lessons from which carry on robustly beyond the moment or context of instruction (see figure 1.1). One writer relates a scene where she has spied a young child, all alone in a room, who dutifully made all the correct gestures and said all the correct words for evening prayers: "Never, till this occurrence, had my mind dwelt upon the momentous fact, though so oft-repeated, that the future characters and the eternal destinies of children, are usually, at a very early period, stamped by parental example; and I now felt what an amazing influence must be exerted upon young children by the manner of performing family prayer."[84] The stamp of character often was made not with the force of precept and harsh sermon so often the practiced by previous century Puritans and strict Protestants, but by forging pleasing associations with prayer, scripture, and holy acts.[85] Ministering with and through affect in this way is most characteristic of what Greven identified as "moderate" Protestantism, whereby love "provided the foundation for the obedience and dutifulness of children."[86] Here, as Douglas has analyzed, the "feminine" virtues of affection and sentiment were making inroads into religious practice—in the sphere of the home rather than of the church—crowding out the masculine approach of invoking the fear of damnation through "fire and brimstone" allocutions when addressing the pre-literate, malleable child.[87] The virtues of sentiment also manifested, according to Doyle, in depictions of mothering that seemed to indicate "less a form a labor and more a way of being."[88]

The first object of female influence, if these writings are any indication, is the child, who must be bent like a sapling toward an affectionate, but no longer authoritarian, relationship with the Word. The strong emotional bond between mother and child, however, can be misguided if not directed toward the ultimate aim of securing a child's interest in and warm disposition toward the Savior. In clear dialogue with ever-popular Lockean notions that favored children's powers of reason beyond infancy, a writer in 1836 eschews the idea that the child's mind be "kept entirely unbiased until it is capable of judging and understanding for itself." In a move that anticipates Freud by nearly two generations,

Figure 1.1. *The Mother's Magazine* advised women to engage their children in prayer from an early age and to offer themselves as pious examples. Source: *The Mother's Magazine*, May 1852, 129.

the writer makes it incumbent upon the mother, who has the "most unbounded influence" over her children, to transfer the object of an emotional bond from herself to the Bible. The way to a child's soul is through its heart, and maternal affection paves that path to "feel the truth."[89] But mortal, maternal accountability remains elusive and contested when child depravity sits at the tip of the tongue of collective memory and is the subject of sermonizing in church on Sundays, as a "Christian Mother" in 1837 attests: "We are aware that it has been asserted, that the mind of a child should be left unbiased to choose those principles of religion which may appear most consistent with reason, on its arrival at the years of discretion; but to one habituated to behold in his child that decided predilection for that which is evil, which the scriptures of truth have described as inherent in every child of Adam, it must be unnecessary to enter into any lengthened argument to prove the fallacy of such assertions."[90] With evil ready to spring from the child at any moment, the idea of waiting for the age of reason to commence moral instruction made no sense, eschatologically speaking.[91]

A clear, though gradual, turn away from the determinism of predestiny, in the form of depravity, and toward an ethos that embraced the idea of child influence can be read in the promise of maternal example and its affectionate aura. Mother's aura—and, indeed, authority—was seen as extending beyond the starkly behavioral realm to encompass the power mothers have and may wield in terms of discipline and obedience, enunciated in the following passage (also partially represented in the epigraph to this chapter), which is worth quoting at length:

> With their feeble capacities and inexperience, they contemplate only present wants, and are wholly improvident of the future. And as indulgence would, in many cases, come in direct conflict with their good, it becomes the duty and privilege of the mother to whom they are entrusted, and who loves them as no one else can, to cross their wishes often, in order to secure their lasting benefit. She must not only withhold some desired favors, but must require and enforce the performance of various acts, the reasonableness of which they are not able to comprehend; for children, left to follow their own ways, endanger their health and lives by their indiscretion, and become unhappy members of the family and of society . . . If the mother is their oracle in all matters of right and wrong; if she is their umpire in all their differences; if she is their comforter in all their trials, and their chosen confidant, into whose ear they may whisper all their secret griefs, she possesses every desirable advantage for doing them good. She may almost entirely counteract the influence of every other person, and thus secure her children from the debasing influence of immorality with which they must necessarily come in contact. That she should thus be the centre of love and confidence to the forming minds under her care, is manifest to all who rightly prize the benefits of fixing early in the minds of children a correct moral sentiment.[92]

The range, depth, and span of responsibility, derived from "maternal authority," imparted here astounds. Ever-present threats must be matched with ever-vigilant knowledge of and attention to the child's every gesture by the mother—the "oracle in all matters of right and wrong." Affection and discipline meld together to serve as a kind of sealant covering the endlessly reappearing moral cracks of an exposed

Figure 1.2. "The proper cultivation of the sensibilities and feelings should be commenced as early as these powers begin to be developed, and never should be trifled with, or tortured." Source: *The Mother's Magazine*, 1853, 161.

child inhabiting a malleable childhood, itself laid bare to a world of risk (see figure 1.2.). The risk can be countered if a mother can produce a pious home environment (see figure 1.3) where piety and example can be passed down through the children (see figure 1.4).

Note the incitement to leverage a mother's unique, intimate relationship with her young child and to mix it with the power of resource allocation by "withholding desired favors" so as to fix a "correct, moral sentiment." Maternal duty, here, requires the exercise of material-economic power and some measure of duplicity, as the window of influence is small, narrow, and closes quickly. Depravity looms. Logic and "education" may arrive too late for lasting effects. A "Christian mother" advised the readership in 1837 to seize upon opportune moments "when children are more open to conviction than others" to exert influence that does not appeal to the rational mind. At these moments—which may be recovery from sickness or during enjoyment of "anything that

HOME EDUCATION.

Figure 1.3. The Christian family circle, superintended by the mother, was thought to serve as a counterweight to the "influence" and "evil tendency" of the outside world. Source: *The Mother's Magazine*, August 1859, 226.

Figure 1.4. "The Instructed Should Instruct": An older child is depicted as offering Bible instruction to two younger children, who have set aside their playthings to listen intently to verse. This "cunning act hints at a duty that devolves upon members of the family already instructed," as the author of the accompanying article notes. Source: *The Mother's Magazine*, May, 1852, 179.

has afforded it pleasure"—the child is ripe to be "taught the language of gratitude, and encouraged to thank his heavenly father for the mercies experienced."[93]

Mothers, in these scenarios, occupy a strategic site—a space of knowledge and relationality—where intervention has a fighting chance. Intervention is dependent on a mother's facility in conceptualizing and theorizing the subjectivity, the interiority, of her child. Being able to identify "opportune moments" and act to steer feelings of pleasure and enjoyment toward desired associations involves a deep identification and capacity for empathy. Decidedly gendered, this capacity mitigates traditional Evangelical dispositions that seek to invoke damnation and replaces them with one that favors motivating moral malleability through affective means. Mother's influence most strongly asserts itself at the pre-logical level—from the heart, not the head. It might be thought of as a kind of affective persuasion. The logic of the tactics here advocated appears remarkably similar—nearly identical in form and attitude—to those championed by commercial actors regarding selling children's goods in the early twentieth century (see chapter 5).

Maternal sentiment lies at ground zero of moral education. It serves as an answer to and an antidote for the malleable child, which promised nothing but uncertainty—uncertainty of the effectiveness of a mother's interdictions, uncertainty of its own salvation, uncertainty of the doctrines under which both resided. Personal, guided, and concentrated empathy could counteract harmful influence by becoming a kind of super-influence, one that contextualized and framed all others, aiming the interpretation and response in the direction of a particular disposition. This emotional configuration of the child can be found in Evangelical Protestantism, independent of and somewhat predating the Romantic movement,[94] where a mix of love and authority was thought to address concerns about the moral waywardness of the young. Child malleability necessarily extended to the emotional, affective realm—a place prior to and beyond that of the cognitive and rational—where fears regarding social "vices," poor exemplars of Christian virtue (like children of "unchristian" parents), and undisciplined passions planted their roots.[95] Mothers, in this community of discourse, appear to be not so much idealized as they were in men's writings of the time[96] as they were understood as imperfect, fallible devices for faith and community reproduction.

Horace Bushnell and the Doctrinal Turn

The concerns and machinations bandied about in *The Mother's Magazine* presented challenges to what was a waning Calvinist orthodoxy in the early- to mid-1800s. The publication of Horace Bushnell's book *Christian Nurture* in 1847 can be seen as an attempt to codify this doctrinal complex—which included depravity, conversion, election, and education—in reference to the problems posed by emergent conceptions of the malleable child. Bushnell, a Yale-educated theologian and Congregationalist pastor in Connecticut, sought to make the notion of nurture central to Christian theology by repositioning innate sin, or depravity, as something that is not "hereditary"[97]—i.e., not passed from parents to children—and is not entirely an individual condition or struggle.[98] Written at a time and in a context when male religious authority and patriarchal governance of the home were on the wane[99] in hardline and liberal branches of Protestantism alike, Bushnell dodges the gender politics of child-rearing. He studiously avoids making mothers the central actors in the enactment of Christian nurture, usually referring to "parents" when addressing the social action required to bring up children in the correct way, often referring to "mothers" and "motherhood" euphemistically or when quoting scripture or relating stories and parables.

The best course to "remedy" the evil into which everyone is born, according to Bushnell, is to counteract it when it is "young and pliant."[100] Depravity, here, like the child, has a development that calls forth a response to effectuate a spiritual gradualism undertaken through moral education (rather than through sudden adult conversion). By giving sin an ontogeny that is isomorphic with the child's (presumed) spiritual development, Bushnell effects something of an epistemological transfer whereby evil or depravity appears not so much the solid essence of the human condition after the Fall—not a predetermined state and destiny—and more as an incipient attitude or disposition that can be countered on its own terms; it is as if the Devil in the young child is also something of a weak "passive lump"[101] like the infant and can be exorcised, as it were, through nurture: "And when, in fact, is the human heart found to be so ductile to the motives of religion, as in the simple, ingenious age of childhood? How easy it is, then, as compared with the stubbornness of adult years, to make all the wrong seem odious, all good lovely and enjoyable."[102]

Again, it is a ductile heart, not the impressionable mind, that is of concern here. Bushnell offers a dialectic of good and evil through organicism. Both evil and good exist in children as seeds that can be either cultivated or pruned. God would not have emplaced sin as the only character of His creation, it is reasoned, but rather wisely allowed for the potentiality of good to be brought out from the first moments and years of existence. Hence, the family becomes the site of Christian nurture where a "steady, new-creating power . . . ought to be exerted by holiness in the house."[103] It is a view that switches the terms of moral dynamic without overturning doctrine. That is to say, moral failing or spiritual piety arises not as a condition of an individual child or of childhood in toto, but as something accomplished in the course of upbringing. Sin and unchristian life are not inevitable and are not simply changed through radical conversion in adult baptism, but are things that can be counteracted in daily life, even by parents who have been sinful. In the same vein, Bushnell inveighs against those (read: Romantics) who assume the "radical goodness of human nature,"[104] which only needs to be drawn out of a child. Producing a Christian being, rather, is a contested, dynamic engagement between good and evil that, moreover, constitutes the condition of the child, of childhood: "The growth of Christian virtue is no vegetable process, no mere onward development. It involves a struggle with evil, a fall and a rescue."[105] The spiritual journey of a child, then, recapitulates the spiritual journey of all people, or at least that of the Chosen People, in Judeo-Christian tradition. Unlike the famous and enduring form of recapitulation theory put forward by G. Stanley Hall sixty years later,[106] Bushnell does not insinuate an inevitability, biologically or otherwise, of one particular trajectory.

In offering his conceptions, Bushnell effectively rejiggers the Calvinist algorithm of spiritual risk. Predestination and election for Baxter, Wesley, and especially Calvin tended to minister on the side of presuming predetermined election for salvation and then acting as if it were so—even though the "odds" of being one of the Elect were few, as Weber emphasized. Bushnell's rearticulation of the doctrine posits a new calculation of risk in the sense that each child was seen to have the nearly fifty-fifty odds of a flipped coin and, on top of it, the coin could be made unbalanced to favor election by luck of the parental draw. The more pious and spiritually attentive the parents, the better the chances not only of salvation, but also of continuing Christian lives themselves that, in turn, would produce a new generation of parents and children—social reproduction of faith and a faith community at its most basic level.

Importantly (and consistently), it is not the parents who exert some unilateral power to renew the child, but rather they are energized to do so by the same source (he calls it a "solar heat," consistent with his organic metaphors) that will also grow the child into piety. Switching the traditional terms once again, Bushnell places the child (one might say today, the child's "welfare" or "best interests") at the center of his theology, asserting that it is because of the parental ability to raise a Christian child they then have a responsibility to do so, which includes living Christian lives themselves:

> Goodness, or the production of goodness, is the supreme end of God, and therefore, we know, on first principles, that He desires to bestow whatsoever spiritual grace is necessary to the moral renovation of childhood. . . . Thus, if nothing were hung upon parental faithfulness and example, if the child were not used, in some degree or way, as all argument, to hold the parent to a life of Christian diligence, then the good principle in the parent might lack the necessary stimulus to bring it to maturity. Or, if all children alike, in spite of the evil and unchristian example of the house, were to be started into life as spiritually renewed, one of the strongest motives to holy living would be taken away from parents, in the fact that their children are safe as regards a good beginning, without any carefulness in them, or prayerfulness in their life; and their own virtue might so overgrow itself with weeds, as never to attain to a sound maturity.[107]

It is thus part of the divine plan that children be susceptible to some form of evil and depravity so as to give parents or, more accurately, parenting and the household a reason to exist.

In this way, the sacred and profane of childhood arise in a cogenerative fashion. One makes the other—and makes the other

necessary. Bushnell's solution to the moral problem of childhood confronting Calvinistic Protestantism was turn the child into a moral project—in the first instance, for the family. Childhood, in this sense—in
this configuration of thought—arises as compromise formation, a structure of mediation between good and evil, between sacred and profane.
In the same breath, Bushnell does not posit Christian nurture merely
as a neutral force. The child, born in and of a Christian life and circumstance, should not require the sudden or dramatic conversion as
would a "heathen" of an inferior race. Such a child already has within
him- or herself the seeds for "regeneration" of the spirit toward the Lord
and the Word—a potential too often ignored or held back by parents
and ministers, who presume the child is in need of radical break or
transformation, rather than a nurturing or cultivation.[108] In this way,
Bushnell de-"Others"—or de-alienates—the white, Christian child and
makes of it an incomplete, but non-foreign version of a desirable adult
self, thereby reorienting child ontology in the process. Heathens, here,
require significant intervention to effect conversion; unlike the white,
Christian child, they did not seem to possess the "seeds," the source, the
"solar heat" that can be activated only by a loving household.

Throughout the book, Bushnell configures the child as the seedbed
of opposing forces that are not struggling for dominance but lying fal-
low awaiting germination and cultivation. The struggle is elsewhere,
outside the child. Hard and fast pureness—pure goodness, pure evil—
disassembles any notion of regeneration as it essentializes *both* terms of
the opposition, thereby essentializing the child as one kind of being or
another. Pureness, of whatever kind, leaves no room for intervention or
education because it denies the malleability of the child's character. It
is the world, in a sense, which makes the child good or unchristian by
drawing out of him or her what, in some form, already exists, somewhat
similar to the Transcendentalists of the time.

Nothing less than a confrontation with conceptions of human nature,
the Protestant tussle with depravity and predestination materializes as
struggles with contingency and essentialness. The child, situated at the
interface of these contestations, emerges as an accomplishment—an accomplishment of human effort and purpose. Success or failure, salvation
or damnation, piety or profaneness, the resultant being derives from
and instantiates a production process, a socially configured production

process, to which women, mothers, and parents generally prove central and indispensable. What makes this refiguration monumental has everything to do with the cosmological and theological significance of the effort. The problem of the child became a problem of the faith such that the nature of deistic intention could be retooled to respond to an increasingly impossible and unacceptable situation whereby infants would be damned outright through no commission or omission of their own. If the babes were to be damned, they were to be damned not by the hand of God alone but by the inadequate effort of mothers and parents. This child, in a sense, was crafted to remake God lean toward benevolence.

A Moral Architecture

The child reworked in the imagined community of the *The Mother's Magazine* and transformed into a new theology by Bushnell did not replace the innocent figure of Romanticism, for it retained the capacity for evil or, at least, for abject non-piety. Nor was this child simply some neutral, halfway stepping stone in a linear transformation from a Puritan conception toward a Locke-Rousseau mix of education and moral primitivism.[109] Historian John Tosh notes the strong formal similarities between Evangelical and Romantic approaches to childhood to the extent children in both conceptions required protection, encircled within the family and home.[110] Competing and differing notions of children and childhood can and do exist more or less side by side in various configurations of thought through long stretches of Western history and philosophy[111] as well as within Protestantism itself as differing "temperaments"[112] and as different conceptualizations of the "child."[113]

In the discourses that circulated among a defined dimension of white, Christian, Evangelical advice-givers and receivers of *The Mother's Magazine*, one finds the ingredients for an attitude and posture of what Sharon Hays would describe as "intensive mothering." Hays placed the origins of this ideology in the post–World War II context, which produced hegemonic expectations on women to engage in emotionally absorbing, child-centered, individualized caretaking. Taking a wider view, intensive maternal responsibility arguably manifests in the demands of and responses to the moral project arising from encounters with an increasingly malleable child.

Liberal Protestant redefinitions of childhood clearly incorporated an inspired sense of early influence over and against a kind of determinism. At the same time, as Bushnell's text seems to indicate, the wholesale acceptance of the innately, completely innocent child of the Romantic imagination was not in the offing. Evil, or perhaps depravity, remained latent as a necessary component of human/child nature. Preserving this potential as constitutive of childhood implicated mothers as more or less culpable for a vast swath of the badness or goodness their children may manifest and, in this way, ensconced motherhood as the keystone to a moral architecture of childhood. It is an architecture that situates mothers' intensive obligations regarding empathic identification in relation to the moral and emotional pliability of the child, holding these in tension with each other and thereby ensuring their co-dependence and perpetual interaction. And it is this architecture, this dynamism of tension, that makes for the base, fundamental elements from which the moral project of the child consumer arises in a later century.

2

Productive Materialities

Making Bourgeois Childhoods through Taste

The malleable, morally educable child of a new liberal Protestantism, as we have seen, was entangled with virtually the same dynamics that produced the "spirit of capitalism" of Max Weber's conception. This child, unlike the contemporaneous child of Romanticism, was construed not as wholly, originally, or naturally innocent, but contained within it a potential for evil even if it was not, in itself, "evil." The Romantic scheme in the nineteenth century attempted (and, in many ways, its remnants today continue to attempt) to return the child to an "Edenic state," as Anne Higonnet puts it—a place unknown to and unattainable by adults.[1] That the Eden of the Old Testament had temptation contained within it—something forbidden and evil—as part of its very constitution often is lost in the invocation of the natural innocence of childhood. Indeed, the impossibility, the distance, of Eden comes to be signified in the late nineteenth century in visual conventions made to depict natural childhood innocence as plants, small animals, and angels—as unthreatening nature[2] but not as humans. The Romantic child had to be transformed into something else, something other than a child, to portray its[3] "natural" state.

It is worth considering, then, as I do in this chapter, how the growing prominence of and increasing attention paid to middle-class childhood in the mid- to late nineteenth century were not clearly matters of bringing an extant, innocent childhood under the protective cover of the home, which then symbolically turned its back on the vicissitudes of the marketplace. Rather, as I argue, writers crafted a version of the middle-class family that turned itself toward goods—toward material objects—as a way of making and locating childhoods, and often particularly girlhoods. Conceptions of and discourses about taste helped mothers in particular regulate the potential dangers of idleness, distraction, or most any sort of pollution arising from the world beyond the home that might compromise social reproduction and, to a much less explicit extent than Evangelical Protestants, spiritual salvation. The ideology of taste progressively formed on the pages of women's periodicals and parenting advice tracts during this time interweaves surveillance, gender construction, pedagogy, aesthetics, and discipline in an effort to navigate confluences among the emerging commercial materialities of an industrial order and appropriate childhoods. The implication here is that the Victorian middle-class "child" arose less in opposition to a rising and dominant marketplace than in interaction with it; in this way, modern childhood—including the "child consumer" and children's commercial culture—stands not as a mutation of or an exception to a pre-capitalist formation of an innocent childhood but manifests as a site of value calibration.

As will be discussed below, mid- to late-century Victorian middle-class concerns with taste—with the child's taste in particular—drew on and wrestled with virtually the same constellation of tensions evident in the struggles with depravity and salvation regarding the Protestant child. Ever-present and ever-looming child malleability imperiled social-faith reproduction and implicated mothers as those responsible not only for the material well-being of children but, more importantly, for their appropriate disposition toward things and the world of things. Both cases, in this sense, worked toward fashioning a similar moral architecture whereby the making of social persons, and of consequent subjectivities, guided the counsel imparted on the pages of periodicals, and is evident in the machinations about dress, food, amusements, and children's rooms discussed below. Taste operated as another way to theorize or otherwise configure the interiority of the child—i.e., to discern the consequences and arrangement of things regarding the making of character and self.

Engaging the Material World

Middle-class Victorians of the mid-nineteenth century understood and lived the push and pull of the particular moral tensions enveloping children, recognizing that the child in their midst—innocent or not— was not so much a ready-made gift as an accomplishment in need of constant renewal through training and education. This sense of malle-ability, growth, and accomplishment rested, unmarked, as a privilege of race, social position, and social class for the audience, actual and implied, of women's periodicals. Situated as an unnamed backdrop, the figure of the poor, often enslaved black child offered an omni-present counterpoint to the problem of malleability faced by elite and middle-class parents. In dominant racist and nationalistic ideologies, non-white, foreign-born people, including those of a "heathen race," were not regularly granted the presumption of the ability to engage in higher learning. "Normal" development, as Nazera Wright shows in her history of nineteenth-century black girlhood, was neither casual nor natural and had to be motivated by either harsh circumstance or dedi-cated Biblical tutoring.[4]

Here, the world of material objects and commercial goods constituted an arena where questions of who children are and what they should and should not be—as gendered, raced, and classed beings—came into play on an everyday basis: in the materiality of the home, in personal display, and in the practices of living such as eating, learning, and playing. It was a world undergoing transformation. The meaning and nature of "things" changed, according to Leora Auslander, during the transition from mer-cantile to industrial then to consumer capitalism, from being "relatively static symbols around which hierarchies were ordered to being more directly constitutive of class, social status, and personal identity."[5] Old, inherited objects no longer stood as the unambiguous signs of inter-generational wealth they once did for this class fraction, in part due to the mass manufacture of goods and to the class ascension of some that was made possible by new sources of wealth during industrialization.[6] The various kinds of "democratization" brought on by a new economic and material order during this time implicated children strongly and directly as the harbingers and carriers of potentially new forms of social difference.[7] Childhood, for some, became the site of social prospectivity, rather than only an anchor of tradition or a timeless container for the struggles of good and evil. Indeed, some childhoods may have incorpo-rated all of these.[8] To be sure, the varied public renderings of ideal, sym-bolic childhoods—visually, literarily—expressed an array of personae offering shared and shareable renderings of how both the meanings of things and of childhood were in flux.[9]

In this context, it is often emphasized, the Victorian home folded in on itself in its retreat from a world of incessant industry, progress, and monetary measures of value. In place of that world, women commandeered the production of family life, combining sentiment and "economy" (the contemporaneous word for thrift) in the creation of the private world of the home—a world marked by emotional bonds, obligations of gift-giving, and the celebration of domestic ritual.[10] Here, in this physical and moral space, the non-laboring child was sequestered, it is thought, from the polluting influences of commerce, and sheltered from the "cash nexus" of the generic marketplace, residing in a "haven in a heartless world."[11] Late-Victorian parents, argues Gary Cross, "could escape the outside world of economic calculation when they showered their children with gifts."[12] Nissenbaum, in his celebrated history of Christmas in America (1620–1900), points out how the holiday—as it was being domesticated from a rowdy, public, carnivalesque, and working-class based celebration—assisted in the creation of a gift economy alongside the monetary exchange characteristic of a rising market economy.[13] The figure of Santa Claus, he argues, came to stand as an anti-commercial icon that allowed many families to enter the world of commercial consumption by reconciling oppositions between market and sentiment.[14]

The social locational origins of something resembling the contemporary child consumer most assuredly have significant roots in the Anglo-European middle-class feminine sphere of the private home of the nineteenth century. One would be hard pressed, however, to locate depictions and discussions of children and childhood in the middle-class, public culture of the mid- to late nineteenth century where the child stands in singular, stark opposition to—or is thought intensely threatened by—everyday consumer items or practices. To be sure, ideologies of gendered domesticity urged women to make home a "haven" for working *men* who, on a daily basis, had to deal with the "corrosive" atmosphere of market life.[15] But the idea of the "market"[16] from which the home was to serve as a refuge did not yet commonly extend to include what would later become recognized as consumer practice. When one finds concerns expressed about children's "consumption," they often referred to issues of the quality of the goods in question and to the place of material life in relation to spiritual life, and not to the child's interface with the market sphere itself. Marketplace enactments and engagements—such as acquiring and displaying finery and furnishings, giving gifts, and generally making a home—largely fell outside what was considered to be the core, toxic essence of the money economy: instrumental self-interest. Women of the emerging bourgeoisie were thought to consume and display only as representatives of their families.[17] Consumption could be carried out "properly" by "proper" people for "proper" ends. The wild and boisterous consumption of the "lower classes," crystallized in rituals such as wassailing around Christmastime in mid- to late-nineteenth-century Britain and New England,[18] put into stark relief the received, domestic forms of consumption and celebration of the elite and middling classes.

Taste, for these classes, provided a crucial avenue for the incorporation not simply of material things but also of materialist values into the economy of the family as a cosmology of the self. Indeed, when bound in sentiment and performed with decided moral purpose and direction, material life could serve as a kind of uplift—personally, spiritually, and in terms of class standing—and thus could work to buffer various sorts of "incursions" into the home and family. Hence, it becomes evident that concentrated effort was expended on the pages of periodicals for women, especially *Godey's Lady's Book* (1830–1878), to render these children and these childhoods confluent with the world of goods. In so doing, they sought confluence also with the social relations into which they were born and toward which they were projected to be headed—a convergence, that is, of a racialized class temperament toward things through the display and ownership of things.

Discourses of taste—of inculcating, discovering, or facilitating children's taste—operated to help produce particular notions of childhood through domestic materialities. For, in this context, children did not represent a withdrawal from things and from the value of things. Rather, white, privileged childhood confronted mothers as an unavoidable site for studied, purposeful engagement with the material world and, in the process, a cultural-moral locale for theorizing interiority. The thrust of this situated middle-class ethos and practice hence sought reconciliation of a different sort—not just between sentiment and calculation, but between object and character.

As many attest, the middle-class Victorian home was awash both in newly made commodities and in inherited goods, garnering much of its social cachet through the conspicuous display and waste that

Thorstein Veblen[19] would instantiate as the hallmark of the leisure class a few decades later. "Victorian ladies" served as the readership for the first consumer periodicals and as the initial, robust customer base of the emergent and transformative retail institution of the department store[20] toward century's end, particularly in the US, England, and France. Rather than a retreat, many apprehended the world of goods as an inescapable environment in which the self or character would dwell and develop, as well as a site for the expression of class and national identities.[21] Yet, efforts concentrating on creating a private domesticity were often also attempts at exercising some measure of control over children's material-moral socialization. The "pious consumption" of Victorian households that Lori Merish analyzed (discussed in chapter 1) addressed the role of taste in the creation of a female consumer subjectivity.[22] She, as earlier noted, de-emphasizes, and often ignores, women's roles/identities *as mothers* and, in so doing, largely presumes the place of children in relation to the meaning of things. As well, Brown's notion of "domestic individualism" speaks to varying and emergent forms of selfhood of women who were traversing the spaces between home and market, but does not engage with the presence and consequences of children, thereby leaving motherhood virtually unexplored.[23] Similarly, deGrazia[24] and Auslander[25] sidestep the place and presence of children in these dynamics, often enfolding them into the "family."

Children needed to manifest taste, too. Their untutored presence and indiscrimination of objects and practices both challenged and problematized any notion of taste as being innate, inherited, and self-evident. White, middle-class, and largely urban-dwelling children of the US Northeast were made not so much to be innocent of the world of goods, which were necessary to their social becomings, as to be sheltered from the world of labor (though not from household tasks and everyday "industry"). Much of the "sheltering" that was enacted manifested as a default sheltering from socially undesirable others like laborers, "unwashed" immigrants, and people of color.[26]

In the coming pages, I follow some threads of public discourse offered by women regarding taste, childhood, and motherhood over the mid- to late-nineteenth-century middle class, bringing to light how malleability and concerns about desire combine to align childhood with material life and, in the process, form an indispensable dimension of the moral project of childhood

Figure 2.1. Sarah Josepha Hale (1788–1879) merged her *Ladies' Magazine* (1827–1836) with Louis Godey's *Ladies' Book and Magazine* to become editor of *Godey's Lady's Book* for four decades, 1837–1877.

and of the child consumer. In particular, I examine taste and its implications in a number of national and local periodicals, chief among which is *Godey's Lady's Book*. Established in 1830 in Philadelphia by Louis A. Godey, whose parents had fled France in the wake of the 1792 revolution, the periodical sought to capture a rising female market for luxury goods, ultimately becoming the organ and premiere periodical of and for a rising middle-class fraction of white, free, urban woman and mothers. In 1837, Godey brought in Sarah Hale, a novelist and pioneer in women's magazines in her own right, as literary editor (see figure 2.1). Godey and Hale, according to historian Elizabeth White Nelson, understood that the female readership of the time not only needed to be made aware of the available goods, styles, and practices appropriate to their social standing, but had to be educated to these ideals as well.[27] As will be demonstrated below, the conception of the "lady" addressed in the pages of the periodical regularly and increasingly included mothers in the pursuit of a moral project of childhood.

The insights hopefully gained from the readings and analyses to come position children, childhood, and the "child" not as appendages to women and their domestic roles and practices but as positively constitutive and figurative of them.

Epistemologies and Pedagogies of Taste: Childhood and Domestic Materialities

Pierre Bourdieu conceptualized taste in terms of, among other things, deeply learned—one might say internalized—dispositions that enabled the selective acquisition and deployment of knowledge about cultural goods and practices which, in turn allowed one to inhabit particular social spaces through acts of social distinction.[28] He, like others, never attempted a theorization of children or of childhood, leaving any focused consideration of the transmission of dispositions—of the generative elements of the habitus—to a presumptive set of reproductive mechanisms.[29] Consequently, his scheme of social reproduction rests precariously on a simple, transparent, and unconsidered notion that culture is, in some deep sense, rather unproblematically transmitted through child-rearing. Yet his famous dictum that "taste classifies, and it classifies the classifier"[30] finds both substantive support and conceptual relevance in nineteenth-century Victorian discourses regarding children and childhood. For Bourdieu, taste materializes not simply in the particular objects one has or in their display, but in the practice of making distinction itself: "Social subjects, classified by their classifications, distinguish themselves by the distinctions they make, between the beautiful and the ugly, the distinguished and the vulgar, in which their position in the objective classifications is expressed or betrayed."[31]

For many middle-class Victorians, matters of taste sat at the core of everyday life. Emergent concerns of mid-century parents and pedagogues regarding the place and processes of education, early learning, and play in many ways become expressed not simply through the things themselves but a moral ordering of things. The idea that the child herself would become ordered—i.e., that her life trajectory could be adjusted and retuned—in conversation with the material world around her drew upon and referenced a Protestant proclivity to seek congruence between internal and external life. One writer in *The Mother's Magazine* put the matter in this way, referring to the natural world, in 1845:

> It may be thought by many that a child is not capable of admiring the beautiful or sublime; but God has made a world without, and a world within, to correspond. He has not spread out before us this magnificent creation, without giving us a capability of admiring and appreciating it.[32]

It is the task of the mother to teach and motivate this sought-after correspondence between internal and external early and often in the child's life, not for the sake of correspondence alone, but to enable a life of happiness—something which the "heathen" cannot know because they have not been taught to appreciate God's creation.[33] As "no impression, how trifling, is lost" and when "a look or a word may leave an impress which time will never wear away,"[34] a pedagogy in and of distinction seems as necessary as that of education in literacy or Biblical verse.

Skirmishes rage on at the juncture where the internal and external intersect—the space also where malleability, specifically the malleable child, resides. For many conservative, Evangelical Protestants, the gateway between the "world without" and the "world within" demanded resolute attention as it represented the site where life pathways—seemingly irreversible—become forged. In this view, it was not so much any singular act of sin or identifiable moment of pollution that would prove to be consequential for the child's pathway; rather, as we have seen, concerns centered on how the personal example of mothers and caregivers, and the material surrounds of the home, would figure in crafting a child's overall disposition. These were understood as essential to undergirding a child's lasting temperament toward the world and toward the things in this world, which could be consequential to the next: "We do not know and cannot know, to how great an extent we are indebted in after life to the influences about our childhood's home."[35]

It is here, at the level of disposition and temperament—and thus in the register of "taste"—where I see significant isomorphism between the posture of religious Protestantism toward the malleable child and that of emergent Victorian middle-class views toward the production of subjectivity. In published works on housewifery and domestic education and in the local and national women's periodicals of the mid- to late century, invocations of taste as regards children were cast broadly across age ranges and genders, making for some variation in meaning and use of the concept across texts and contexts of discussion. In 1831, *Godey's Lady's Book* reprinted a tract from *The Mirror of Graces*, a "treatise" on "female attire" written by "a Lady of Distinction" originally published in 1811 and directed toward a British/European readership. In the excerpt quoted, one was instructed that "taste requires a congruity between the internal character and the external appearance and the imagination will involuntarily form to itself an idea of such a correspondence."[36] These words, apparently oft-repeated at the time, were taken from a 1790 *New York Magazine* article penned by Vicesimus Knox, a British moral philosopher of the eighteenth century.[37] They reasserted a dominant view of the day (at least among the leisured and well-to-do classes of Europe), which put the "inside" and "outside" in communication with one another. In Knox's formulation, inside and outside not only should correspond, but will be made to correspond in the mind of an observer. Hence, appearance—the "outside"—must be attended to so as to give a true reflection of the "inside," or character.

Note that the desired congruity between internal and external is something sought after, something of an aspiration, rather than a given. This dictum of taste enunciates, in essence, a semiotics whereby signifier (appearance) and signified (character) combine to form a singular sign, into which the "imagination" will make a correspondence. That is, one's character will be read off one's appearance by observers, some of whom will take the sign as a true, transparent indication of character. The coordination between character and appearance presents itself not as a static state of affairs but as a project to be engaged in by women for themselves and as an aspect of "education," especially for girls, who are emerging into womanhood and who therefore must learn "the true state of the world with which they are to mingle."[38] It is a world where women's bodies serve as signs of their class position and sexuality and as a prospectively imagined place for girls in a system of gender capital.[39]

This epistemology of taste—which, in many ways, continues today in some form through the dynamics of commodity aesthetics[40]—enables manipulation of its elements and is therefore both admired and abhorred. One can become fixated on the externalities of appearance in the hope of hoodwinking the observer into accepting these as indicative of a deep, true aspect of self or, alternatively, in the hope of being transformed internally by the reactions to the performances and displays of observers. In the case of the latter—i.e., that things also in some sense produce the person or character—the goods themselves become agents of sorts, a hallmark of contemporary actor-network theory.[41]

The Victorian domestic sensibility of surrounding oneself with fine materials extended beyond matters of public display and the performance of proper femininity and domestic sentiment;[42] these also were to act on one's character as well as that of family members. Goods and materials, rather than being external to or an invasion of home life, sat squarely in the production of selves, relationships, generational trajectories, and gendered imaginings.[43] The slippages of interpretation afforded by the polysemy of signs inserted issues of taste into the everyday considerations of child-rearing and household management. The uncertainty expressed above about the effect of "influences" on a child addressed something more than an outcome, be it this-worldly or otherworldly, as important as they are; it also acknowledged an inability to know which acts or objects matter most to the bearing of the pathway under construction. Prayer, a pious household, and Christian example seemed insufficient in and of themselves. In a system or set of arrangements whereby appearance can convey multiple meanings, where things can act as well as indicate, home commodities and home consumption served as a training ground of sorts in the art of value calculation and moral calibration.

A malleable, educable child encountering the conceptual vagaries and social hazards of taste required attention by mothers whose own character, as one writer put it in 1831, is revealed by "the internal appearance of her house, and the dress and manners of her children."[44] The writer continues: "If her children, notwithstanding the fashion or richness of their clothes, are dirty, or carelessly dressed—if their minds are uncultivated, and their manners rude, the mother will most generally prove to be both ignorant and indolent, or which is worse, wholly indifferent to the wellbeing of her children."[45] Care for well-being arises as attention to the elements of taste: "In the dress of her children, she unites simplicity with taste, and attends at once to the improvement of their minds, and the cultivation of those graces which, in a greater or less degree, according to their respective stations in life, will recommend them to society."[46] Taste, here, not only classifies—and classifies the classifier—it also educates. A child can be, in a sense, delivered over to the collective gaze and judgment of social class scrutiny—of "society," as it was often called—whereby the parties, promenades, and appearances at church all occasion an opportunity for display and "recommendation." Note how the author takes pains, in the latter passage above, to universalize the underlying logic of good taste as something untethered to monetary wealth.

"Good" taste, as many would insist, exists in a realm beyond the material conditions of existence—beyond the ownership of this or that dress, this or that table—and, theoretically, could be possessed by anyone, wealthy or unwealthy, adult or child. Always plagued by contradictions, as Auslander points out, taste can be both innate and learned, self-evident and mysterious.[47] At once the key to character and an expression of it, good taste resides not in the things themselves but in their arrangement, their suitability, and their simplicity—all characteristics of beauty. Yet the beauty of taste cannot exist completely apart from the materiality and industry of the world, which would increasingly threaten "pure" taste with vulgarity. Lydia Sigourney (see figure 2.2.), a noted poet of her day, writes in *Godey's* in 1840 that taste, when "combined with a vivid imagination . . . colours like a passion-tint, the whole of existence; and if surrounding scenes are devoid of its favourite objects, peoples for itself, a world of ideal beauty."[48] Such imaginative capacity, she notes, is also a companion of good moral character and mental health. The ability to "see" the beauty of the world beyond its physical objects, interestingly enough, becomes an argument for the accumulation of things:

> Assuming therefore, that a pure taste, is one of the tests of a healthful moral condition, we shall prize it, not only as a source of pleasure, but as an adjunct to virtue, an ally of religion. Shall we not then, seek to multiply the objects, which it is legitimate to admire? Shall we not familiarize our children, with the harmony of colour, the melody of sound, the symmetry of architecture, the delights of eloquence, and the charms of poetry? The fragrant flower, the whitening harvest, the umbrageous grove, the solemn mountain, the mighty cataract, are they not all teachers? or text-books, in the hand of the Great Teacher?[49]

Figure 2.2. Lydia Sigourney (1791–1865), poet and writer, penned advice for mothers and concerned herself with the education of women, including in *Godey's Lady's Book*. Source: *Godey's Lady's Book*, June 1838, last page.

"Legitimate objects," so construed, can be put to the service of instructing children about the intangible virtues of the world, their acquisition thus made acceptable as kind of educational supplement. Indeed, most any thing can be seen as providing instruction in beauty and intelligence—a notion presaging Matthew Arnold's explications of the "sweetness and light" of "good culture" by about three decades.[50] In this way, having or desiring things is not, in itself, antithetical to good taste or good mothering. Taste—a "pure taste"—is revelatory in its moral propinquity to virtue and religion. Taste, in fact, counters the "avarice of Mammon" as well as the vulgarity of relentless progress with, as Sigourney puts it, its railroad machinery, political ambition, and steamboats "rushing to the thousand marts of wealth."[51] Here, one encounters something of an anticommercial rhetoric enfolded into the celebration of domestic materiality—not a turn away from objects but a sensibility about discerning appropriate things.[52]

Mrs. Sigourney articulates an emergent sense of what I call the "soft pedagogy of things,"[53] a cover term for a variety of beliefs and expressions that objects can and do impart lessons by and through their very materiality. The idea that things teach, or can teach, I suspect exists in some form in many social worlds throughout culture and history. The severe distinction between subject and object, as Daniel Miller discusses, tends to be one imposed by researchers and observers who, upon attentive inquiry, often find it not to be operative for many as a strict dichotomy.[54] The notion of a pedagogy of things, it seems, courts a particular resonance in and for the world of the middle classes of this Victorian era as the cultural coordinates of material-economic life continued to shift, making for semantic disruptions that spread beyond particular objects and into configurations of being and becoming (see the discussion of children's rooms below). With the proliferation of objects in an industrializing society and shop-oriented social world, the ability to be cognizant of and drawn to the correct and beautiful ones does not necessarily come easily or even wholly naturally, especially for influenceable children whose taste is not yet developed or refined or for mothers whose every choice and non-choice portended irreversible "influence."

Indulgence represents one threat to taste, vanity another. Mothers, it seems, are susceptible to both, according to one writer, as they tend to acquiesce to the "whim" of children's desires in an effort give pleasure in the moment. Such indulgence never opens the "moral sources of enjoyment" to them, leaving them in their later years with "fragile health . . . dissatisfied temper . . . peevish indifference . . . [and] revolting selfishness."[55] The misplaced, well-intentioned desire to make a "happy childhood" results in unhappy consequences over the life course. That it is parents who can commit the "sin" of indulgence onto their children manifests in pleas for simplicity in children's dress, where lavishness of child adornment is thought to forge a path to vanity and undue self-consciousness (see chapter 4).[56] One writer explicates a kind of "zero sum" notion of children's taste capacity and the cascading consequences for girls and their unfolding womanhood. Addressing mothers, the unidentified author instructs them that childhood has its "natural graces" and that "you" should never "overload with adornment," which not only subtracts from the visual, artful display of taste, but incurs a price as well. When over-adorning children, she writes, "you disfigure the pure tablet of the child's mind, by writing upon it, in line upon line, 'vanity and vexation of spirit.' There is small room for anything else."[57] Poor taste—here in the guise of indulgence and vanity—it seems, crowds out other lessons, other influences; it arrives and manifests as pollution.[58]

Dis-taste materializes, not simply in the articles of dress, but in the wrong colors, the inappropriate bows and strings, the needless details that make children—particularly girls—excessively mindful of their external appearance. Other children and adults alike reinforce sartorial preoccupation by calling attention to dress and finery whenever possible. Without the ability to sort the correct from the incorrect, when the young lady "comes into the world," she apparently is doomed to repeat her fate:

> Is it strange that her brain is filled with French fashions and jewelry, and her heart a "moving toy-shop?" She marries; and what hope but in having wealth to gratify her love of dress—what aim beyond excelling in her fashions of attire will she naturally consider important to her happiness? Will she not train her own children, should she become a excellencies of character and that knowledge of useful household accomplishments which are indispensable to the enjoyment and improvement of domestic life?[59]

Boys, she continues, unlike girls, can shake off "the shackles of finery that foolish mothers impose upon their infant sons."[60] The danger in cultivating lifelong vanity lies in the fear of creating an intergenerational chain of women without a proper sense of taste and without a proper, reserved attitude toward the nature and meaning of things and their display. Attention to apparel should matter only to the extent that it is an "outward sign of an indwelling spirit" and should never distract mothers from attending to "foundations of Christian virtues" whereon the future character of the nation rests.[61]

Indulgence weakens the nation by weakening the middle-class child with short-sightedness about the importance of immediate appearance and desire. One writer quotes from Lady Morgan's (1829) tracts, which instruct that the perfection of motherhood lies in the qualities of a good citizen—in an abnegation that "lays every selfish consideration at the feet of duty."[62] Some of the presumed maternal selfishness arises from the mother's weakness to resist the temptations of the market-place of fashions. A mother's vanity can be for herself or can be the result of her "natural" sense that her daughter is pretty and so she must show her off to others.[63] The ability to instruct a correct balance between appearance and character served the requirements of class through taste, those of citizenship through selflessness, and those of religion through self-control. As models and embodiments of these virtues, the vectors of discipline intersected at mothers' bosoms with the governance of appetite, theirs and their children's, being the guiding mode and motivation.

Surrounding children with correct, beautiful things—often in appropriate quantity and accompanied by the proper attitude—here functions as a kind of prophylaxis against the seemingly inevitable incursion of the vulgar, the overwrought and the extravagant, which surely will arise in their world. In the context of the white, bourgeois childhoods at issue in forums like *Godey's*, taste arises as something prospectively oriented as a kind of ontological forecasting of the child's disposition in the service of both personal happiness and cultural reproduction, rather than mainly a retrospective sign of lineage and heritage. It becomes something to be inculcated as anticipatory defense, as is all education at some level. The increasing availability of goods of all sorts and the specter of the untutored, untrained tastes of immigrants and those of the underclasses generally[64] appear not only as external threats in and of themselves. When placed astride the conception of the young child as an influenceable being whose appetite must be trained, the outlines of the moral project of childhood comes into focus as one that grapples with the problem of appetite, desire, and attitudes toward things and their meanings.

Malleability and, indeed, innocence cut many ways—as portals for the "good" and also as opportunities for pollution of all kinds—but the solution, the response, was not the formation of a clear, unmitigated opposition between child and object, between childhood and material goods, between sentimental value and market value. The response, rather, incorporated the ethos of taste into the exigencies of malleability of childhood so construed. Taste, in these discourses, operated as pedagogy in an evaluative register configured to engage with the world, not as a retreat from it. At this point and in these contexts these women held fast to a confidence in the power of sentiment, of domestic culture and of maternal and family influence[65] to handle or otherwise deflect "external," polluting incursions.

It was not the goods themselves or their potential market origins in and of themselves that constituted an immediate danger to childhood at the onset of a culture of consumption, but rather how the goods or products—and attendant desires and appetites—were to be handled. The world for these and other Victorians was organized in and through goods and objects that served as counterpoints, as external measures or signs, and so were not so much to be shunned as to be sorted, organized, and put into proper relation to each other. With a gradual acceptance of industrial, market life by liberal Protestants as a kind of "secular religion of progress," as Herbert Spencer put it,[66] taste offered a vital link that helped manage a changing commercial-symbolic-material landscape alongside the promises, threats, and uncertainties posed by the malleable child to social reproduction. In this way, it formed a key term in what today is referred to as "parenting" for mid- to late-century Victorian middle-class mothers to the extent that it served to organize narratives of becoming—becoming a proper adult and, for girls, becoming a desirable mate, good housekeeper and, eventually, mother. When viewed through the lens of childhood or parenthood, taste enacts its morality prospectively as a form of training; it is not something necessarily to be mastered in the here-and-now, but an ongoing project (see Figure 2.3).

In 1832, the domestic economist Lydia Child remarked how "neatness, tastefulness and good sense" can be demonstrated through good household management, that "ingenuity and economy" can serve as an antidote to "excessive concern about appearance and finery," and that children can be taught avarice.[67] The uses of amusement and ornament were always to be subservient to the larger effort to form character. Catherine Beecher, in her widely read *Treatise on Domestic Economy* (1841), sought to advise housewives on the proper focus of attention of their duties: "Every woman, then, when employing her hands, in ornamenting her person, her children, or her house, ought to calculate, whether she has devoted as much time, to the intellectual and moral wants of herself and others."[68] The "object of life," she continues, "is not to secure the various gratifications of appetite or taste, but to form such a character, for ourselves and others, as will secure the greatest amount of present

Figure 2.3. Young children, especially girls, were thought to be "taught" by the externalities of "taste," which could reflect, or even shape, internal character and disposition. Source: *Godey's Lady's Book*, September 1855, CII.

and future happiness."[69] Acquiring "handsome" furniture, clothes, and a "variety of tempting food" is a secondary pursuit to be subordinated to the duty, here particularly a parental duty, to aid in developing "social, intellectual and moral nature."[70]

Manufactured goods did not in themselves threaten innocence; they threatened taste to the extent that they enabled and encouraged extravagance. That is, they threatened to disrupt the mechanisms calibrating the value relation between character and appearance, between subject and object. Taste—the discourse of taste—in its polysemous variants

Figure 2.4. Taste, many insisted, could be cultivated regardless of financial circumstance, although the depiction of white, free, well-to-do children and families expressed a particular, ideal disposition. Source: *Godey's Lady's Book*, July 1855, CII.

functioned as an orienting and regulatory apparatus giving indication of how to sort the proper from the improper, the good from the bad, and, in the same instance, instantiating the imperative that such distinctions be made (see figure 2.4). The insistence that "people of the best standing and taste never follow [the] excesses" of overdressing their children[71] turns on itself as self-evident cultural tautology that, in a contradictory way, must be stated to be rendered not so self-evident.

The classificatory work accomplished by taste, emphasized by Bourdieu, blends with the disciplinary injunction that one's enactments of taste be surveilled, noted, compared to others' and, as Michel Foucault instructs, judged against a normative ideal. Discipline and governance, like taste, begin with the parent.[72] Note the parallelism of the injunction below about parental discipline from *The Mother's Magazine* in 1837 with the discussion above on training in taste:

> The parent must possess unwearied patience, and a never-tiring interest in the welfare of the child; but particularly must he learn to discipline himself, and to subdue his own selfish feelings and desires, his love of ease and self-indulgence, if he will either instruct or discipline his child. And here it may be remarked that the proper training of children not

only includes instructing them in those things that are necessary for their conduct in this life, and the knowledge of a future, but also in carrying forward that system of discipline which is absolutely necessary to curb the natural propensities of the human heart, and fit the mind for that subjection to the Gospel of Christ without which it cannot be a partaker of eternal blessings. Few parents are aware how much they prevent the Gospel having its full influence on the hearts of their children, by not forming in them habits of obedience.[73]

Self-governance, a hallmark of Calvinist Protestantism as Steven Mintz notes,[74] is the first step in fabricating a proper, lifelong, and consequential conduct aimed at curbing the "natural propensities of the human heart." The consequences of taste, for some, were no different and constituted essential components of discipline. What is "natural" is inferred from and imputed to the child; so too are the devastating consequences of failing to provide timely and proper governance in these matters: neither God nor good taste, apparently, can enter a child's "heart" if crowded out by unchecked impulse or bad example.

In a particularly virulent tract in 1845 on "moral poisons," "FCW" (thought to be perhaps Francis C. Woodworth, editor of the *Woodworth's Youth Cabinet* periodical for children), draws a heavy line between taste and fashion, which are "often at antipodes" with the latter lacking in "moral principle"[75]

> Fashion is subject to the whims and caprices of men and women not under the influence of moral principle. It is unstable as water, and fitful as the wind. Taste, though arbitrary in some of its details, is, in its essential elements, governed by fixed principles and accords with the immutable laws of mind. Fashion may harmonize with morality and religion, or it may not. Taste has no affinity for vice, and coalesces with nothing so well as with the religion of the cross.[76]

Taste, true taste, manifests an isomorphism with the "religion of the cross." Both are immutable and not subject to the whims of the fleeting externalities of day. "Parents," unsurprisingly, must "labor" to craft correct literary taste,[77] just as the implied "she" needs to endeavor to produce a proper relationship between the internal and external.

"Parents"—again, more likely, mothers—themselves, however, can confuse securing the cooperation of their children via bribery with gaining their obedience (also see chapter 4), as this *Godey's* writer proclaims:

> Regard, for instance, the children of those fond and indulgent parents who seem to forget that there are any other claims upon them than those of parental love. Look into the nursery strewed with fragments of costly toys, remnants of the whim of yesterday; observe the varied appliances which nurture them into feebleness, the delicate food which pampers diseased appetite, the rich attire which awakens selfish vanity, and the unlimited devotion to their caprices which governs the whole household. Every day brings a new pleasure, something is constantly in prospect for their gratification, and the time, the wealth and the talents of those fond parents are lavished to confer happiness upon their idols.[78]

Another writer warns parents that "there is much danger, from an amiable wish to gratify a child, of counter-ordering your own orders."[79] Anxieties about failure to train children properly extend beyond mothers to include teachers, nurses, and servants whose main concern is pleasing the child to make their job easier—all the more reason, according to one author, to educate children early, prune bad habits, and bend the sapling the right way before handing them over to others.[80] Materiality, desire, and the dangers of indulgence intersect with discourses and practices of child punishment, as discussed in the next chapter.

The cultivating of taste as a discipline against "whim"—i.e., indulgence represented by fashion—here stands as the stitching of a seam joining the virtues of religious injunction with the material, sensual life of the world. If rich attire "awakens" vanity, and delicate food pampers an already "diseased" appetite, as in the passage above, then the implication is that these conditions are extant or latent in the child, activated by indulgence through commissions of gratification and omissions of denial. This configuration resembles that of Horace Bushnell's conception, where good and evil lie dormant within each child until some force takes hold of one or the other. Interestingly, innocence here manifests not as a separation from or flight from the world, as Gary Cross discusses regarding late-nineteenth-century views (although that aspect of it surely is ascendant), but as an initial (and perhaps naïve) openness to all the world—to the "natural propensities of the human heart," as the Calvinist quoted above put it.[81]

Room for Children[82]

These period writings seek integration between the malleable child and the realm of mothers, both intimately tied to the material world through issues of discipline and desire. What is not so evident—either in the Calvin-esque views presented in the last chapter or in the writings by women in this chapter—is any strong indication that either the market origin of things or particular kinds of goods, in themselves, necessarily contain or portend moral pollution for children. Indeed, the world represents an incessant source of new desires and temptations where, as one author said, something is "constantly in prospect for their [children's] gratification."[83] Properly cultivated taste ultimately enables the child to filter the fit from the unfit. In large part, children's moral trajectory and fortitude derives from their engagement with material goods through the trope of taste. To the extent that "taste," in this way, favored a certain morally ascetic attitude toward material things—i.e., things were to be subservient to character—it also allowed and encouraged a lurch in the direction of a kind of hedonism. That is, if the proper attitude is cultivated, as one writer above put it, then there is nothing wrong with surrounding oneself and one's children with many such things. Indeed, as the author above presented the matter, the child, rather than the world, is the project and becomes a proper subject through that world.

Proper things, in fact, can themselves educate. They can carry the lessons of taste long past the moments of specific instruction. In so doing, objects and materials can serve socialization roles and functions as children grow toward maturity. Over the course of latter third of the nineteenth century and into the twentieth, the question of how and whether to accommodate a separate children's room or rooms in both urban and rural households in US contexts arose with increasing frequency; consequently, the "child's room" serves as an opportune site for investigating material socialization. Problems of gender and décor and questions about the extent to which children should be allowed to decide the contents of their rooms organized much of the public discussion around "children's rooms" (here the "children" appear often to be in their early to mid-teenage years).

The details of decoration, of the contents and, importantly, of their arrangement turned several functions, including both a training in and a revealing of class-infused notions of taste and character. Taste and social class took distinctly gendered forms. The gendering of rooms at this time and in these depictions arises less as a matter of content—e.g., color or decoration—and more as a differentiated disposition toward things and the order of things. For boys, their rooms were said to provide an opportunity for them to appreciate and care for things that they may otherwise lack. One writer in the *Ohio Farmer* in 1875, reprinted from *Scribner's* (a national magazine), relates a story of how some boys "claimed" an old loft over the farm's woodhouse, offering the view that parents should give "over to boys as soon as they turn 12–14 a room, not a sleeping chamber, which they will take reasonable care."[84] It should be decorated and furnished plainly "according to the boys' own fancy; if the taste is bad, they will be interested after a while in correcting it."[85] Parents and sisters should refrain from entering the room except "as guests."

A narrative of the favored daughter–neglected son arose repeatedly during this period.[86] It attempted to correct the gender presumption of female curation of family and class taste by allowing boys into the word of aesthetics and material appreciation. Writers challenged the belief that boys are "naturally" inclined against attending to things domestic. A September 1881 opinion from a reader in the *Ohio Farmer* called for "fair play" when it comes to boys' rooms.[87] The author made the case that although boys are neglected and dismissed as "careless" and as "only boys," the way to teach them to be "neat and particular" is to allow them their own rooms. Boys "of course" are "naturally careless," the writer continues, but this makes sense when they have only a "forlorn quilt." Compromises could be made, as it is not practicable to keep white spreads on the bed on a farm, but "it is reasonable at least to have neat whole furniture carpets, curtains, mirror, combs and brushes so the boys will feel somewhat civilized, and look so too."[88] Here, as elsewhere, the kinds of things that surround a child are made to be consequential to the fabrication of their character.

The faith in the self-correcting nature of "taste" expressed here recurs throughout these writings during this period and can be found inform-ing prescriptions for both girls and boys, albeit usually in a different register for each. For girls of this age, according to one writer, rooms and their decoration serve as expressions of an inner character, a no-tion in line with an ethos of materiality described above. Rooms inform whether the girl is "neat or unneat," "orderly or disorderly" and give a sense of her "disposition" as "sunny or gloomy."[89] The care of these rooms and the sense of taste, beauty, and disposition they reveal, the writer continues, does not come from the amount of money one spends for furnishings and decorations. Indeed, it is at this age—still living at home with her parents—when a girl will expect to come to have a "new standard of values in the matter of spending money, as soon as she be-gins to want to buy things to make rooms pretty."[90] The enemy in this scenario is ugliness born of an untrained or unmotivated sense of beauty and aesthetic "fit." The writer pleads: "No! It is not a question of money; it is a question of taste; it is a question of choosing between good and beautiful things which last for years, and do you good every hour of every day, as often as you look at them, and things which are gone in an hour or a few days, and even for the few days or the hours do harm rather than good."[91]

Monetary cost is raised, it seems, as if to dismiss it as irrelevant to the ability to make a place beautiful. The existence of the room itself teaches about responsibility and taste, but it also reveals character, which is supposedly independent of wealth or financial standing. From an 1891 article in *Harper's Bazaar*: "A young girl's room may be as full of costly articles as wealth can make it, or it may be the result of taste and ingenu-ity with but trifling expense, but the one who looks on it can, if choosing to take the pains to do so, tell at once the character of the occupant by the mere arrangement or disarrangement of the place."[92] The gaze of the judgmental observer troubles this discourse and coaxes the female reader into the self-same critical perspective—toward her daughter and thus toward herself. The intended reader for this advice surely is not the girl herself but her mother, the housewife, who is told, in effect, that one cannot buy one's way out of bad taste or inferior character and that such flaws are on display as conspicuously as an imperfectly hidden blemish on one's face. The room is to be for the girl, but it will never be only hers,

Figure 2.5. Illustrations of girls' rooms submitted for a *Ladies' Home Journal* sponsored prize competition. Source: *Ladies' Home Journal*, February 1903, 26–27 [two-page spread].

as it reveals something much wider than individual preference. By the early twentieth century, the character of middle-class, presumably white girls' rooms rose to the level of advice features and competitions sponsored by women's magazines (see figures 2.5 and 2.6).

The lessons thus imparted by things derive not simply from the things themselves—the wallpaper, the furniture, the carpet, etc.—but significantly from their placement in relation to one another. A writer in *Arthur's Home Magazine*, acclaiming the girls' room to be "her little kingdom where she reigns supreme," notes that the room tells the "story" of a girl's character and perhaps gives "a stronger clue" of "its occupant than in the study of her handwriting."[93]

The syntax of this "story" again locates girls' character, taste, and class standing not in the amount of money spent but in the arrangement of things:

Let the furniture be the most costly and luxurious that can be purchased, or consist only of the most meagre requirements of the bedroom, the owner's individuality is there, and something of her character is stamped upon what those four walls enclose . . . but the girl who can make her room expressive of the harmony in her life, which recognizes that order and neatness must go hand-in-hand with artistic grace and beauty, will have invested it with a charm which is not dependent on the actual furniture and fittings.[94]

This writer makes explicit for girls that which is implied in similar tracts for boys' and younger children's rooms of this time—and which stands as a key presumption of material life for the mid- to late-century Victorian middle class—namely, that rooms and their making are integral to a training in taste through a soft pedagogy of appropriate things and of their proper arrangement.

Conclusion

The Victorian middle-class home of the mid-nineteenth century could not and did not shelter itself in toto from the machinations of the capitalist economy and, in many ways, did not attempt to do so. The trick of taste and materiality resides in their duality—that they behave like

AN ARTISTIC STUDY IN BLUE AND GREEN.

Figure 2.6. An artist's rendering of an ideal girl's room in 1906. Source: "Girls' Rooms," *Harper's Bazaar*, October 1906, 936.

portals as much as borders, exhibiting a blend of porousness and separation or distinction necessary to their existence. Victorian middle-class understandings of taste decried material life while living off of it, with materiality providing the substance to craft non-material virtue. Threat and promise, grace and pollution assemble at these borders and in these interchanges, unavoidably transporting something of one side to the other, making for an integration of difference.

Sociologist Emile Durkheim wrote of the sacred and profane as "profoundly differentiated" and "radically opposed" categories that, nevertheless, required some sort of contact between them if, for no other reason than to reaffirm the ultimate necessity of their separation.[95] Likewise, at every turn of the well-appointed home lurked the potential to encourage materialism itself or, perhaps, to demonstrate an inner virtue independent of things. In every meal, in every donning of finery, in each toy or form of amusement, existed opportunities to instruct children in correct dispositions toward the world—and toward the world of goods. They also, of course, portended the possibility of failure. Understood in this way, the middle-class Victorian home of the mid- to late nineteenth century served not so much as a reprieve from commercial life as it did a sorting mechanism for the meanings and values of things—including an emerging sense of market value itself, where it extends and should not extend.

As classificatory scheme and moral prophylaxis, taste and personal discipline operated as homologies working to knit children, childhood, and material life together. In this middle-class culture, taste mattered because engagement with the world of things was both unavoidable and desirable, constituting the cultural space where character was made and revealed in conversation with a disciplined attitude toward things. The child imagined in and by the public discourses of taste resided in a world separate from wage labor, from being held as the slave property of others, and from pauperism. Labor value consequently stood several steps removed from their immediate life worlds, transformed into the household of things and the moral lessons they were thought to hold. The sentiment of the household, of women's and mothers' efforts, maneuvered through the expanding world of commercial goods and meanings with children in mind, not in spite of them, and hence not apart from economic value and valuation.

Taste here made the interiority of the child available by laying bare the interiority of the "mother." Mothers were to understand, intervene in, and direct the taste of their children by self-reflexively consulting their own preferences, their own self presentations, and their own "character." Unlike Carolyn Steedman's conception, this kind of interiority derived from a moral necessity of mothers to theorize the dynamics of selfhood with regard to the child's encounter with the world.[96] Discourses of taste enabled a conception of that encounter and how it might be handled by and through domestic materialities. Many writers quoted above went to lengths to stress that the amount of money spent on a garment or on the furnishings of a room should be subordinated to considerations of taste, but not because these children or others were to be removed from participating in consumer market relations, even if that participation was vicarious. Monetary measures were dismissed so they could be taken up as distinction.[97] If one purchases or values some things because of one's taste, and that taste happens also to be congruent with the fine pottery and linens that nearby social others also acquire, the congruence is fortunate. The child, consequently, will be fortunate to be exposed to and trained in good taste, even if that training does not manifest itself until years later. The less monetarily fortunate, pleaded many writers, can also exhibit taste.

The homology between taste and discipline offers one clue to the underside of Weber's Protestant ethic problem of being unable to account for the rise of consumer culture and for the growing importance of goods and self-display that seem to arise out of belief structure that privileges a form of this-worldly asceticism. Weber concentrated on the world and practices of industrious and industrious-minded *men* who, almost by definition, were setting the boundaries between work and domesticity, between production and consumption. Weber's idea of labor did not extend to the domestic work of women[98]—including child-rearing as well as the aesthetic work thought necessary in making a household—because these were not part of a rational, calculable system of free labor.[99] Hence, he did not consider the education, care, discipline, and experiences of children as impactful to his key notions of election, the calling and asceticism, as discussed in the previous chapter. Weber consequently did not account, in any serious and substantive manner, for the ways in which the domestic worlds of these men were produced or, importantly, reproduced. His conjecture of an "unprecedented inner loneliness"[100] plaguing those who closely followed Calvin's teachings presumed and individualized an adult male actor whose concerns were about his own election and salvation.

The labors increasingly left to women as the nineteenth century progressed centered largely, though not exclusively, on grappling with the dangers and possibilities of the malleable child—be they concerns about ultimate salvation or about the formation of character—both of which were undertaken by many with religious attitude and purpose. The classificatory labor demanded and allowed by taste, as Bourdieu theorized, here encounters an equally robust and increasingly demanding apparatus: the malleable child, which embodies the risk of a particular, classed social reproduction in ways that no other social institution could. It is not surprising, then, that the voiced concerns of mothers, observers, and pundits of the time centered on the profound moral bearing wrought by the implications of the malleable child—i.e., in the progressive realization of the problem of making human beings. Taste, in many ways, provided interpretive-moral ballast, a possibility for balance and uplift, to offset the notion that the trajectory of human life appears, more or less, ductile and plastic.

3

From Discipline to Reward

Reworking Children's Transgressions

The punishment which the four-year-old child does not understand is thrown away. It is not worth my while to say that
the practice of indiscriminate scolding, cuffing and whipping shows far more viciousness in the parent than in the
child. Parents who follow or allow this practice can never
establish the sympathetic relations with their children essential to helpful discipline.
—Philip Hubert, "The Punishment Ledger," *Babyhood,*
January 1888[1]

Through the malleability of its character, desires, and ontological trajectory, the child became manifest as a new sort of dynamic problem of
social reproduction. With the waning of depravity, white, free Americans living in the latter half of the nineteenth century witnessed a
progressive, if uneven and incomplete, sequestration of the Devil from
everyday life. Spiritual destiny continued to migrate, generally, from a
determined fear and assuredness of damnation toward a sense that evils
could be countered, even avoided, by good work upon this earth.[2] The
object of that good work often focused on the child's education, character, and behavior. Taste, for bourgeois Victorians, enacted part of that
earthly good work through material means. Yet this-worldly sources and
locations of "evil" continued to multiply, requiring vigilance on the part
of parents and adults. Depravity, it seems, jumped from within the child
into the world over the course of the century.[3] Heathens, immigrants,
exploitative industrial labor, poverty, unchristian parents, cities, and
nursemaids in different ways came to constitute various sorts of threats
to the increasingly uncertain pathways of an ever-unfolding—and perhaps narrowing—sense of a good childhood.[4]

Notwithstanding the banishment of depravity from within the child as Horace Bushnell intended (see chapter 1), the child remained a problem to its own ontology in the form of the passions, i.e., of impulse and desire. As Satan stepped away and as inborn degeneracy receded, the nature and substance of children's wants, needs, and dispositions came to the fore, particularly with regard to the practices of parenting and education for bourgeois Victorians, liberal Protestants and Calvinists alike. An emerging attitude forged an amalgamated conception of the child based on an epistemology of development, whereby children's likes and dislikes came to be understood less as indications of sources of evil and increasingly as cues to its extant, perhaps "natural" and always gendered, desires and inclinations, which could be countered or, at least, directed. "Household management" more and more encompassed attention to children's desires regarding such things as food, play, and the objects and spaces surrounding them.[5] Locating sources of enticement as potentially external to the malleable child made possible the production of a subject whose pleasure-seeking—in Campbell's terms—was, at once, a "natural" and therefore legitimate facet of development (or education) while also serving as a site for surveillance, regulation, training, and discipline.[6]

In the latter decades of the nineteenth century, the issue of the discipline and punishment of children surfaced as an ongoing discussion and debate on the pages of periodicals devoted to mothers, such as *Babyhood* (1884–1909), the first national publication of its kind dedicated to the intersection of child development and children's welfare. With the fading of child depravity, severe corporal punishment also gradually fell out of favor in Northern, white, bourgeois circles. By no means extinguished, corporal punishment, rather, came under scrutiny. If the "Devil" no longer exists within the child, then it does not need to be beaten out of her. But since the Devil—or, at least, devilishness in the form of disobedience and mischief—did not depart completely from childhood, some calculation was required to determine how much of it remained and thus how much and what kind of a thrashing it needed.

Often at odds with the "old" ways of severe physical discipline intended to elicit unquestioned obedience, discussion in *Babyhood* evinced a decided turn in conceptualizations of the "child" and in a constellation of related matters and ideas. Questions of discipline and governance relate directly to notions of children's nature and their state of knowledge about the world—understandings of right and wrong, of willfulness, of deceit—and hence to the locus of control among young infants and young children. Children's disobedience calls into question childhood innocence; it provides evidence of potential discord between child and adult and, in so doing, brings underlying power dynamics to the fore. Disobedience demands an explanation of its origins, impetus, and systematicity, and also calls for a commensurate response. In this way, disobedience and considerations of punishment require an investigation, a theorization, of interiority—both the child's and the parent's.

The deliberations put forth in editorials, features, and letters from readership over the 25-year run of *Babyhood* etch an arc of a process of grappling with a fundamental re-evaluation and re-ordering of children's personhood—that is, their moral status vis-à-vis their ontogenetic trajectory. At issue were problems of epistemology and ontology: what kinds of beings are children and how does one know? Do infants and babies occupy a continuum of being with older children, and they with adults, or are they separate and distinct and thus in need of a transformation of some kind? How does one read the actions of infants and babies in terms of their motivations, desires, and their knowledge of the world regarding disobedience?

Throughout these interrogations lurked the question of the child's perspective—its way of knowing—particularly with regard to the meaning of acts of physical discipline. Debates and discussion about the proper kind of punishment and how and whether to administer it at all could be found on the pages of periodicals intended for women and mothers, which increasingly devoted space for advice, letters, and discussion (see figures 3.1 and 3.2). Unavoidably, and it seems increasingly, these discussions and debates incorporated the presumed or imputed point of view of the "child" both as evidence for the effectiveness of one method over another and as moral grounds for taking up or refraining from various kinds of punitive action. To consider the child's view meant taking the child's standpoint and entering into its interiority in an effort to see, feel, and understand as the child might. To engage in empathy in this way dismantles, in some measure, the absolute power of the parent or adult who would necessarily take steps to evaluate the effects of disciplinary measures on the child's behavior and attitude. As one door opened on the child's perspective in issues of governance, so

Figure 3.1. By the 1880s, space devoted exclusively for maternal concerns had become a standard feature of many women's periodicals, such as this one from the *Ladies' Home Journal* in 1890. Source: *Ladies' Home Journal*, January 1890, 17.

too did others on the span of the child's world in terms of desire, reward, punishment, and motivation—themselves moral-epistemological gateways to the child consumer.

Memory, Empathy, and Analysis: Late-Nineteenth-Century Discourses of Punishment and Governance

In the February 1885 issue of *Babyhood*, the third of this new publication, the editor responded to a reader inquiry about when it was proper to punish a two-year-old child who "desires to have his own way" by advising the reader to use "other methods" first before resorting to corporal punishment: "While it would seem that some children can be conquered by no other means, the specific effect of the old-fashioned orthodox whipping is too often to harden and brutalize."[7] As the child gets older, the response continues, "beating is undoubtedly demoralizing, because it lowers his self-respect." Above all, the author (and readership) is admonished to "keep your own temper." Recurring regularly in discussions on child discipline, pleas for parental self-control contained within themselves an implicit requirement that parents understand the nature, origins, and contexts of their children's behavior—that they make the effort to know their child on its own terms and from its point of view. The realm of this "knowing" could reach from contemplating the consequences for the punishment (or threatened punishment) on immediate circumstances, which may include the present behavior and feelings of the child and its relationship to the parent. It could also encompass consideration of the physical pain inflicted, if any, the long-term effects

Figure 3.2. Women's periodicals like *Ladies' Home Journal* (top) and *Babyhood* (bottom) provided regular forums to print selected letters from mothers asking for advice or sharing their views. Source: top: *Ladies' Home Journal*, December 1890, 16; bottom: *Babyhood*, September 1887, 345.

of harsh or inconsiderate disciplinary action, as well as the moral and social integrity of the child, noted in the quote above.

Patience on the part of parents, especially mothers, mattered also for imagining how the child sees its own actions, and therefore for grasping the motivations behind these actions, thereby making the study of the child requisite for effective, responsive mothering. Another letter writer relates a story of a boy who was made to stay in his room for two days for failing to say "please."[8] Though this mother could be extolled for her willingness to devote herself to this "phase of childish willfulness," notes the letter writer, perhaps a lighter penalty would have sufficed. Writing tactfully, it seems, to a presumed skeptical audience, the author continues to note that sometimes an unwanted behavior arises from origins one cannot immediately see. Since no two people are equal in capacity and understanding, she argues, the "unformed mind of a child" cannot always be expected to accept parental wishes: "Put yourself in his place, and, while insisting upon the child's acceptance of cardinal principles on your *ipse dixit* [a dogmatic expression of opinion] until he develops intelligence enough to adopt them as his own, give him as few of tears as may be necessary."[9]

What Ought John Sr. Have Done?

A telling illustration of the interchange between obedience and punishment, on the one hand, and the conception of the child, on the other, populated the pages of *Babyhood* in its first year. Beginning in May 1885, an extended discussion ensued after a letter published in the section "The Mother's Parliament" described a standoff between a father, John Sr., and his two-year-son, John Jr.[10] Penned by "X," presumably the wife and mother of those involved, the writer presents an account of a confrontation: the child pushed a paper off of father's desk and refused to pick it up after several insistent commands by John Sr. Sprinkled with dialogue and "baby talk" (e.g., the boy says "Junior-'ont-pick-it-up!"), the drama unfolds when the mother tries to intercede in the boy's whipping at the hands of his father, who was to make use of whalebone, only to find herself struck by the obstinate child. After being commanded to leave the study, she describes the screams and sounds of the child heard through the closed door. Apparently John Jr., after a first round of spanking, kicked the piece of paper in question, which somehow wound up landing on the desk. Unhappy with this gesture, John Sr. put the paper back on the floor and whipped the boy again, saying "'Papa' (the blood welling unseen with every stab the parent dealt himself) '-will-whip-his-boy-until-he-picks-that-paper-up-with-his-hand-and-lays-it-on-the-table!'" The boy finally complied, this time bringing the paper to the father by holding it between his teeth and on his knees. The author asks, "What, dear reader, *ought* John, senior, have done?"[11]

The story of John Sr. and John Jr. attracted many responses for months, continuing into late 1885. One writer, "Z," suggested that John Sr. could have made a game out of it coaxing the boy to return the "poor little paper" to its home on the desk, or shut the child out of the room and told he could not return until he agreed to pick up the paper. For "Z," not the act but the disobedience of not complying should be punished, and not with such severity "except as a punishment for willful lying."[12] Another respondent, an "M.D.," remarked that John Sr. could have used politeness to request the paper be returned. Instead, what "really happened" is that the father incited anger through arbitrary power, which only strengthened the child's resolve in the wrong direction, as the child never did pick up the paper with his hands.[13] In that same set of letters, "L. P." acknowledged that it was the "sacred duty" of parents to exact obedience from their children but vehemently disagreed with the method, asserting that children must be trained, not broken, and that the object of parenting should be not to govern the child but to "teach him to govern himself."[14] Recalling her own whippings as a young girl, L. P. notes that they were "neither many nor severe, but to everyone which comes within the scope of my memory I look back with pain, tracing the harm it did me." The memories fill her with "humiliation and degradation," which she sees as "common to all sensitive, high-spirited children." For these reasons she is opposed to all whipping of children, except for the rare "extreme offences," and never babies or young children.[15]

The story of and debate about John Jr. and John Sr. apparently spread beyond the confines of *Babyhood*, as the June issue contained a response from Mark Twain, reprinted from the *Christian Union* (originally July 16, 1885). The famous writer admonished the father for stubbornly and unthinkingly escalating the situation by calling the child names and making immediate demands on him. If he were John Sr., Twain suggests, he would have realized that calm reasoning away from the situation would have helped, something for which the mother is best suited.

If after a period of calm and reason the child does not comply, other actions might need to be taken. Spankings, in his house, are never given in anger or out of revenge and the "child never goes from the scene of punishment until it has been loved back into happy-heartedness and a joyful spirit."[16] Next to Twain's response was that of John Sr., who derided the respondents for contradicting themselves and allowing sentiment to override reason. Correcting the record that he did not use whalebone but an open hand, John Sr. goes on to express the view that children cannot be taught too early the "necessity of implicit obedience" even if comprehension of the punishment is not possible, as the "discipline alone will be of incalculable benefit to him . . . not only in babyhood but in later years."[17] The inability to restrain a child of a feeble effort at discipline, he continues, is the "greatest mistake that can be made in the education of children." Furthermore, it is "folly to assume they do not understand victory over us."[18] Wrongful, unrestrained acts of children, where they are allowed to handle and enjoy things they should not have been allowed to touch in the first place, are what "fill the penal institutions."[19]

The instigation of and replies to the question of what John Sr. ought to have done draw out dynamic interchanges between conceptions of childhood, of the "child," of parental authority, of "appropriate" responses to disobedience, and of its effects. Here, the infraction of insubordination eclipsed any other wrongdoing (like touching something one shouldn't touch) because it brings into relief and questions the power relation between child and parent. For John Sr. and for those who sided with him, the severity of the punishment ultimately matched well with the seriousness of the act, or refusal to act, to the extent that the whipping was thought to correct the behavior, if not the attitude and outlook, of the child. Expressed opposition to how John Sr. handled John Jr. drew upon and deployed something akin to the child's perspective through the use of personal memory, conjectures of long-lasting effects on the child (or on children in general), appeals to empathy regarding pain and personal dignity or through writing in the voice of a mocking, "talking back" child who is "asking for it."[20] The battle here being waged was over the very definition of the child, over what kind of person or being it is. In this way, the moral project of childhood manifests not only in what children may become, but in how they become.

The Ambiguities of Deceit and Truthfulness

Representations of willful disobedience register tensions in authority relations between parents and children; they also implicate the what and how of the ways in which the child "knows." "Disobedience," in the late-Victorian, middle-class world of the *Babyhood* readership, also centered on the question of children's "truthfulness." In an 1888 anonymously authored article, a (perhaps staff) writer acknowledges the frustrating situation that children are not always truthful but turns the attention directly on the response of parent whose methods used to "correct the fault" often make matters worse. Parents often lack an understanding of the child's "nature" and so often are unable to adopt a kind and intelligent treatment suited to its wants. Instead of seeking the cause of the untruth, the writer counsels, the first effort is to press upon the child's mind the "enormity of a lie and its direful consequences—something entirely beyond the child's comprehension; then it is made to understand that severe penalty must and will be meted out for such offences."[21] To understand the child is to understand the immaturity of the child's mind[22] and that spoken untruths are sometimes not known or understood by the child to be untruthful or to be offences. In fact, it is the strictness and severity or threatened severity of the punishment that may actually contribute to, if not cause, untruthfulness and other acts of child disobedience in young children. A child may "lie to hide an offence," hoping to escape the "dreaded punishment." It is painfully true that parents, through "inflexible sternness and undue severity often cause their children to lie."[23] The discipline necessary to bring up a child can draw out a sense of awe and fear of the parent, making the child afraid to confess to what he or she has done.

Lying—purposeful, knowing deceit—nestles the child a little too closely to a thickly lingering aura of depravity, of being inclined toward evil. From a *Babyhood* editorial in 1890: "There is a general feeling among mothers that when a child has been guilty of telling an untruth it has manifested depravity that it must be made to understand the enormity of its crime, and that punishment summary and severe must be administered."[24] The editorial continues, "How many mothers stop to reflect upon the probable causes which lead children to tell falsehoods, or to veer away from the truth?" The writer restates the notion put forth above that children might lie from a strong "instinct of self-preservation" when they fear the "consequences of an untruthful confession"[25] Untruths told by a child cut holes in the veneer of innocence unless they can be explained as something other than outright falsehoods. However, all untruths spoken may not necessarily derive from nefarious sources. One writer in 1885 explained to the *Babyhood* readership that young children actually are not liars but that their "imagination often outruns [their] capacity to select the proper object on which to exercise it."[26]

Uncertainty about the origin and meaning of untruths speaks to underlying questions about children's being and knowing, the responses to which can carry consequences in terms of how harshly to "correct" the child, or whether to do so at all. It matters a great deal to parental action and governance if untruths, or other forms of disobedience for that matter, are understood as indicating a disagreeable "nature" or a stage or moment in a child's growth. In the white, Northern, middle-class world represented in later nineteenth-century writings in *Babyhood* and elsewhere, the preponderance of discourses evinces a palpable shift of burden from accounts that locate the essence of deceit (and disobedience) within the child to those that see untruthfulness and disobedience as arising from sources external to the child proper, or to those that reconfigure falsehoods and the like as evidence of the benign working of a young child's mind like "imagination." They represent a collective attempt between readers and writers to figure out a sensible place for disobedience in an emerging modern moral order of childhood, something that required discerning the viewpoint, the positionality, of the child. The multiple and multiply configured forms of seeing and knowing increasingly expected of mothers required seeing the world (and hence oneself) from the child's perspective and grasping how that world may be apprehended—i.e., what consequences one's actions may have on how the child understands right from wrong. In order to accomplish this feat, the mother would have to be willing and able to engage in a multi-perspectival analysis of the situation, which here included a theory or insight about the baby's understanding of the mother's actions, the baby's form or level of knowing about the world, and the long-term ramifications of the perception or misperception of all of these.

Sympathy, Empathy, and Memory

Letters to *Babyhood* regularly and, it seems, increasingly advocated for some effort to take the child's view in terms of punishment as well as in terms of the affective contextualization of the punishment. One writes in 1887 of the "need for sympathy" in punishment to keep pace with "home training," adding that "parents' fear that speaking their compassion will counteract the discipline or lessen their authority." Sympathy can follow the administration of punishment by introducing a remark like "It's pretty hard to remember everything, isn't it, dear?" to a forgetful child. Such measures will assure the child that mother's heart is not "turned away."[27] Along these lines, a writer protesting against whipping in 1891 suggests that children strike back at parents when beaten due to an instinct of self-preservation.[28] Parents, according to the writer, sow the seeds of this reaction when they begin to reprove a young child's effort to investigate the world when they tend to grab "whatever is in its reach." The slap on the hands is likely to defeat its own purpose, as the "active, quick brained toddler may be inspired by this removal to devise a better means for taking the same object," when a "suitable toy" would keep the boy's hands busy. "Rule by love, and not by fear," because "nothing compensates a joyless childhood."[29] The child here manifests as an active, knowing, agentive being whose reactions and sensitivities require consideration and adjustment on the part of the mother who is striving to govern.

Evil becomes a matter of intent and not so much a matter of the constitution of children. For mothers and others endeavoring to sort out and grasp children's intentions—especially those of infants and babies—the most readily available material is derived from observation of one's children, others' children, and from one's own memory. Indeed, writing from and of one's memory remained a staple literary practice in letters and articles on discipline and on childhood generally. In June 1888, Lucy White Palmer penned a feature moving in and out of a first-person account in relating a story of her being falsely accused of wrongdoing when she was four years old.[30] She relates that "(e)very time that memory has conjured up this vision . . . my heart has been stirred with great pity for that unjustly treated little self, and a burning indignation on her behalf." She continues on to make her case for patience, understanding and leniency ("Better pass by nine transgressions unpunished than to punish unjustly one") to avoid lasting moral injury. Palmer beseeches the maternal readership to swallow their pride and give apology when it is due the child for, in doing so, "your dignity will not suffer in his eyes: rather will his respect for you be embraced and the courteous justice which you show to him will surely engender the like in him." Memory and maternal experience here grant authority to speak for and from a childhood past, yet present, and thus in a sense for "all" children. In so doing, Palmer garners empathy for this injustice in support of the idea that children generally deserve justice in the home.[31]

Taking into account the child's emotional reaction—including the specter of carrying the same kind of memories into adulthood as did some of the writers—discussion ventured into a range of practices adjacent to physical beatings that were thought to elicit the same, contradictory results. Hence, a child can be lied to by a parent just as the child can impart a falsehood. Exaggerating children's faults by calling them thieves or liars for committing "misdemeanors" of childhood so as to scare them away from unwanted behavior, as a frequent writer to the journal argued in 1893, "makes the insignificant terrible and creates a sense of false standards which diminish the child's ability to judge the degrees of wrong doing."[32] Similarly, threatening a child with tales of "ghosts, bogies, the black man who comes down the chimney to catch children who will not go to sleep quietly," complains a *Babyhood* editorial in 1884,[33] makes for incalculable mischief and perhaps long-term repercussions of timidity and a damaged nervous system. There is, unsurprisingly, no mention of inculcating insidious, endemic racist fears by invoking the specter of the "black man" invading the home via the preferred route of Santa Claus. Another mother relates the sounds she overheard on a hot summer evening along her street of "average means and culture" where one mother threatened to put a disobedient child in the cellar and another silenced her child by lying to her that a policeman was downstairs wanting to know what was causing all the noise. The writer conjectures that "later, when the full-grown plant of disobedience confronts these mothers, they will murmur at this 'degenerate age' and wonder at the influence of 'bad companions,'" unaware that they had planted this seed with their own hand and unsure why later education cannot undo these early mistakes.[34]

To see with the child's eyes is to think through the child's experience, an experience of subordination, dependency and, in the context of this discussion, often of fear.[35] Writers and readers sympathetic to this attitude delivered story after story and example after example illustrating the various ways that the impatience of parents toward children's trespasses compounded the problems of governance and, in so doing, potentially contributed to reinforcing the very problematic behavior in question. Whipping the child out of anger or out of sheer performance of adult dominance became suspect, in one regard, because observers began to question its utility, suggesting that such measures may quell an immediate situation but, in the long run, do not produce obedience behaviorally or, perhaps more importantly, emotionally. Administering swift, unthinking "justice" to children represented a mode of parenting that was quickly falling into disfavor among a rising cohort of middle-class observers, and many sought to dramatize its harm by representing and voicing the child. The malleable child continued to represent a problem not of "order" per se, as in the Hobbesian tradition, but of ordering, i.e., of shaping and molding. It was something organized not so much over and against an overbearing sense of depravity and evil, but rather oriented toward grasping and finding ways to guide the inner workings—the generative principle—of the child. Here, this child offered a glimpse and demonstration, as Carolyn Steedman discusses, of human "interiority."[36] That is, the figure of the child in these textual transactions exclaimed a depth of historicity within individuals as in, for instance, the deployment of memory—of specifically mothers' memories—and the subsequent pleas for sympathy and empathy noted above.[37] In this way, it is altogether worth considering the extent to which the public explication and deployment of mothers' memories of their childhoods undergirded the exploration of the landscape of children's interiority and subjecthood in this context and beyond. The style in which this community of mothers imagined itself, to return to Benedict Anderson's point, here accepts shared memory as a basis for parental action.[38]

It is equally significant to attend to the ways in which "the child" acquires a self and gains a right to a selfhood. A sense that the child has or can have a self that can be affected, injured, shamed, propped up, and torn down informs the changing public, middle-class attitudes about child discipline and, as we shall see, child sanctions. As such, an emergent sense is that a child who possesses a self—or can possess a self—can be put at social risk, in addition to having a soul that remains subject to spiritual risk. The women writing and debating in *Babyhood*, as well as in *The Mother's Magazine*, *Godey's*, and other similar public forums, contributed to reinventing morality as something which, like the child, has a development. Anticipated in and expressed by Bushnell (see chapter 1), human moral understanding for many of these female writers could be seen as something that arises through experience and would be subject to circumstance and influence. Not simply a sequestration of evil in the religious sense, the thrust and trajectory of discourse regarding disobedience and governance sought explanation from considering the child itself—its experiences, the basis of its motives, and the natural or expected teleology of its development. If selfishness or impetuousness or "lying" be observed and experienced as naturally occurring in children, these become figured as tendencies that can be steered and handled through a complex algorithm of nurture enacted in the everyday here-and-now of parenting.

Appropriate Punishments: Authority and the (Un)making of Future Selves

The governance of young children remained a kinetic moral discourse as observers and commentators sought to calibrate causes, responses, and responsibilities for misbehavior. For many, punishment stood as the ultimate practice of child discipline in the way that it marked and thereby enforced a boundary of authority, a boundary thought essential to producing well-behaved children, a well-governed household, and a well-regulated nation.[39] The first precept of "Thoughts on Home Training" noted by a letter writer to *Babyhood* advises: "Don't wait to govern your child until he governs you. Begin when he first recognizes your face or the sound of your voice, when the little lip quivers at a cross word or the little face dimples into smiles at an endearing one."[40] Writers relate many a story about children who obviously had not been trained well—i.e., early and regularly—by their mother, as evidenced by both the child's and the parent's behavior. For instance, in response to the "Baby's Plea" letter discussed above, one person responded by criticizing the father's apparent hesitancy to ever punish his child again, arguing that such dis-engagement would deprive the child of "wholesome discipline."[41] The practical benefits of teaching children "prompt and absolute obedience" were related by way of stories or anecdotes of children avoiding death from moving trains by unthinkingly listening to their mother or, less dra-matically, by vignettes of fussy and disobedient children who would not, for instance, sit in the dentist's chair upon command.[42]

The idea of making the punishment "appropriate" to the misbehavior and making the effort to explain to the child the reason for the punish-ment further moved in the direction of instantiating the child's perspec-tive, the child's experience, as both legitimate and consequential. The view of discipline emerging in *Babyhood* in particular takes both the process and the child to be rational, or at least able to be guided by ra-tional principles. As constructions of the child, including infants, moved toward a model or continuum of rationality,[43] and as the notion and practice of child study gained hold among the class constituency of the readership of *Babyhood*, rational methods of punishment appeared—a marked divergence from the affective, sentimental approach pursued by the mid-century Victorian and Evangelical women encountered in pre-vious chapters.

Men's voices, it must be noted, appeared central to debates about punishment to a far greater extent than for any other topic in these woman-oriented periodicals—often amplifying the notion of "reason" in punishment and "logical" ways to enact punishment and often serv-ing as counterpoint to the view that women pursue an overly sentimen-tal, soft approach. One person, a man, proposed a "punishment ledger" based on Herbert Spencer's writings, whereby the parent systematically recorded the child's offences, the types of punishments used in response, and the reactions of the child, so as to govern by "scientific principles."[44] The author, Philip Hubert—quoted in the epigraph at the head of this chapter—recommends explaining the reason for the discipline but warns that sometimes a child is "born vicious" and thus its reasoning power is weak by inheritance. The system he proposes will help parents know what sorts of actions work for which kinds of children. The notion of the inheritance of a contrary disposition held its philosophical cache against other arising views of complete, initial child moral neutrality (or "innocence") at this time.[45]

For others, establishing a direct connection between the imposition of a penalty and the precipitating action was thought to enable the child to learn not only to associate the action with an unpleasant event, but also to understand that the painful experience arises out of love and concern, and not out of enmity. For this reason, the time between action and punishment should not be delayed lest the cause-effect connection be lost.[46] One writer in the "Mother's Parliament" section lays out the problems with delayed punishments, which include a "weakening of the child's belief in the parent's truthfulness" and an unnecessary anxiety aroused in anticipation of the promised reprimand, recalling her own painful memory of waiting to be spanked when she was a child. She cautions, however, that exceptions should be made to avoid acting out of anger. One must not "get into a habit of hitting a child when it is offend-ing," noting that a boy she knows winces in anticipation of being struck whenever near his mother—a mother who "loves him tenderly" but is "quick and impetuous" in this "habit."[47] Yet doubt continued to be ex-pressed by others that appealing to a child's "higher motives"—i.e., that he/she "owed" obedience to parents—usually did not succeed and, when such appeals failed, there was little recourse other than administering some form of reasonable, relevant, and limited punishment.[48] Discipline delayed is governance denied, so it would seem in this worldview. Once a child gets a taste of unchecked willful behavior, it is difficult to turn it around into obedience.

The emergent sense of discipline found in *Babyhood* served civilizing ends, but only when done so properly. Appeals to the child's present and future civility can be found woven throughout the ongoing and changing justifications for the use of discipline, including corporal punishment. Strict routines of sleep, feeding, and exercise—staples of the Child Study movement and of Emmett Holt's rubric for child care—had their coun-terparts in the ongoing negotiations about the appropriate ways to pro-duce, or at least not impede, the production of a proper child, a proper *bourgeois* child.[49] If the child could obey within the family, then it would most likely find "success" in the world beyond. At the same time, the use of corporal punishment potentially brings parents, the disciplinar-ians, closer to the "savage" and to uncivilized ways of maintaining order. Echoing the discourses of anti-corporal punishment reform efforts that began in the antebellum era,[50] writers in *Babyhood* sought to connect the

unthinking and impulsive whipping of children with practices of flog-
ging that took place aboard ships on the high seas (whereby "it has been
proved that a more excellent discipline can be maintained by means that
appeal to the man within the culprit, and that couple possibilities of future respectability with present subjection").[51] "Whipping" is something
a Southern slaveholder did to his human property; it was not a behavior
congruent with white, free Northeast civility and upbringing. A "Papa
who reads *Babyhood*" excoriated the "well-intentioned correspondents"
of the magazine who extolled the virtues of strict discipline and harsh
punishment as being not savages but rather unengaged apathetics: "If
you know no better, of course, command and whack; but do not flatter
yourself that your laziness is kindness and your selfishness wisdom."[52]
Attitudes toward corporal punishment in many ways encoded multiple
notions of civility and savagery regarding both children and adults, and
in this way expressed a kind of "taste."

A formal expression of the view that parents need to be mindful of
their actions and the consequences of their actions made the pages of
Babyhood in 1895 in a reprint of an *International Journal of Ethics* article on "The Punishment of Children"[53] wherein the author writes of
"conscientious parents" who "can have no interest in life higher than
the wellbeing of their children."[54] Well-being springs from the "moral
empire" of the home, wherein order must rule, order being "born of authority and obedience."[55] If adults treat children as equals and let "natural consequences" for action rule, then they will "treat us as inferiors."[56]
One must "appeal to the mind," to the child as rational being, in punishment and not resort to corporal punishment: "It is the savage, who has
not patience to reason or explain, who strikes. Corporal punishment
can seldom be administered without passion. When we show excitement
we give signs of weakness."[57] Self-control, another letter writer writes in
1893, is needed because the everyday incidents of disobedience and their
response

> become a part of the warp and woof of the character of those who are
> growing up to fill places of importance and trust. When through the
> country appear riots, strikes and discontent, who thinks of the little 'in-
> cidents' which occurred in the nursery? Who thinks of the impatient
> words, jerks, shakings that children have received . . . ? Self-control is an

essential to wise government in the home. Words uttered once will not be unsaid; blows administered will leave a scar.[58]

The fate of the child, of the family, and of civilization itself, it would seem, rides on the minute, impassioned or passion-less actions and reactions of mothers in directing their children. Indeed, society's ills—the "riots and strikes"—appear as positively *matriogenic*.

The entire trajectory of the life course of the child, it seems, hinges on maternal attitude, posture, and a weakness for indulgence, as it did in discourses of piety for Evangelical mothers and in discourses of taste for Victorian middle-class mothers. It is clear that "intensive mothering,"[59] while taking on particular forms in response to social, economic, and cultural historical configurations, also manifests a cultural circuity and ideological template emergent in the late nineteenth century around the formation of the middle-class child-mother-punishment nexus. These meld with and arise from an impetus to dodge notions of innate depravity while endeavoring to inhabit, in some way, the perspective of the child.

Punishment here and elsewhere manifests as a complex form of communication—a way of imposing an authority of office while simultaneously proposing a relationship of love and care. It is a tricky business that somehow must isolate the act of punishment to the specific act of wrongdoing and connect the two in a timely, explicit, and reasonable manner, whereby mother and child both potentiate "rationality." With corporal punishment falling out of favor over time, and particularly within the class faction represented by the learned, relatively liberal readership of *Babyhood*, the readily available means to compel a child's behavior likewise underwent a general shift from prohibitions toward the direction of incentives.

From Punishment to Reward

If parents were increasingly willing to spare the rod, as they appeared to be, they also worried about spoiling the child and, in so doing, becoming governed by it. Yet, with a decreasing acceptability of severe disciplinary action, combined with a growing sensibility of and sensitivity toward children's perspectives and dispositions, the most readily available avenue to having influence over the malleable child came in the form of incentives and rewards. Recommendations for providing recompense for a child's cooperation or good behavior often appeared astride the discussions of discipline and punishment in *Babyhood*, increasing in frequency, scope, and acceptability with time. In November 1888, a letter to the journal offered assistance to an "Ohio Father" who, in a previous issue, had presented his woes concerning the difficult governance of his children by noting the use of a "system of credits" and debits, each worth ten cents, tallied weekly and kept in an account book. On Saturdays, the weekly record is shown to "papa . . . when he goes over the mishaps, thus recalling and preaching a little sermon, and then paying the amounts due." The writer added that the ease with which one can form the word "credit" with one's mouth if "the child is near strangers" has a "magical" effect on behavior.[60]

Subsequent responses found little merit in this system. "M" from Baltimore conceded that it is "not as bad as spanking" but a system of rewards and punishments is a "confession of impotence on the part of the parents." She elaborates that the "natural, healthy way" that children are led into good conduct is through firm, gentle, unbending guidance whereby the child, like everyone else, can seek appreciation from those whom we "feel instinctively . . . to be our moral superiors."[61] Another writer, also finding the system unnatural, speculated on what would happen if the child fell so far behind in owing credits that he or she would give up and have no incentive.[62] One mother had found merit in the system, relating how giving her child a "prize" for ceasing the habit of nail-biting worked so well that she instituted the practice in other areas of the household, like encouraging the child to keep her play corner in order.[63]

Yet the preponderance of views expressed in the late 1880s into the 1890s were unfavorably disposed to offering external or material incentive to cajole desirable child behavior. The question of the place of enticements in parenting unfailingly nestled against concerns of the development of child morality. In the most basic terms, parents and observers worried that giving rewards would draw the child out of the circumscribed world of its immediate governance or immediate context to seek compensation and motivation elsewhere. A reprint in 1888 from *The Atlantic Monthly* speaks to the parental responsibility for infant goodness, complaining that a "false morality" is being taught to children by "respectable and educated persons."[64] The problem, it appears, is that many are putting the "expedient before the right" in using bribes and other forms of enticement to do the "right thing" that deflect the source of motivation away from seeking the right, as (hopefully) exemplified and explained by loving parents who stand in for "God himself." Such acts teach the child to "do right" because performing them would "bring him some advantage."[65]

Acknowledging that it is "a much easier thing to reward children than to punish them," a regular columnist in *Ladies' Home Journal* opines that "bribery" of children occurs in families where training had "not begun early enough" and is thereby implemented as a problematic, retroactive fix that focuses not on the root of the problem but on "some special manifestation of it."[66] Another reprint in *Babyhood*, this time from *Macmillan's Magazine* in 1891 on education, explicitly deprecates the use of prizes rewarding success in schoolwork because such a motivation distracts the child's attention from the focus of study.[67] Rewards train attention on the comparative aspects of one's effort and detract from the "harmony of life" and "peacefulness of heart" that nineteenth-century German educator Friedrich Froebel had sought.[68]

Rewards can come wrapped in many packages, from comments on how well a child is dressed[69] to overdressing a child[70] to giving "too many" toys,[71] or the wrong toys, at Christmas and other times,[72] to the everyday acts of giving in to children's slight requests or ignoring their refusal to cooperate on the little tasks like dressing or eating.[73] Rewards, here, serve as something beyond the simple inverse of punishment. As incentives to obey or to behave in certain ways, rewards inflect and activate a different sense of self, a different model of engagement with the world, than do relationships based in discipline and punishment. Those subject to acts of punishment generally seek ways to avoid an undesirable outcome or feeling, often by refraining from some proscribed behavior or another. The dynamics of a reward structure, on the other hand, center the presumed wants and desires of the subject—the child—who is to receive the reward, making of them prospective longings.

A number of ills seem to follow this manner of centering children's desires—most significantly, that of selfishness abided through invidious social comparison of material things. In an 1887 article, Christine Ladd

Franklin asserts that "keeping down the growth of self-consciousness of children" is second only to the maternal duty of developing moral qualities in children. "If [children] are left to stand idly in the room and see themselves looked at and talked about when there are visitors present, they have nothing left to do but to think of themselves and the impression they are making."[74] Indulging children's efforts to attract attention to themselves—i.e., when they are allowed to interrupt adult conversations or to show off to the benefit of others—deprives them of the "wholesome neglect of mother and friends" which they need to acquire the attractive and charming "grace of modesty," as one writer put it in 1888.[75] For some, avoiding the encouragement of self-consciousness in children was of paramount importance, the concern often arising in conjunction with discussions of dress and finery. Clothes that do not match one's social status, that are elaborate and call attention to the refinement of the wearer, were often regarded as out of step with the supposed simplicities of childhood[76] (see chapter 4) and reflect not the desires of children but the idiosyncrasies of adults. As one 1888 *Babyhood* editorial put it, it is "reprehensible to trick out children in unsuitable clothing simply to gratify the taste of their elders."[77]

Contributors to *Babyhood* expressed concern about fostering a sense of social comparison through things and thereby committing Evangelical Protestantism's "chief sin" of encouraging pride in a child.[78] Christmas morning often served as the prototypical moment when "too often disparaging remarks are made by some child of larger possessions" to those with smaller ones.[79] One mother bemoans the implicit pedagogy of Christmas observance in her circles, where children usually expect an "undue amount of attention, an unlimited amount of injudicious feeding, and a selfish expectation of unneeded presents. Thus egotism, greed and selfishness are fostered."[80] Parental culpability in producing selfishness, asserted a *Babyhood* editorial in 1890, arises from their "zeal" for seeking the greatest good for children.[81] The remedy could be found in demonstrating to children that they are part of a "harmonious whole" of a family by giving them daily responsibilities. The maladies of offering extrinsic rewards can be located in most any endeavor, including games, asserts another *Babyhood* contributor: "There is hardly a fashionable novelty more dangerous than giving game prizes. It is bad for children to have the desire of gain connected with their innocent sports.

Probably nothing sows seeds of pride, envy, hatred and malice, in little hearts sooner than this custom."[82]

The issue here involves not simply concerns about selfish, egoistic children and the feeding of their potentially insatiable desires; it is, as well and perhaps most critically, a dangerous parental disposition to quench those desires. The analogy between appetite and generalized desire comes through in a physician's dissertation in 1888 on the use and abuse of feeding children. He identifies animal crackers as a telling case of the confusion between hunger and appetite, noting the commercial dimensions of the problem: "The cracker-maker, detecting this propensity in children [being anxious to eat a number of animals], furnishes a wonderful assortment of animals, and the child is eager to eat one, at least, of each kind purchased. The mother thinks these animals are so nice for children to play with that she gives them to the child to keep him quiet as he is trundled along in his carriage."[83] Perversion of appetite and a starchy dyspepsia can follow the over-consumption of these treats. Responsibility again resides with the mother, whose daily minute decisions are presumed to be consequential to the regulation of the libidinal, metabolic, and social systems of the child. The increasing number of things, and the greater options for consumption and possession, becomes the basis for their devaluation in everyday life, a dynamic unfavorable to children who will grow up unappreciative of the world around them. One writer took it upon herself to speak to the *Babyhood* readership directly about how "feeling poor" is a matter of comparative lack, arising from unmet expectations.[84] She writes that "a healthy, natural child wants very few things he cannot have. . . . If you can stop the orange, banana, pineapple or ice-cream for his benefit to once in a while, he will have the sense of absolute luxury, whereas if you keep the cooky and doughnut jars constantly full . . . your child will soon catch a dissatisfied, longing, envious spirit, and may begin, in his third of fourth year, to murmur at his hard lot."[85]

If parents enable the expression or development of selfishness in children, they do so in a new age, an "age of rush,"[86] where material goods abound and where both child and parent lose perspective on the dear value of things. It is the parents' desire to please the child that drives overindulgence and threatens to produce impertinent adults. In a severe critique, Caroline Le Row connects what she sees as the "decline of sentiment" in children with a growing materialism of the age. Children, she tells the *Babyhood* readership in 1891, are born into a material world unheard of in human history where the "surfeit of picture-books gives far less pleasure than the one single volume, fingered perhaps into tatters, and kept at night under the child's pillow. Christmas brings children so many and such varied gifts that their heads are turned literally, as well as figuratively; they are bewildered, wearied, and too often disgusted with the confused, and consequently unsatisfactory assortment." She concludes with a "grave question" of whether there is "great risk of fostering in our children a hard, cold and indifferent spirit . . . a calculating and selfish disposition" which could "seriously hinder the moral and spiritual progress of the race."[87]

Hatred, malice, envy, selfishness, self-consciousness, a calculating disposition, weariness, bewilderment, a cold and indifferent spirit—these seem to threaten to arise when the child, in terms of voice, perspective, and desire, lurches toward the center of consideration in parenting and "education" generally. Abundance threatens not simply because of its materiality, but because this materiality fuses with the stark realization that the malleable child—that unfinished moral project—might be turned toward decidedly un-childlike and, to be sure, unchristian trajectories. Home discipline and maternal practice form the moral pivot of this potential turn whereby the growing ethos of valuing and perhaps valorizing the child's perspective—for instance, enacting sympathy and empathy for young children in terms of the pain they might feel when punished—also nourishes a disposition to participate in their pleasures and see the world in that delight.

For historian Gary Cross, this delight arrives in a new form of innocence arising in the late-nineteenth- and early-twentieth-century American culture of capitalism. Alongside the familiar notion of sheltered innocence, where children are to be cut off and protected from threats posed by the adult world, stands a "wondrous innocence." Wondrous innocence can be found in the image of the "delighted child" who expresses a "look of wonder" that arises from pleasures that are "unsought" by the child.[88] Rather, it is a pleasure mainly of, by, and for adults to be evoked in and through the child as a way to stave off the "sins" old age. For Cross, the threat of a loss of a pastoral past that associated children with nature made middle-class parents long nostalgically for their own childhoods. With the rise of a consumer culture in the late-Victorian era, he argues, commercial interests and parents' desires converged in the wondrous child, which gained expression through invocations of the "cuteness" of children in dolls and other products, in stories and iconographic representations in advertisements and popular venues like the cover of the famed *Saturday Evening Post.*[89] In this way, the cute, wondrous child at once draws upon pre-capitalist imagery and associations while also providing a vehicle for consumer participation on behalf of children.

However, when examined in the context of the intermixture of and tensions between concerns about discipline and rewards in the governance of children in the home, as expressed in public discourses in the last decades of the 1800s, the impetus for parents who might seek to evoke a sense of wonder takes on a different hue than what Cross theorizes. If it is the case that punishment, including severe corporal punishment, began to diminish as a regularly acceptable, unremarked-on mode of parenting—though the "necessity" for governance remained a key element of daily life—then something was needed to take its place. Unable to govern as strongly, exclusively, and unreflexively through physical discipline as had been practiced (or, at least, as authoritatively sanctioned), these parents' ability to direct or otherwise guide children likewise underwent a transformation gradually in the direction of rewards and incentives—or, as it would be put in a later time, of positive reinforcement. Put simply, rewards of various kinds became readily available and increasingly viable disciplinary tools at the disposal of well-off American families. Indeed, it appears that those thought to subscribe to the "new" childhood and the new, "modern" parenting of the late nineteenth century are those who would incorporate a reward structure into their system of governance, making of it a form of "development."

From this view, the sense of wonder that may have become associated with gifting children, as Cross argues, indicates not so much the presence of a parental longing for their own lost childhoods as it does an absence of—and substitute for—severe punishment of the child. It is likely that the childhood memories of many adults of this time were populated with recollections of pain or the anticipation of pain, as described by several writers above; hence they may have been trying to produce, rather than reproduce or reinstate, a wondrous innocence for their children. The depiction of a wide-eyed wondrous child opening Christmas presents within the gleeful family circle[90] screens out the looming specter of the hickory switch by standing in for it and thereby offers an affirmation of the place of goods and incentives in family life. If there manifests a sense of "innocence" in this scenario—wondrous or otherwise—it comes not in the form of shelter from an adult world of market calculus, but as a buffer from adult, patriarchal power. Hence, the "gift economy" that arose in middle-class Victorian family life[91] in mid-century, centering strongly on children, can be understood as a largely maternal, perhaps maternalist, response to the ever-intensifying pressures to transfer all responsibility for maintaining the patriarchal household onto mothers who, as we have seen time and again, had become subject to the unsettling openness of the malleable child. In this light, the increasingly popular Santa Claus can be seen not simply as a mythical figure deployed to hide the market origins of gifts in order to retain a kind of authenticity to the holy day, as Nissenbaum[92] insists; rather—and perhaps additionally—Santa Claus assisted in deflecting the everyday dynamics of punishment and reward onto an impersonal plane, embodied by a half-deity who stands in judgment of children but does so with a benevolent thumb on the scale. What Kris Kringle may have hidden (and may still hide) is not so much commercialism, but the "adult" or the "parent," who is both present and not present in the gift-obedience exchange ritual culminating for many in late December every year.

"Good and Happy at the Same Time": Making the Right "as Attractive as Possible"

Discourses about the ills of punishment and the ills of rewards both engaged with the child's perspective, making its acknowledgment something of a moral imperative. The ills of punishment arose, in part, from a disregard of the child's view—the pain, the humiliation, the fear experienced. The punished child existed as something of a non-being, a non-person. The ills of reward, on the other hand, seemed to impart an excess of consideration of the child's view—her/his wants and impulses, which were dreaded as productive of the spoiled child and destructive of the parent-child relationship, both leading toward an unsavory adulthood. A third way charted not a simple middle course, but one tolerant, even encouraging, of children's desires while seeking to avoid the pitfalls of an overwrought sense of self-consciousness thought unbecoming of children and destructive of character. An unattributed article in *Babyhood* from 1901 advised that the central problematic of parenting concerned itself with how to make children "good and happy at the same time."[93] Pleasing the child here stands on par with enacting its governance. It is not abundance, not market culture, not commercial life per se that are the antagonists in this narrative of the child's ontology but rather, in a familiar refrain, it is the "parents" who must shoulder the weight of stitching happiness and obedience together: "Parents are greatly to blame for careless over-indulgence or undue severity— whichever form the want of judgment may take—that results in so much that is hard for the young victims of their mismanagement." "Managing" children correctly, the author continues, comes about when adults make a "special effort to see life from the child's point of view."[94]

To see the world with and through children's eyes—to engage in what I have elsewhere termed "pediocularity"[95]—situates the child as a node of knowledge and thus of moral value and valuation. Once centered, the child's view becomes something employable and deployable as an argument for the veracity of its focal position. The author quoted above continues: "In thus trying to realize more keenly what life means to the children, we shall be able to estimate better the extent of the demands we are making upon them."[96] All else responds to the centrality of the child's eye, whether in efforts to affirm or contest. But, in child governance, in the home, in the church, and in relation to the society of relevance, there are rights and wrongs, goods and bads, which must be upheld and demonstrated. "Right must be done at any cost, and it is obviously a duty for everyone, especially mothers, to make *the doing of right as attractive as possible*, more particularly until the habit of doing right for its own sake is thoroughly formed."[97] The mother arises as one who is duty bound to pave attractive, pleasing pathways toward good behavior which, it is assumed and hoped, leads to good intentions and correct reasoning. Child innocence—when and where it becomes manifest—evinces less a positive state of being than a residence in the relative absence of culpability; i.e., not a retreat from desire, but an achieved, cooperative production of appropriate longings.

4

Simplicity, Money, and Property

Moralities, Materialities, and the Didactic Imperative

Ascendant at the turn of the nineteenth century, the figure of the long-ing, desiring child of the white middle-class imagination arose from a now-familiar dynamic between child malleability, maternal responsibility-liability, and the growing centrality of the child's perspective. As a complex of tensions, historically situated and located, this dynamic forms the crux, the generative core, of a rather resilient and generalized figuration of the child consumer recognizable and operative in contemporary practice. The procreant nature of these tensions—and thus this figure—resides in and results from the moral tensions it necessarily produces as a matter of course. Whatever immediate problems the child had posed for Protes-tants or Victorians—be it salvation, taste or governance—these were not solved by the fixes offered by mothers, preachers, and teachers; rather, the increasing insistence of child malleability guaranteed, ideologically and practically, that the child was to remain a problem in perpetuity: the ontological and epistemological core of childhood would produce and reproduce itself as moral vexation.

In this way, malleability ensured, and continues to ensure, moral hazard. Mothers, charged with the Herculean task of anticipating and countering the hydra-headed beast of unending risk, acquired the mul-tiply perilous duty of attending to, accounting for, and ultimately lion-izing children's subjectivities—i.e., their perspectives, desires, feelings. Supported by an admixture diffusion of the theoretical understandings of educational theorists like Locke and Rousseau, as well as Spencer, Froebel, and Pestalozzi, mothers and others of the new middle-class parenting struggled with the impossibilities of governing children ac-cording to social expectation while facing diminishing recourse to strict, perhaps harsh, discipline. Decades of discourse, child study, and the gospel of child development prepared the way for mothers, physicians, psychologists, and observers to appreciate that a young child's disobedience stemmed not from innate depravity or the hand of Satan, but from the workings of as-yet-incomplete, undeveloped mechanisms of reasoning. Simple moral suasion would bear no fruit here. The young child would need to be shown and persuaded away from the incorrect and inappropriate and enticed toward proper attitudes and objects of attention until correct ways became habitual.

Goods, materials, and amusements, as we have seen, composed essential elements of a child's world, not as things from which to be shielded but as ingredients with which to educate, govern, and construct selves and lives when engaged with in proper amounts and durations. From this vantage, middle-class children's middle-class desires were not to be considered necessarily wrong or incorrect in and of themselves, but as ever-present, if problematic, facticities requiring direction and guidance from (mainly) middle-class mothers. The emergent conundrum of an emerging middle-class childhood at this time assembled around the congenital strain represented in late Victorian selfhood—and examined closely in the discussion of taste in chapter 2—whereby true value existed internally and ephemerally but could only be known and accessed in relation to an external world of material things. Moral or sentimental value, in this way, remained perpetually in some sort of communication with pecuniary value. Yet, the children of a growing moneyed and professional class arose in and from material relations—by default as well as by design. From the pedagogy of Friedrich Froebel's kindergarten, which put physical objects at the center of instruction, to the rituals of festive gift-giving, to the increasingly accepted ideas of instructional toys, the materiality of childhood could not stand apart from character training and moral pedagogy.

This chapter examines the cultural-interpretive labor involved in defining right from wrong goods and activities and in negotiating the place of possessions, money and property in the instruction and rearing of children in the latter quarter of the nineteenth century. It is a labor that fell to fathers as well as to mothers, particularly when money was involved. Under such an episteme, and with so much at stake, responses to materiality clustered around a didactic imperative: the necessity to turn all aspects of child's life into an instructional course of action. No moment, it seems, could sit quietly without a lesson to impart. No action or inaction was without some consequence for the child. All objects, including money itself (see below), instructed in one way or another. Indeed, the didactic imperative—operative for generations in different modes in American parenting practice and discourse[1]—manifested in the dynamic of objects and exchange processes themselves, distinguishable from but connected with parenting/mothering efforts.

Observers and commentators invested faith in the self-corrective characteristics of simple goods and money (especially in the form of allowances), and in the notions of children's property rights. Always perched on the tipping point of morality, children and their relation to the material-pecuniary world were thought by many to be not only salvageable but necessarily consequential for the child's, and civilization's, future. The threat to childhood among this particular class fraction arose as much from within the child in the form of innate appetite as it did from the externalities of an emergent form of consumer capitalism. In the process of coming to terms with a growing material-commercial culture and with the inescapable presence of money in middle-class children's lives, observers, pundits, and advice-givers framed their responses in terms of justice and fairness whereby the child's subjectivity, its personhood, appears as an increasingly intractable focal point with which to assess the morality of materiality.

Simplicity

A growing "objective culture," as sociologist Georg Simmel might have put it, incorporated and encouraged a consciousness of childhood, of a new, modern, liberal, middle-class childhood wherein objects—and hence industry and money and exchange—mattered in new ways.[2] Though small in scale and limited in scope, the production of things specifically intended for children's use and consumption took on increasingly purposeful effort in design and promotion over the late 1800s and into the twentieth century. Circumscribed niche industries for children's books,[3] toys,[4] ready-made clothing,[5] and nursery ware[6] varied widely by location and concentration and could be purchased in local dry-goods stores and through mail-order catalogues such as those published by the Sears company of Chicago. Advertisements in periodicals like *Babyhood* and the *Ladies' Home Journal* indicate, in addition, a growing trade and interest in baby carriages and some types of food for children—particularly condensed milk and cereal. BB-gun rifles and model train sets regularly appeared on the pages of specialty magazines for boys such as the *The Boys' World*.[7]

A persistent question confronting many living during the rise of modern consumer society centered on the question of whether and how human character would or would not change in relation to the unprecedented and ever-increasing availability of goods and the widespread material abundance.[8] The proliferation of things in the world ushered in by increased material production and a rising consumerist posture among the moneyed and not-so-moneyed classes posed multiple challenges to raising children according to an ethos of self-control and self-reliance.[9] Material life, burgeoning in both quantity and kind, brought with it ambiguities concerning the worth of things (e.g., the relationship between price and value) and its impact on the ability to forge character. On the one hand, faith in the absolute presence of child malleability—in the strength and domination of "first impressions"—ensured something of an endless porousness to the child, an almost undifferentiated openness to the influences of the world. On the other, long-practiced notions about the training in taste and character were met with the increasingly hegemonic presence of the child's subjectivity—his or her wants and desires—which took on something of an air of naturalized authority.

It is along this latter vector that the child's subjectivity becomes taken up as a measure of verity and where great energy, consternation, opportunity, sense of embattlement, unity, and division accrued. In one sense, children's affinities for things and activities—e.g., the "instinct" of play, the seeking of amusement—gradually pitched toward being construed as likely benign and perhaps benevolent. In this new post-Victorian childhood—a childhood emergent before Victoria had departed—parents and caregivers often enough were advised to follow the child and to seek the places where impulses pointed the way to child-centered insight and where they led astray into selfish indulgence.[10] Each step in the propagation of material life of children instigated concern about the content and direction of childhood and, as well, demanded a requisite response. Parenting this version of the child required not only an eternal vigilance for potential dangers, but also a cunning eye and an astute analysis to undertake empathetic action. Here, a number of adjustments were at work to find some sort of route through opposing tendencies.

At its most basic, the notion of "simplicity" served as a kind of over-arching frame of discourses of taste by way of attenuating the quantitative and qualitative variety presented by an expanding world of goods. Especially for those with means, the number and kind of toys children received, particularly around Christmastime, presented challenges for training in character and taste. One writer, making a "plea for fewer playthings" in 1888, described the marked change in attitude and behavior of her three-year-old daughter after a particularly materially bountiful Christmas, when she received three different dolls.[11] The family "allowed" some of the toys to break (helped, in one instance, by a "number 9 boot"). The solution of (motivated) material attrition was met with a different response a few issues later by a mother writing of how her boy at first shunned a brand new horse for a "shabby" valise, only later to embrace the horse,[12] noticing thereafter his preference for old, basic toys that were not broken. The lesson from this mother, who affirmed the initial plea for fewer things, struck a different posture: "Is not this faithfulness to old friends, albeit only toys, a most beautiful trait of childhood? I, too, would plead for fewer playthings and more substantial ones . . . It seems to me that there is nothing more absurd than to give a child a costly book or toy which he can never use until it is held and manipulated by a grown person, and a child will always resent such interference with his rights with all the sense of justice of which his little heart is capable."[13] A number of ideas unfold in this brief passage: monetary cost and usefulness to the child are put in opposition to each other; the right kind of toy or object is one the child can use on her or his own; and the child displays an inner sense of wisdom and "justice" and understands that its "rights" are tied to an appropriate mode of individualized and autonomous action. Here, the child's innate, practical wisdom enacted through play confronts and defeats the logic of a presumably adult consumerist view that tends to equate value and price. The world—or market—may offer too many playthings, an excess corrected when the observant parent intercedes as an informed purchaser of an appropriate object.

Indeed, any number of writers in *Babyhood* expressed concern that too many toys or amusements, or the wrong kind, would lessen children's ability to amuse themselves[14] and consequently dull the child's ability to appreciate simplicity—a pillar of good taste. One mistake, a contributor (apparently a school teacher) notes in 1893, "lies in expecting children to meet us on our own plane, forgetting by what a long road and roundabout way we reached the plane ourselves." She continues: "A toy that is complete in itself, that calls for no play of the imagination, that allows no scope for the child's creative instinct, fails to charm, while the rude, most clumsy toy with which he can 'do things' is a priceless treasure." What appears as "trash" to an adult ("a bit of board with its nails and strings and colored paper attachments") represents a "brilliant fancy" in which its owner "sees in it wonders of which we cannot dream." Teachers who recognize this brilliance can spell the "prophecy of his future career" of being educated as a future inventor. Froebel's system of "gifts," she continues, tempts the kindergarten teacher to "please her own fancy at the expense of the child's needs," offering evidence of simple games children played with rings and sticks and beads and the excitement that surrounded planting and tending to a garden. She concludes, "Ready-made toys that will 'go of themselves,' ready-made thoughts that are complete in themselves, and are tacked on to the memory, at no point touching the children's experiences, reason or reflection, should form no part of the child's education."[15] In this emergent nineteenth-century version of the creative child,[16] things and thoughts inform each other and inform the shape of the child's mind and experience—all of which are to be directed or curated by an adult, in this case a teacher.

Christmastime seemed to offer the forum to express dissatisfaction with ready-made toys. In December 1894, a mother wrote "Pleas for the Home-Made Toy," striking a familiar refrain that "common everyday resources for amusing the little ones were being lost sight of." Attempting to assuage the anxiety of mothers who worry about not being able to purchase "a quarter of the pretty things which will keep her little one supplied with the requisite novelties," the writer details many traditional games (like pat-a-cake and peek-a-boo) and suggests that many items around the house, like clothespins, can serve well to entertain the children. Indeed, she notes, children tend to prefer basic items: "Do all babies nowadays cut their teeth on an elaborately carved ivory ring, or at least a rubber one, or are there some who still cling perversely to a little earthen-ware butter dish, or even the wonderful celluloid tape measure out of momma's work basket? Plenty of little people will from choice reject the costly rattle for plebeian beans or buttons in a tightly corked bottle." She ends with reassurance that the mother who uses things from her kitchen and sewing basket this way "need never feel anxiety that her baby is not enjoying life quite as much as her more fortunate neighbor who has abundant means to bring home a new plaything everyday."[17] Another writer affirms that that her boy likes her home-made gifts the best.[18] The child affirmed here appears to sport a Bohemian spirit toward the material world.

Not pitched yet as a direct confrontation between commercial producers and the child, the problem of character training posed by a striving world of ever-bountiful and ever-elaborate goods redounds to mothers. The doctrine of early impressions situated mothers, educators, and other adults as moral brokers of sorts between children and the worlds they would encounter, positioned to act as arbiters and translators who would adjudicate between the child and relevant material cultures. It is a position nearly identical—structurally and morally—to that of the new motherhood arising from liberal Protestantism as discussed earlier. In both cases, the mother was to attend to every potential "input" to the child, attend to her own behavior as exemplar, and self-regulate her own weaknesses. Mothers of late nineteenth century middle-class or middle-class-aspirant families additionally had to strive to take the perspective of the child—to enter into its interiority in some way—and to understand the natural brilliance of its play, desires, and wants. The world that is producing ready-made toys also is encouraging dull, uncreative thinking in children and status anxiety in mothers. The threat here, as expected, lies with the mother in her inability or unwillingness to see beyond the surface of the unnecessarily manufactured complication of toys and into an inner simplicity of character a child would naturally exude, if left to its own "devices," as it were.

Simplicity offered something of a solution to the apparent and apparently cumulative density of children's material worlds due, in part, to the remarkable ideological resilience of the narrative equating simplicity and taste. Strongly resonant in the 1840s, equivalences of simplicity and taste remained pedagogically relevant to middle-class mothering practice and discourse as that century drew to a close. One writer, in 1891, opined in the *Ladies' Home Journal* that "people of limited means aspire to many luxuries nowadays that never entered into the imagination of their father as being possible to attain." The anxiety to keep up with the standard set by "our neighbors" can be tempered by the "wife" who "regulates the expenditure and manner of living" for the family and in so doing can impart value lessons to her children about the importance of ministering to the "inner life." To maintain simplicity of the home and simplicity of dress for children and to "have everything in perfect keeping," she insists, is itself "evidence of refined taste."[19] Twenty years later, another *Ladies' Home Journal* writer could not have been any clearer in her "chat with girls": "Good taste is simplicity. That's it, girls, right in a nutshell, and to make it all the clearer to you let me tell you how the dictionary defines simplicity: 'Freedom from complexity; freedom from artificial adornment; clearness.'"[20] Another writer amends that "simple clothes" are not necessarily "plain clothes."[21] The tight relation between simplicity and taste continued reiteration though periodicals and moved into "expert" circles through the 1930s in discussions of clothing.[22] As well, as a number of writers propounded, proper children's rooms must be kept unassuming and furnished with inexpensive, oftentimes cast-off, items[23]—a notion that became, perhaps paradoxically, ingrained into commercial design thinking by 1930.[24]

Money enabled and encouraged the proliferation and accumulation of things—things that complicated the lessons of taste. The more options available to children and parents, in this view, the more likely children will become conscious of externalities and thereby become self-conscious of the gaze of others. Unnecessary expense, fuss, and frill increased the challenge to be able to cut through the artifice of things and enable character to dominate. It is easy enough to read the focus on simplicity in children's things as a straightforward cultural response to loudly voiced contemporaneous concerns about the loss of authentic character, selfhood and, particularly, manhood during a time when bureaucratic organizations, urbanization, and mass-produced, prepackaged goods came to predominate.[25] Complaints lodged at the turn of the century in the *Ladies' Home Journal*—that Christmas had become complicated,[26] that American women had become "rushed" with activities, keeping up with the new age and with ambition,[27] and that happiness may be well-nigh impossible alongside modern achievements[28]—found that a return to some manner of simplicity offered a solution.

Cultural historian Jackson Lears contends that "childlike traits" such as simplicity were embraced by late-century Victorians because the "psychic demands of adulthood grew more onerous" under the onus of capitalist expansion.[29] "Innocent sincerity" and a "primitivist veneration for vitality" could be found in the figure of the child which, he contends, provided for adults an "after-hours escape from the rigors of bourgeois adulthood."[30] Fears of over-civilization stimulated interest in a refined, comforting conception of the child that increasingly stood for the youth of the race itself[31] and provided pointed evidence of "man's" fall from grace. However, what Lears fails to recognize is that for mothers and those for whom the care of children constituted their central life duty, there were no "after hours" to which to escape, particularly when it comes to children. Malleability does not take a holiday, and training in taste, simplicity, discipline, and governance likewise presents itself as ongoing and perpetually demanding. No doubt, childhood as a trope and symbol served to express antimodern sentiment[32] and it is likely that the urge toward "simplicity" in children's lives and things constituted an element of that critique. Pleas for simplicity also operated as critiques of—or warnings to—mothers as well, reminders to remain focused on the inner virtues and inner beauty of her children and not on the surface of passing fads and fashions. Too much frill proffered by mothers to their children, their male children especially, once again was seen as a weakening of civilization, of its feminization, and as just one step away from an original, natural, perhaps "savage" imagined in Child Study recapitulation theory of the time.[33] If a focus on simplicity remained trained on children and their governance throughout several decades of mothering advice and discourse, it did so not because simplicity was seen, simplistically, as a mere "childhood trait"; simplicity maintained its cultural robustness in large part because it continued to offer a pathway for a bourgeois—and assuredly white—moral selfhood to manifest in relation to the world of things while serving at times as an antidote for some of civilization's ills.

Money

From *Godey's Lady's Book*, 1879:

> It is very necessary that children should learn, when young, the value
> and the use of money; they should be taught to spend it, as well as to
> save it. For this purpose, at an early age, children should have a fixed al-
> lowance, proportioned to their years, and to the means of their parents.
> This should be given to them monthly, and at the end of each month they
> should be required to produce an exact account of the expenditure of
> the money. By this plan the parents will have an opportunity of advising,
> reproving or commending the mode in which the allowance has been
> used. The children have the pleasure of following their own tastes and
> judgments, restrained by the prudence their limited means will enforce.[34]

In this passage, the ways in which children ought to be given money
and how their relationship to expenditure should be managed fall in a
clear alignment with the sense of childhood manifest in the discourses
of taste, reward, and simplicity discussed throughout this book. Money
is to be seen as yet another arrow in the quiver of parental guidance, put
upon the child as a system of restraints and rewards, serving as a "valuable branch of education." Money, here, operates didactically, not as an
evil to be avoided or to be kept ritually separate from the child, but as a
set of relations in which to engage such that the varied lessons unfold to
address different temperaments: "The charitable will learn self-denial;
the thoughtless will be trained to reflect, and the extravagant will learn
economy."[35]

Money also figures in "taste," in the sense of preferences, which enable a certain pleasure of individual choice and pursuit. Denying children this pursuit of pleasure by refusing to give an allowance, for the
author of this editorial piece, arises from parents' desire to "keep their
children in subjection." The freedom thereby granted by a regular sum
would be regulated by family means—a moral economy in a rather literal sense—in concert with the ever-watchful eye and behavior of the
mother, who herself must again monitor her own desires and acquisi-
tive tendencies. A "judicious" mother "must give her admonitions and
counsels with gentleness and discretion, giving to example as well as

precept, for if the child sees injudicious and extravagant expenditure with economical advice, the latter will be naturally attributed to meanness."[36] Money and the ability to wield it somewhat at one's own discretion begets a measure of interpersonal equality, a sense of justice, within in the household. The "child," armed with money, reflects back on the mother as a disciplinary mechanism by applying the gaze of equality of relative expenditure.

The *Godey's* article presaged what was to become a site of contention for many contemplating how to coordinate child governance with the thickening presence of money and exchange of what Mark Twain and Charles Warner would dub "The Gilded Age."[37] In 1888, *Babyhood* sought fit to reprint an entire chapter of Jacob Abbott's *Gentle Measures in the Management and Training of the Young*, originally published in 1871. Abbott—who also authored *The Mother at Home: Principles of Maternal Duty* at about the same time (see figure 4.1)—affirms the place of money in "cultivating and developing the qualities of sound judgment and of practical wisdom" and in "its bearing upon the subject of the proper mode of dealing with their wishes and requests."[38] For the noted author, the development of and adherence to a system of particular ways and means of monetary transfer between parent and child is of utmost importance. The child in question, for Abbott, is a boy and money figures into the development of manliness:

If a parent wishes to eradicate from the mind of his boy all feelings of delicacy and manly pride, to train him to the habit of obtaining what he wants by importunity or servility, and to prevent his having any means of acquiring any practical knowledge of the right use of money, any principles of economy, or any of that forethought and thrift so essential to ensure prosperity in future life, the best way to accomplish these ends would seem to be to have no system in supplying him with money in his boyish days, but to give it to him only when he asks for it, and in quantities determined only by the frequency and importunity of his calls.[39]

Abbott here affirms the relationship between money and power for the child—the option seems to be either servility of training or "prosperity in the future"—and does so with a masculinist undertone. Without a system or sense of regularity, the boy has no choice but to rely upon

Figure 4.1. The Reverend Jacob Abbott's *The Mother at Home: Principles of Maternal Duty* and his *Gentle Measures in the Management and Training of the Young*, both published in the early 1870s, helped codify the position of Christian mothers as interposed between God, child, and economy. Source: Jacob Abbott, *The Mother at Home: Principles of Maternal Duty*, 1871. New York: The American Tract Society (inside cover).

"his adroitness in coaxing" parents. Acquiring money through persistent request or sly maneuvering, rather than systematic management, represents "those means which are the most ignoble and most generally despised by honorably-minded men as means for the attainment of any human end."[40]

Setting the boy up to beg or plot, in other words, encourages precisely those actions of practiced street urchins like Oliver Twist, Charles Dickens's cultural icon (1837–39). Perhaps worse, the "lives of men of means" are made "miserable by the recklessness in respect to money which is displayed by their sons and daughters as they advance towards maturity, and by the utter want, on their part, of all sense of delicacy, and of obligation or of responsibility of any kind towards their parents in respect to their pecuniary transactions."[41] Abbott's system requires strict regularity of payment of a decided sum, which encumbers the parent to a contract-like relationship, be it through payment or bank account with credits and debits. The parent must keep an implicit and utmost faith with the child (here he includes girls) not only in terms of payment but also in terms of the ownership of the currency—i.e., to refrain from "borrowing" from the child's savings during an emergency and then neglecting to repay it.

Pecuniary relations—here including those of child and parent—induce commitments and ties, make for trust and power and, as well, contain within them their own form of didacticism. Abbott also urges that parents allow children to employ their reserve entirely at the child's own discretion—excepting of course anything that can be injurious—allowing the natural consequences of their decisions to serve as lessons of consumption and foresight without much intervention on the part of mothers. If, for instance, a boy wishes to buy a kite, and the mother thinks there are too many trees nearby in which it is likely to become tangled, she can explain her reasons against buying the kite, but should not prevent him from obtaining the desired object. When the kite gets stuck in the trees and is no longer of use, she should not "triumph over him, and say, 'I told you how it would be. You would not take my advice, and now you see how it is.'" Rather, she should empathize with him and explain that sometimes spending money incurs losses and that he should learn from his decisions and how to "bear them like a man."[42]

Like taste, the dynamics of money and acquisition seem to contain their own self-corrective mechanisms which, if wielded wisely by the mother and, often, the father, should produce prudent boys (and sometimes girls) who come to understand experientially the "value of a dollar"—and indeed the value of value itself. Money and possessions were not to be denied the child outright, as such actions were thought to highlight the "injustice" of unequal material relations between parents and children—as noted above—or activate the temptation to seek a forbidden fruit. Rather, written advice favored engaging children in pecuniary relations as one remedy for their insatiable and, on their own, uncontrollable desires. Like steering a sailboat, however, a slight change of tack, a miscalculation, can produce long-term deleterious results. One reverend, writing in 1890 for the *Ladies' Home Journal*, warned that mothers must guard against tendencies to spoil their children (boys especially, it seems), which comes about by giving in to his every demand and giving him "plenty of money without any question as to what he does with it." Knowing the worth of money comes by earning it, even if he is overpaid for everyday duties. Being too frugal with him, however, also produces a sense of imbalance, an unfairness, out of which comes temptation to steal from parents to procure the joy "just five pennies can bring."[43]

A regular contributor to *Babyhood*, Grace E. Eliot, echoed a contemporary wisdom of the moneyed classes at the turn of the century. She remarked that children's "eagerness" to spend forms part of their "unconscious desire to assimilate another of the great phases of our modern life, that of the trade world."[44] As such, they should not be denied the ability to earn it—though clearly not as wage laborers, but as helpers around the household, perhaps assisting the maid. Importantly, the child should not be denied the ability to spend it as "he" pleases: "If he spends unwisely, the pennies are lost; he must work to earn more, and that is scant encouragement to improvidence. Too long hoarding defeats its own object. Spending each penny as it comes is relaxing to the child's character. There are few mothers who cannot lift their child's ideals to the point where he will spend wisely, and the best plan is to allow him freely to choose some object that is within his reach."[45]

Whether it is the "child" who seeks assimilation into the trade world, or the adult seeking the same for the child—or both—it is evident that the moral tension manifested here at the turn of the century is not simply between a sentimental notion of a sheltered childhood and the vicissitudes of a market economy, as many have contended and assumed.[46] Rather, the key spindle of contention wrestled with extant, though ever modifying, strains where malleability, children's subjectivities, and maternal responsibility meet and overlap. The kind of presumed male child hewn here was thought cut from economic fabric and his childhood secured on a biographical trajectory into a world of commerce. For pretwentieth-century observers and commentators, as well as those active early in the new century, middle-class children's consumption[47] itself functioned as moral pedagogy. Ms. Eliot continues:

Otherwise he will become careless of results, and when this carelessness is later transferred to wider interests, it will undermine the whole character. And the lordly yielding of those pennies for the object for which they have been earned and saved! It is the child's first insight, perhaps, into the divine law of compensation, balance, justice. It is because men do not recognize this law that they fail to live up to the ideal of brotherhood. Everybody, in these days, seems perfectly willing to get something for nothing. And so we have sweat shops, and gambling dens, and bargain counters, and bread riots, and strikes. They are various results of willful or ignorant violation of this law of absolute adjustment, supreme as it is in the worlds of minds, soul, and matter.[48]

Economy, money, and consumption can be relied upon to teach "divine laws." Parents—here father as well as mothers—need to be active and invasive and, as well, laissez-faire: impossible balances.

Saving and thrift in themselves would not suffice at this time, as the "natural" tendency for children to be spendthrifts[49] was met by the unsavory figure of the miserly child who likes the sound of money rattling in his bank.[50] Teaching savings focuses on accumulation, one writer noted in 1893, "whereas it is quite necessary to know how to spend wisely."[51] The institutional response to the child spender (i.e., banking) in the 1910s to 1930s, as historian Lisa Jacobson demonstrates well, sought solutions with regard to notions of thrift in educational and promotional campaigns[52]—and ultimately advocated consumer training.[53] But these measures drew upon and were steeped in epistemological and ontological struggles about the nature and the provenance of desire and about how childhood figures and prefigures its manifestations. The "insatiability" of children's desires did not arise as a construct of children's libidinal hunger with the onset of consumer capitalism, as we have seen in earlier chapters. Nor did the idea and practice of the weekly child allowance come into being simply as a replacement—or cultural compensation— for the appearance of the economically useless child, as Zelizer[54] seems to contend. Rather, allowances or the piecemeal gifting of money appeared also to address the middle-class family's concern for training in taste and character, whereby the concern was centered not on keeping the child outside of commercial life, but on locating means to usher their mutual integration.

Money, Zelizer instructs, has often been taken by social theorists—Marx, Weber, and Simmel, among others—and observers alike to enforce a kind of leveling of value, whereby disparate things come to be understood as the "same" kinds of social objects.[55] Yet, as she illustrates, an attentive examination of social process will find that people create, exchange, and negotiate a variety of different kinds of monies, earmarked in some way, such that their uses and circulations are enabled in certain directions and prohibited in others. Political contributions, donations of various kinds, and money earned from illegal or illicit activities are but a few of the examples of earmarking of money[56] and hence the constructions of culturally grounded meanings of exchange and consumption.[57] One key distinction between working-class and middle-class approaches to money—besides whether or not the child was a wage earner—centered precisely on the extent of regulation thought to be in place with regard to the child's spending. As David Nasaw's history of working-class childhood in the Lower East Side of New York City (and other industrial cities) in the early twentieth century indicates, (male) child spenders enjoyed geographical mobility, social freedom, and influence with business proprietors on par, or nearly on par, with their elders.[58] These children—working often as newsies, bootblacks, and messengers—could buy what they wanted when they wanted for the most part, and did not have to wait to go home to fill their bellies. How much of the earned money "belonged" to the boy (or girl) earner and how much to the family, and to what ends, defined a significant element of working-class family at this time, speaking as it did to intergenerational relations, the expression of self in a consumer economy, and gender dynamics.[59]

For the middle-class child discursively bandied about on the pages of advice publications, the "earmarking" taking place occurred less at the level of currency—i.e., which money could be used for which purposes—and more at the level of the transaction and the prospective contemplation of transactions. Didacticism at the child-economy nexus—i.e., the supervised and guided working out of natural laws or tendencies—fits rather snugly with questions, issues, and epistemologies of taste. To spend "wisely" included being able to discern price-value relations; it also meant overcoming the lure of the surface of things, of the pull of novelty, so as to obtain things that are lasting and of beauty.

The morality of money and simplicity spoke not so much to material things themselves as to the character of how things might be acquired and used. The lessons to be imparted are intended to operate prospectively, in the register of anticipated purchases and anticipated wants, which were to be disciplined and guided according to a pedagogy of taste and thrift.

One writer tells a story of a girl "whose taste was supposed by her mother to be really superior" who was allowed to go shopping with a gold piece given to her on her birthday. The result was that she returned with an "appalling array of cheap jewelry, perfumery, and ridiculous trinkets." The lesson to mothers is transparent: "One should not take it for granted that children are born with a clear sense of the artistic, but should strive to develop one that is latent."[60] If outward instruction does not yield the desired results, a mother can rely on the auto-corrective dimensions of taste and economy to impart the lesson by experiencing the limits of a budget whereby the child "cannot spend its money and have it too. Better let the bank remain empty for a time than to refill it and let its owner feel it has unlimited means to draw upon."[61] In the kind of historical working-class contexts scholars have studied, the ability to "let the bank remain empty" was not a viable option for moral instruction. Mothers and parents did not have the leverage of disposable income for everyday pedagogy.

Although employed here and again over the subsequent decades into the twentieth century, faith in taste—in the pedagogy of taste (chapter 2)—appeared to be loosening a bit among those employing and creating a new-middle-class ethos of parenting. The sense this author offers is that taste, rather than being active and in need only of the "correct" object to be exercised, requires motivated and active intervention to awaken it from some "latent" state. If indeed "taste" and all that it has signified in the materiality of the Victorian, late-Victorian, and perhaps post-Victorian middle class cannot be relied upon to become manifest without intercession, then a vital feedback mechanism in the reproduction of class through childhoods ceases operating, or ceases operating as once hoped. Moving in to compensate and supplement the (slow and gradual) waning of taste is a reliance on the quantitative limits of money in relation to a marketplace—i.e., what the child can buy given its limited means. Here again, the parent finds herself as gatekeeper—or, better, bank teller—to the child's wishes and desires to which she must minister wisdom by precept and example.

As numerous writers testified, the ways in which children came to acquire money framed its social and moral meanings, and therefore its didactic, character-building value. From the late 1880s into the first decades of the twentieth century, public advice on children's allowances and monetary gifting coalesced around the idea that children must earn some of their money and must also be assured a certain amount of allowance, proper to the family's means and the age and gender of the child.[62] The trick of paying children for household duties, as Zelizer points out, lay in the difficulties of avoiding the confusion of household work with wage labor.[63] To make household chores subject to compensation by payment or to make a capricious allowance—thereby making the child "beg" and bargain for every hand out—is to render the home a workplace guided by the "principles of the shop floor,"[64] as a writer in *Harper's Bazaar* put it in 1900. One way past this merging of market and home was to frame the middle-class child's "dignity" as tied to the sense of equality and, I would say, personhood that arises from pecuniary participation—i.e., when consumption and ownership of possessions come to be apprehended as a right rather than a privilege.

Property

Guided money acquisition and management enabled the child to exercise judgment and to learn from the structure of pecuniary relations and dynamics. In the eyes of many turn-of-the-century parenting advice-givers, the material-moral being of middle-class childhood resulted from the Original Sin of desire, the direction and momentum of which must be controlled and directed in situ by mothers so as to enable a proper adult to emerge. Day by day, case by case, mothers were the ultimate governor—the key servo-mechanism—in the feedback apparatus of children's encounters with the world of goods and economic value. Here, the small-scale purchases involved, the low numerical amounts of expenditure, and the nature of things to be purchased enabled mothers/parents to allow money to instruct by providing a kind of play arena for the development of an entrepreneurial or, at least, fiscal self.

Discourses and notions of taste coupled with the measured, and clearly uneven, transition from punishment to reward in child governance affirmed, in their own ways, the place of goods and possessions in childhood and parenting. In the process, these asserted the child's subjectivity as authority in both mothering practice and in the maternal voicing of children's perspectives in publicly offered discussion. With the sense of an arising subject and subjectivity, the figure of the child also acquired a growing sense of social personhood, whereby fairness of treatment would accompany the recognition and valorization of the child's view. A significant swath of the consideration of severe punishment, as discussed in chapter 3, arose in concert with the appreciation of the child's experience, regardless of whether it was remembered, invented, or observed. In a structurally similar way, the incorporation of money—its acquisition and management—into character training at once acknowledges and plays off of the child's conception of value, a conception into which the thoughtful, responsible parent should enter. The admonishments to parents—both mothers and fathers—to deal squarely with children in matters of money indicate that elements of fairness accompany and inform the valorization of the child's world and understandings.

Questions and considerations of children's rights stewed in this milieu of taste, money, reward, and punishment. Writers asked of readers if children were behaving obstinately by refusing to be kissed by strangers or relatives, clearly a common practice at the time,[65] with many in favor of the bodily integrity and the right of children not to be kissed and of the "respect due the young," even if such refusal upset those present.[66] Respecting the young was an oft-repeated refrain and included, among others, the right to be instructed, the right to be governed by fixed— rather than capricious—rules of conduct,[67] the right to be treated well in public,[68] the right to be dressed well,[69] and the right to be born of good parents.[70] On top of and intertwined with the pleas and invocations of these varied rights, the notion of property and property rights garnered attention, discussion, and elaboration.

Ensconced in an expanding, increasingly dense world of goods, parents and educators sought to make sense of the materiality of childhood. The idea that a child can "own" or possess "property" in the parenting advice and consultation literature took a number of forms and reached out from typical or expected philosophical positions and into the emerging world of consumer culture and post-Victorian childhood. One early statement by Emma C. Embury, writing in 1844, did not note the idea of property specifically, but emplaced the materiality of childhood into her notion of rights:

> One of the first rights which children are disposed to claim, is that of being instructed and enlightened. As soon as they begin to take note of objects, their inquiring looks tell what their imperfect organs of speech fail to utter; and as soon as they can frame language for their thoughts, they ask questions. Every thing is new and strange to them; objects of curiosity and interest surround them on every side, and they demand the information which is best adapted to their unfolding faculties.[71]

Instruction and education arise from children's engagement with the world of objects, objects about which they have a "right" to be informed. Parental attention and care, integral to this process, must be given with the young child's view in mind. Embury beseeches the readership to think back on their own childhoods when "light was poured into our own souls" and note that the moments recalled were ones "of the mother who threw aside book or work at the call of her child, and seated on the floor amid our heap of infant toys, would share our sports, while she imparted the golden treasures of daily wisdom."[72] Part of the right due children includes being attended to on their own terms—with their own things and on their own spatial and temporal planes.

Writing in 1892, Ruth Ashmore, in her column "Side Talks With Girls" in the *Ladies' Home Journal*, affirmed the links between mother's duty, children's desires, and their God-given rights:

> You have no right to withhold from your child any innocent pleasure; grief and unhappiness come soon enough and the playtime of life ought surely to be when one is young. You have no right to demand from your child to do, and do for you, without any regard to its happiness nor its hope for the future. You have no right to consider that your child is not an independent being; it should be allowed to think and to reason out, with your assistance, the problems of life, but your assistance should be

so sweetly given that is will never seem an impertinence. You toss your head at the idea of a mother being impertinent to a child, yet it is possible. A child has a right to its own belongings, to its own thoughts and to its own life . . .[73]

Addressed to the adult female readership of a successful national periodical—specifically "a talk aimed at my married girls"—the child's rights take the form of negations, of disapprobation to mothers about what they should not do. Pleasure and ownership interlace with independence and happiness to weave a necessary part of an ideal of a modern, bourgeois subject. Here the unmarked white child, despite its age, is presumed or invoked to have rights—and to have a right to have rights—that should be "respected as religious as the rights of parents."[74]

Specific discussion of property and property rights came into focus beginning in the late 1880s during the post-Reconstruction, Jim Crow era when contributors and letter writers alike noted that, at times, white children were treated like the "property of others" or as "public property" and displayed concern also with a sense of public respect, or lack thereof, shown these children.[75] To be able to hold property indicates that one is not the property of others and will not easily descend to that status. Instructing children on their property "rights" or privileges in this way served as a symbolic and practical wedge of a specific sort of social distinction—one not simply of class, but also of personhood.

Commonly, property referred severally to a child's "possession," a developing sense of ownership, and the social right and wherewithal to possess. A child should be taught which toys are hers and which are those belonging to other children as well as which things are hers and which are mother's. Toys most often took on the possessive case, as the materials most readily available to children and most readily identified as "children's."[76] The notion of property bespeaks an individualized self, a person recognized as capable and worthy of exercising ownership. In the 1890s, the increasing attention paid to the sense of ownership in children understood the "property sense" as developmentally emergent and, like money, subject to being steered in different directions with desirable and undesirable consequences. In this way, the desire to own things begins to appear as a "natural" characteristic and impulse of a proper, emerging middle-class self—a trait vital to participation in a capitalist cultural-economic order. As naturalized in this way, the "property sense" also forms a foundation for children's rights.

Writing on "The Property Rights of Children" in 1895, Lavina Goodwin enunciates an ongoing discourse, thereby reaffirming its fortitude: "Instinctively children have a lively sense of ownership, and with it are associated strong convictions of justice concerning the protection of their rights."[77] To recognize a child's sense of ownership is to recognize it as a person cognizant of and deserving of justice. Along these lines, to recognize children's personhood requires appreciating that their view of things and of value arise from their comparatively restricted experience: "If they overestimate the value of small possessions, according to their limited capacities, it is not certain they fall so far below our plans to merit reproof or ridicule."[78] The piece is a plea to parents, made through several examples, to take seriously the seemingly insignificant tussles among children about the ownership and possession of toys and small things in which children regularly engage. Children's property rights must begin from an acknowledgment of their subject positions regarding the valuation of things and the consequent enactments of justice in and for their worlds: "A principle of equity in what possesses little or no intrinsic worth is as true, if not as momentous, as where it involves the cattle on a thousand hills or the commerce of nations. How shall they weigh with our balance who have never been in our place, when we, who have occupied their place so often, fail to observe a just balance between child and child?"[79] How parents handle these very incidents—"from the time an infant is able to recognize its cup and rattle"—contributes mightily to forming ideas of justice for the "coming man or woman."[80]

Subsequent responses to Ms. Goodwin's salvos came from many directions, with one parent asking at what point respecting property rights turns into supporting selfishness.[81] Others concurred that parents should help children understand not just their own property rights but also those of others—to come to learn the difference between "mine and thine"—which, at once, serves as a sign of responsible upbringing and would likely produce respectful and respectable citizens of the future.[82] Cognizance of property relations, for some, begins in the micro-ecologies of the nursery and the dinner table where a sense of ownership, and thus a responsibility for maintaining order, can be instilled by giving children real, quality furniture in their rooms[83] and in the helping of home tasks, like sewing.[84] As with other elements of the child's world, many readers and authors concurred that attending to property and property rights formed an important aspect of discipline and governance,[85] while others warned that instructing too closely on "mine and thine" in the nursery might become demoralizing for children and difficult for parents to enforce.[86]

For all its pedagogical promise, the notion of children's property rights would not shake suspicions that untutored and perhaps unlimited desire—as supposedly found in the youngest among us—can be explained with reference to an original depravity or evil. As one letter to *Babyhood* in 1897 puts it, "That children are conceived in wickedness and brought forth in sin is the firm belief of many good people." The writer continues on to relate how an incentive to collect fir (tree) tips around the house for piece payment curbed, but probably did not cure, the instinct of acquisitiveness in a son who had the "habit" of stealing family members' money. "Legitimate acquisition" seemed to offset the desire of the boy to "misappropriate the property of others" but, the writer cautions, "'acquisitiveness' is a characteristic unusually strong in some children" which can only be guided and not suppressed.[87] Indeed, the idea that children by nature are desiring, consuming, voracious beings took on new language and framework as the twentieth century opened, with the work of G. Stanley Hall and the Child Study movement promoting the conception of the human lifespan as replicating that of the entirety of the evolution of the species and, with it, the march of civilization. Such a view is noted in *Babyhood* by long-time contributor Grace Eliot: "It is a truism among educators that the child is somewhat of a savage. He comes into the world without ethical or intellectual ideas. He wants to be kept warm, well fed, kept comfortable, at the expense of others as far as possible."[88]

Eliot, who just three years earlier had written that children's eagerness to spend money stemmed from their desire to assimilate the trade world (see above, this chapter), found the contemporaneous discussion of property to be misplaced and counterproductive. Accepting the voracious, even "selfish" nature of the child, she argues that a distinction must be maintained between matter and spirit,[89] the former limited and divisible, the latter unlimited and expansive. Children must learn what is theirs and what is not with regard to limited material resources at their disposal. When this is accomplished, the child "will have taken a long leap toward citizenship." However, a "material conception of the human soul" might educate it but never satisfy it. It is on the spiritual plane where human insatiability can be made productive and creative (i.e., music, art, philosophy, ethics). She beseeches parents to lead the child out of a "personal self, with its likes and dislikes and its dangers, into the greater self, the Oversoul."[90]

Conclusion

The didactic imperative of the malleable child—evident in the discourses of simplicity, money, allowances, and property—strongly resonates with the epistemological and ontological anxieties animating concerns about and approaches to punishment and reward, discussed in chapter 3. The sense that the child deserves equality and justice—and thereby has or deserves "rights"—in matters of money and property also underlies emergent notions about governance, the two linked together by the preoccupation of seeking to know and feel as the child knows and feels. Matters of taste and simplicity provided a basis, vague as it may have been, for discerning and guiding judgments about the relationship between the material and nonmaterial and, in so doing, continued to function as a this-worldly, secular basis of sacredness. In a world where the God of one's parents and grandparents was rarely conjured for specific direction in matters of parenting in these tracts and where goods, pecuniary relations, and material life swelled in influence and proportion, a belief in taste as something of a divine direction must have helped grapple with the emergent uncertainties of value and valuation. Taste, governance, and money/property—while in no way simply isomorphic with one another or functionally interchangeable—represent distinctive strands of a braided dynamic that together wrap around the tri-helix structure comprising the malleable child, maternal responsibility/liability, and the child's voice/perspective.

The moral project of the child consumer arises from and draws upon these interlocking, ongoing compositions and negotiations. At opening of the twentieth century, neither a strong sense of innocence nor of the pecuniary pollution of a sacred child dominated the public understanding of children's involvement in and relationship to goods and consumer market. Rather, discourse, practice, and attention reached for a moral amalgam whereby goods, children's subjectivities, and mothers' imperatives found mutual resonance, often with the interlocution of market actors.

5

Think and Feel like a Child

Pleasure, Subjectivity, and Authority in Early Children's Consumer Culture

Public and publicly directed discourses helped forge a childhood wherein playing with toys, engaging in a certain order of amusement, receiving allowance money, and having a stake in property relations did not, in themselves, constitute moral transgression. The fear of the middle class, rather, was bad taste—i.e., not only wanting and choosing the wrong things but also inhabiting an incorrect disposition toward possession. It is a fear borne of the facticity of malleability, that is, of the daily, evident uncertainty regarding which influences, infractions, or incursions would make an indelible imprint, thereby altering, perhaps permanently, the child's moral biography. This ever-present concern regarding influence was informed by and derived from the Protestant response to the problem of salvation, as I have argued throughout (but see especially chapter 1). Malleability acquired additional layers of significance and complication as mothers, educators, advice-givers, and others came to regard the child's experiences, perspectives and, as we would now say, subjectivity as legitimate sources of expression and thereby worthy of consideration. Positioned precariously, but nonetheless enduringly, at the intersection of external influence and child subjectivity, mothers and motherhood came to bear the brunt of steersmanship, of navigating appropriate passages through difficult straits.

This moral dynamic—the symbiosis at play between malleability, maternal responsibility or liability, and child voice and perspective—constitutes the "child" and is also a key element of the "child consumer." These two figures differ neither in origin nor in cultural morphology. Distinguished by the focus on capital, commodities, and the materialities of the self, the "child consumer" arises in the late nineteenth and early twentieth centuries not as a being apart, a figure apart, or a

category apart from the "child." Rather, the child consumer materializes as a systemic partial of a (particular and expanding) middle-class
version of childhood. It is a figure, as we have seen, forged in the dis-
cursive machinations about material practice and maternal practice,
punishment and reward, property and money, simplicity and taste—all
of which accepted (some embraced) the place of things in the making
and unmaking of selves and of life trajectories. Indeed, the child and its
consumption stood not simply for "child consumption" but represented
a palpable embodiment of the interlacing of biographies and materialities and the moral perils thereof. In asserting the near isomorphism of
"child" and "child consumer," as has been built up in previous chapters,
I do not intend to discount the powerful, pervasive weight of a churning capitalist system that was in the midst of distributing some of its
momentum toward the consumption side of economic life. Likewise,
it would not be useful to elide the differences in the varied notions of
childhood in circulation at the turn of the century. A key problem in
this chapter is how "child" and "consumer" came to be put into cultural
conversation with one another in the 1900–1930 period—a conversation that comes to resemble a dance as much as anything else, a dance
of value and of modes of valuation. In the process of articulating the
place of commercial life in childhood, and of childhood in commercial
life, the discourse of parents, teachers, advice-givers, social observers,
economic actors, and institutions pursued measures of truth, of the
correct and proper reciprocation between the material and moral.

Follow the Pleasure

> [Children] are inclined to be ashamed, at least in a slight degree, of un-
> cleanliness, vulgarity, and brutality, when they see them in broad contrast
> with beauty and harmony and order. For the most part, they try "to live
> up to" the place in which they find themselves.
> —Kate Douglas Wiggin and Nora Archibald Smith, Children's
> Rights, 1892[1]

We have even as children an embryonic, aesthetic nature. Things beautiful have a fascinating effect upon the unperverted individual. We need
but to have objects of beauty brought to our attention and we desire them

without being taught their desirability . . . Furthermore, the beautiful af-
fects us without our knowledge of the fact. We stop and look at a beautiful
advertisement, but may not be aware that it is the beauty which attracts
us.
—Walter Dill Scott, *The Psychology of Advertising*, 1902[2]

The two remarks above, published within a decade of each other at the
turn of the twentieth century, together enunciate an easy confluence
of some contemporaneous aspirations of a bourgeois childhood and a
growing ideology of commercial practice. Here, Adam Smith's postulate
of the human propensity to truck, barter, and trade meets the human
propensity to desire and seek the good, the beautiful, and the orderly—
and, ultimately, the pleasurable.[3] The latter of these also can be found
in the natural state of human beings who, as children, have an "embryonic, aesthetic nature," according to Walter Dill Scott, an early leading
thinker in the psychology of advertising. The Benthamite dictum of
a deep, instinctual, and guiding utility—to seek pleasure and avoid
pain—is at work here, bridging the aesthetic realm with that of the commercial.[4] As essential and normative, the aesthetic sense operates on
and derives from most any object in the world: a flower, a tidy nursery,[5]
a well-executed advertisement. This instinctual sense, as well, functions
prospectively as a basis for biography, i.e., for what might be motivated
in a foreseeable future. As noted author and educator Kate Douglas Wiggin implies in just a few words, there is a pedagogy to beauty for the
child she construes; the child will not simply recognize and revile vulgarity, but will try to "live up" to the beautiful, the harmonious—echoing
discourses of taste discussed in chapter 2.

Like taste, the power of aesthetics here operates largely outside of re-
flective, willful consciousness. But Scott speaks of the effects of beauty in
a neo-Lockean accent, at once affirming the power of early impressions
while making of these an opportunity for "suggestion":

In pleasure our minds expand. We become extremely suggestible and
are likely to see things in a favorable light . . . In pain we are displeased
with the present experiences and so withdraw within ourselves to keep
from being acted upon. We refuse to receive suggestions, are not easily influenced, and are in suspicious attitude toward everything which is

proposed. When in pain we question the motives of even our friends and only suspicious thoughts are called up on our minds.[6]

Hence, the "modern business man does his utmost to minister to the pleasure of others"[7] and the advertiser must also do so by making use of a key device at "his" disposal: aesthetics. Drawing on the psychology of William James and taking it into the realm of commercial relations, Scott conceives of influence or suggestion as a cumulative, interactive process occurring over time. Not all "impressions" or suggestions for Scott are equal[8]—early impressions have no memory to draw upon, no basis for comparison; hence, their import lies in the way they set a template for the construction of subsequent experience, of a second conception.

Kate Wiggin and Norah Smith walk a path remarkably similar to Scott's psychology in their discussion of children's rights. Their effort brings Friedrich Froebel's kindergarten pedagogy into the fore by looking to those things and activities that engage and keep children's interests, with the idea of turning these into opportunities for education and training. In large part, it is through prescribed and circumscribed play that a true and most desirable childhood will blossom. Of Froebel, they relate:

> It was while he was looking on with delight at the plays of little children, their happy, busy plans and make-believes, their intense interest in outward nature, and in putting things together or taking them apart, that Froebel said to himself: "What if we could give the child that which is called education through his voluntary activities, and have him always as eager as he is at play?"[9]

In addition to its "voluntary" nature, play enables instruction because the didactic intent and relationship (between mother and child or teacher and child) remains relatively hidden, as it is subordinated to pleasurable activities and interactions. Wiggin and Smith quote what would become an oft-cited passage of the time from Malleson's *Notes on the Early Training of Children* (1885):

> "We cannot tell how early the pleasing sense of musical cadence affects a child. In some children it is blended with the earliest, haziest recollection

of life at all, as though they had been literally 'cradled in sweet song;' and we may be sure that the hearing of musical sounds and singing in association with others are for the child, as for the adult, powerful influences in awakening sympathetic emotion, and pleasure in associated action."[10]

Play, here in the form of musical activity, produces pleasurable, albeit unknown, effects on the child that can be extended by way of association into other realms so as to influence attitude and behavior.

Linking the pleasurable (for the child) with what is desirable (of the child by the adult) provides for an ideal realm where the didactic needs and objects of social life blend seamlessly: "Let us unlock to him the significance of family, social, and national relationships, so that he may grow into sympathy with them."[11] The world of children and adults here encounters no externalities in Wiggin's voicing of the Froebelian approach. Indeed, as she continues, "If we could make such education continuous, if we could surround the child in his earlier years with such an atmosphere of goodness, beauty, and wisdom, none can doubt that he would unconsciously grow into harmony and union with the All-Good, the All-Beautiful, and the All-Wise."[12] Recall in the last chapter the strong linkage made by mothers and commentators that "fitting" the toy or object to the child involved a sensibility which was, at once, moral and developmental. In Wiggin and Smith's approach to children's rights, explicit, conscious instruction—moral or otherwise—stands in an inferior position to the soft pedagogy of things, of play, and of the presumptively didactic bourgeois sense of beauty. Beauty, pleasure, and play, in essence, could very well re-establish the divinity of children and do so without their awareness—restoring them to something of a pre-conscious, pre-capitalist Edenic state—and yet accomplished with their unspoken consent by virtue of an unbroken linkage connecting children's subjectivities with their moral ontogeny.

For Wiggin and Smith, the right of the child is, firstly, to be recognized as a child and to recognize that the child has "a right to his childhood"[13]—a right that is known and exercised in the acknowledgement of the child's individuality, unencumbered by "our [i.e., adults'] artificial standards."[14] Beyond being a courtesy or maneuver, centering the child and centering the child's view here arises as moral duty—a duty requiring a decentering of one's own self while paradoxically stepping in to organize education for children. This movement is trained on enacting and encoding maternal self-effacement[15] as necessary and as necessarily correspondent to the first right of the child. Mother and child subjectivities co-relate in a yin-yang kind of way— where the undertaking of one unavoidably implicates the character of the other, a dynamic ingrained historically as definitive and productive of children's consumer culture.[16]

Commercially speaking, in this way the benignly malleable child of Locke, Rousseau, and Froebel gave a kind of a cultural permission for market actors to speak to it, through it, and on its behalf. In the process, ideologies of motherhood became entangled with the growing visibility and legitimacy of the perspective and voice of the child. Here, child-rearing and commercial interests found agreement with one another other. Producing beauty, or contexts for the realization of beauty, arises as both an obligation to help produce proper bourgeois subjects domestically and an occasion to specify and concretize the realization of pleasure in specific products and things in the market. As Scott notes,

> We have an intellectual nature, but in the case of the child the intellect is little more than a spark which, however, is sufficient to indicate the presence of that which may be developed into a great light. The child is prompted by curiosity to examine everything that comes into its environment. It tears its toys to pieces that it may learn their construction . . . The public wants to know what is offered for sale. It wants to hear the story which the advertiser has to tell.[17]

The advertiser can be ready with the kindling of suggestion to catch this spark of curiosity in order that it may be "developed"—the child here also stands as a prototype of the "public." In Scott's terms, the child's "instinct" provides bearing—a directionality—in support of the efforts to guide it. The advertiser, like the mother, would do well to attend to the child's interest.

Mirroring a general shift in parental governance away from punishment and toward reward, discussed in chapter 3, both the language of children's rights and the psychology of advertising—as here represented in these texts—at the turn of the twentieth century embraced a demeanor of ingratiation. In this mounting worldview, gaining the favor of the child, the consumer or, as we will see, the child consumer, required a tactical pursuit of the agreeable—a stealth motivation of desired behavior enabled by the intimation of the pleasurable. Thought innate yet ductile, taste and beauty in this sense appeared less a matter of conscious inculcation than a perpetual effort to steer children away from the corruptible and vulgar, and toward desirable things and environments that would work the quiet magic of suggestion and intimation. In the same gesture, the impetus to ingratiate the child or otherwise defer to children's interests and pleasures positioned the young ones as a kind of authority over these interests and pleasures, leaving parents ever in danger of sliding into indulgence and positioning market actors as key figures in child guidance.

The Pleasure of the Advertisement

Pleasure, beauty, training, and commercial culture tie together in literary historian Ellen Gruber Garvey's studies on children and advertising in the late nineteenth and early twentieth centuries. In *The Adman in the Parlor*, Garvey argues that girls in particular became "trained" toward consumption and consumer society in the 1870–1910 period.[18] In scrapbooks most likely made by girls, Garvey finds a playful, often inventive, engagement with print advertisements and trade cards that often elided the distinctions between home and market. Juxtapositions of images and copy often took the form of humorous commentaries on the adult world, thereby exhibiting children's access to and facility with popular commercial visual materials and themes.[19] The training made and remade gendered practices of the time through collecting advertisements and trade cards that encouraged the application of a domestic, genteel curatorship over the objects of the world, including those arising in and from the marketplace. As Garvey surmises,

> The female compiler brought her aesthetic skills as an arranger of materials and as a decorator—skills produced by her gender-specific training—to bear on the arrangement of the cards on the page. She learned to create attractive and individual displays from mass-produced articles—applying "taste" to make something unique from goods everyone else owned.[20]

Garvey comments on the notion of taste with the use of quotation marks, indicating her distance from this contemporaneous interpretation. Yet, when this kind of scrapbooking is placed alongside a variety of similar taste practices, or taste dictions, surrounding children, domesticity, and materiality, it would be reasonable to conceive of it as another arena where commercial life and everyday practice of the middle-class childhood, here girlhood, converged.

Advertisements and trade cards can be seen as being subsumed into existing gender practices and accompanying ideology as taste brings these into a known framework of identifiable and largely non-threatening female leisure pursuits as a kind of "domestic containment" in Elaine Tyler May's sense.[21] In *The American Girl's Handy Book* by Lina and Adelia Beard (1887)[22]—also discussed by Garvey[23]—the authors write of the "fashion" for trade card scrapbooks and offer numerous suggestions for how to reuse and remake the old ads in new configurations. The Beards' text encourages fanciful musings and combinations of old advertisements—e.g., the reader will be "delighted at the strange and striking pictorial characters that can be produced by ingenious combination"[24]—and does not indicate anxiety about the commercial origins of the images, contrary to Garvey's interpretation.[25] Children may have constructed these scrapbooks of their own accord and under the scrutiny of the parent, but the surviving compilations—as well as their elaborateness—speak to a milieu in which the consumer market per se was not, to any great extent, objectionable for *fin-de-siècle* middle-class girls (and apparently for their parents or those, like the Beards, who encouraged them) when confined within known cultural shapes and understood as gender-appropriate "play."

In another study, Garvey discusses the efforts of the editors of *St. Nicholas*, a popular children's magazine, to engage children with the comparatively modest amount of advertising on its pages through a series of advertising contests beginning in 1900.[26] The training that children were thought to have undergone by participating in these contests, in contrast to scrapbooks, was purposefully engineered rather than simply taken up by children of their own accord. Garvey found that the magazine endeavored to use the contests to demonstrate to their advertisers that children (girls and boys) were paying attention to the publicity placements located in the back of the monthly publication. With an eye toward inculcating an "appreciation" of "good" advertisements, the contests sought to employ children as makers or creators of advertising copy, awarding prizes to individual children and offering incentives to schools to encourage their pupils to participate.[27]

Drawing on psychologist Walter Dill Scott, discussed above, Garvey notes how the *St. Nicholas* editors made the case that the strength and import of early "deep impressions" would create lasting dispositions toward the products and companies brought to children's attention through playful, creative practice, and that the "intensity of response"[28]—i.e., level of engagement—would also serve as an indicator of the potential effectiveness of contests. Garvey points to the ways in which, as with scrapbooking, children engrossed themselves in the texts, images, and projects set before them, seeing in this deep engagement an integration of children's play and creativity with and through the semiotic materials of a growing consumer culture. In particular, she argues that through such contests, "children learned both to enjoy ads and play with them, and to look to ads for some of the same pleasures of fiction." In running the contests, *St. Nicholas* did not instruct the children to believe or not believe in the truthfulness of the advertisement. Children, rather, "learned that the issue of believing or not believing the ads was irrelevant to the pleasures of participating in advertising."[29]

Garvey's work helps illuminate how a bourgeois child, so constructed, thickly manifested threads of continuity with the child consumer. Play and fiction, along with a preoccupation with training, with guidance, and with an "appreciation" of things that are "good" (good advertising, good art, etc.)—together with presumptions of lasting, deep impressions—coalesced around the enactment of pleasure for and by children. The pleasure of the text, of making texts, of the mashing-up of various images and narratives in scrapbooks into commentaries—these appear as decidedly belonging, in the cultural sense, to children. Indeed, play and pleasure speak directly to children's subjectivities as authoritative. Unable to be forced or coerced and still retain their integrity, play and pleasure position children's subjectivities centrally as moral objects and moral projects. So positioned, it becomes incumbent upon teachers, mothers, advertisers, reformers, and others who act with and on behalf of children and to consult children's pleasure and play as proxies of their voice, agency and experience.

Centering the Child: Subjectivity as Authority[30]

Historian William Leach writes of a new, "child-world" of goods, spaces, and iconography exploding onto the American retail scene in the first decades of the twentieth century.[31] Department stores like Marshall Field's in Chicago began to target and address children in a purposeful manner in advertisements, window and shelf displays, promotional materials mainly for toys and dolls, and services. Some urban stores provided areas where middle-class mothers could "check" their children with store personnel while they surveyed the offerings; others provided barbershop services for children; some built indoor playgrounds to interest and occupy the little ones.[32] By the 1930s, entire floors of some stores were dedicated to outfitting children from birth through teen years, and in addition to dedicated areas and staff selling toys, different parts of the store sold furniture and other items for children.[33] Radio programs, comic book characters, juvenile clubs, and contests—many of which far outpaced the efforts by *St. Nicholas*—combined to fabricate and support a morally infused commercial infrastructure of goods, spaces, personae, and meaningful associations.[34]

The core of this consumer culture of childhood, as it would come to be known, lay not simply in an economic dynamic made up of increasing incomes of a newly minted middle class, nor only in an ingrained drive of capitalism to expand markets, nor primarily in permissive parents displacing wonder onto their children through goods and purchases. Arguably comprising aspects of all of these, children's consumer culture at base manifests as a problem—a moral problem wrapped around the question of who and what a child is and should be. In the making and remaking of material and pecuniary relations about and around children, market actors—along with parents, designers, educators, and reformers—wrestled over the puzzle of how to know the child, i.e., how to know as the child knows and see as the child sees. Hardly a novel problem in itself, the commercial impetus to inhabit and theorize the child's interiority here bears remarkable similarities to the efforts of Evangelical Protestants in the early to mid-1800s who sought to bring children's ontological understandings of right and wrong into a theology relating child nature with salvation. Seeing the world through children's eyes also formed the basis of empathy for those who worked to consider how their middle-class children experienced punishment, understood the concept of property, and apprehended the materialities of their worlds in terms of taste. In important ways, advertisers, retailers, and psychologists of the new commercial world appropriated a similar ontological scaffolding and brought it to bear upon consumer-material-pecuniary configurations unfolding in the early decades of the twentieth century.

In the first decades of the twentieth century, stores would come to devote increasing resources and energy to producing pleasing sales environments where children shopped. One writer in 1923 asserted that the psychology is the same for children as it is for parents but that it was important to realize that, as an adult, the child "will find himself or herself influenced unwittingly by advertising done years before."[35] Malleability—here manifested as impressionability—reaches prospectively into the child's biography, conceived as a consumer biography. The advertising message—beyond the known dual appeal to both parent and child—speaks also to a presumed conjectured self, one that is conjured through the figure of an imaginative and imagined future customer. Hence, the "child represents a market infinitely worth going after. To capture that market however, the advertiser must carefully consider the individual that makes it up and psychology of the child." Once these facts are understood thoroughly the advertiser can be sure that advertising still "pays sales dividends."[36] To be sure, the writer himself is selling advertising itself—i.e., the notion and practice of advertising—to advertisement sellers in pitching the investment potential of the child market. At the same time, he is voicing a position whereby those who promote consumption need to "consider" the individuality of the child, which constitutes one part of the market.

Advertisers and marketers began to realize that turning children from intermittent customers who episodically make purchases into more or less continuous consumers required, among other things, seeing the world through their eyes. Some retail establishments strove to orient their practices to the presumed and imputed view of the child as consumer. The choice of sales personnel, the accessibility of store fixtures and displays, the installation of child-height mirrors in clothing departments, and the decoration and design of store layout itself were among some of the efforts to respond to the "child consumer" as construed through memory, immediate observations, rule-of-thumb understandings and, eventually, systematic market research based on applied developmental psychology.[37]

Take, for instance, a piece in 1920 in *The Dry Goods Economist*, a trade periodical, which instructed the commercial-oriented readership to "Put Yourself in the Child's Place to Learn the Toy He Craves."[38] The unnamed author implored "Miss Toy Salesperson" to "look around you" and "pick up the toys there and study them," and to query herself: "What are they for? What will the child who may ultimately possess them think of them? What would *you* have thought of them as a child—not as an adult looking back on your childhood—but *as a child?*"[39] Success in selling depends on recalling one's own self as a child, transforming those memories into a sympathetic posture toward children today and, crucially, studying children in one's immediate sphere:

> Watch the children around you. There is no one so secluded or separated that she does not know a few children. See what they like, how they play, what they seem to do with the things they have. If there is a playroom in the store where you work it would pay you to spend a few minutes of your noon hour, if you have no other time, watching the children.[40]

Here, again, memory and the ability to know the child are made to co-relate. Aided by one's own memory—of making oneself into a child again, if only momentarily—it is incumbent upon the presumably unmarried and childless saleswoman[41] to observe children and see the world they might see. She is encouraged dissolve her view into the child's in the service of sales for the store and, as it is implied, for her own self-interest in the form of her own sales commissions.

Once in the posture of becoming confluent with the child's view, while also reflexively studying children, the writer instructs the saleswoman to classify the children (as mechanically minded, physical, active, etc.), to play with or handle the toys herself, and to think about the kind of mother who may enter the store. She should be ready to suggest the "educational" toys to "educational" the mother—i.e., the one who has "gone to college in her youth and learned bookfuls of the theories of life, the meaning of play in man and the child."[42] This woman is easily served if she comes in looking for an educational toy. If it is unclear what "kind" of mother has entered her department, it is advised to ask about the children first and glean whatever information can be from their response—i.e., if they have a play room, what color it might be and whether it is more of ruckus room than a genteel space. When a child enters the store with a grown-up, the saleswoman should treat them as "entities" and with all seriousness, watching their eyes, which "can generally be counted upon to follow their interest."[43]

In the same year, *Printers' Ink Monthly*, an advertising trade journal, volleyed a similar inquiry to its readership: "What Kind of Advertisements Do Boys Like?"[44] Horace S. Wade, a novelist of the time, chastised copy writers for not thinking like a child, specifically like a boy: "Boys read advertisements, a lot. But there are some advertisements which they don't read at all, and I'm going to tell you why I think they don't read them. Men who write these advertisements have forgotten what boys like. They use words boys don't understand." The inability to think, know, and see like a child—here, a boy—again stands in the way of the realization of exchange value. Not only a fall from grace, and perhaps from innocence, adulthood—i.e., manhood—stands as a barrier to commercial practice. Wade continues: "It is strange to grown-ups, unless you remain young, what queer heroes boys chose. Outlaws, Captain Kidd, Rob Roy, Jesse James . . . Boys live in a 'make believe' world, and when you come down off your high horse you can reach them every time." The remedy, again, is to observe the target audience by, for instance, watching a boy read a newspaper where he will "read every line of a hold-up, but skip over [a story] about the high cost of living." Learning to (re)become a boy in this way will aid in writing copy in his own language that will "get" him, and so his mother, or perhaps motivate him to earn enough buy the product on his own.[45] Significantly, writers counseled mothers along the same lines as saleswomen and copywriters when selecting children's toys. One writer in 1926 suggested that mothers "watch the occupation of a little boy or girl" to get an "indication of the qualities a toy should have for him."[46]

Gender, child study, and commodification interweave in a single gesture to privilege the child's view as observed with a market eye. Whether the primary focus of selling bears upon on mothers as consumers or upon children as consumers, the effort in the first instance uses the child's imputed, gendered subjectivity as a center of gravitational pull. The child's attention—be it drawn in the co-presence of children or from personal recollection—gave indication of its presumably untutored, naturalized interests, the existence of which guide the saleswoman or copywriter in triangulating mother's concern, commercial practice, and the child's pleasure. In this pecuniary trigonometry of perception, the invoked child looks back at the mother through the gaze of the retailer and advertiser, apprehending the goods as a copywriter, merchandiser, or designer might beseech. The problem here lies not in the child's desire as imagined—for he or she wants to possess things as much as the merchant wants to sell them—but in fabricating a metacommunicative frame that positions the relationship between buyer and seller as collaborative rather than antagonistic.

A key to enacting positive social-commercial relationships rested in appreciating and treating children as customers and readers in their own right, rather than as necessary appendages to the pocketbook-wielding mother. Time and again, the trade press entreated merchants and advertisers to recognize children as individual beings with a distinctive perspective who, nonetheless, should be accorded the same treatment as any other customer. A *Dry Goods Economist* writer discusses the gendered aspects of salesmanship in a story where a "salesgirl" talked down to a boy by using baby talk (e.g., "Put your hannies into the coat sleeve"). The writer explains that neither mother nor boy was pleased with the treatment. "Just as mothers and fathers want their little girl babies to be sweet and dainty so they want their little boy babies to be sturdy and manly—'real boys.'"[47] Boys' and girls' clothing sections should be segregated as early as possible, the writer continues, and no later than age two. Gender and subordination are directly linked, specifying the kind of interpersonal relationship a salesperson should develop with each sex: "Salespeople for the baby boys' section should be chosen with regard to a slightly different angle than that needed by those who serve the baby girls," whereas "little boys particularly appreciate matter-of-factness in a salesgirl."[48]

Salesclerks and retailers echoed the virtues of this differential treatment for boys and girls in apparel departments and sections as early as 1919: "Take her seriously and sincerely. . . . Don't patronize or talk down to her. Don't call her 'my dear' or 'girlie' or 'honey' or any similar expression. Don't override her evident preference in order to sell her mother. If possible in such a case take a tactful middle course."[49] The buyer and merchandise manager for the children's department of L.S.

Ayers & Co., Indianapolis, related to the *Dry Goods Economist* in 1921, "We treat the children as much like grown-ups as possible. . . . And we find that it pays. It takes a special type of saleswoman to please little girl shoppers, and to hold boys at all, as the latter are invariably bored to death with the whole process of shopping."[50] As customers or, perhaps, consumers—albeit often in a secondary sense as enacted through the parent—children were thought worthy of being accorded a kind of personhood, an interactional dignity, likely unavailable to them in other adult-dominated spheres like home and school. Their views on goods and, especially, on "customer service," it seems, mattered enough to be given attention by retail trade observers.

It is within the realm of goods and arenas of consumption that the bourgeois subject, in the apparition of this composite child consumer, comes to the fore as subjectivity and social person. Alice Mason Johnson, a writer for the children's wear trade publication *Earnshaw's*,[51] avows to department-store clothing buyers and managers the moral integrity of children who eschew used, hand-me-down items:

> Watch any child who is clothed in the cast-offs of older brothers and sisters. He is different, embarrassed and shy. He is altogether unsure of himself or of his place in the world. Conscious only of misfit, and of wearing things not of his childish choice or to his childish liking, the youngster's mind knows no feeling of proud assurance which comes with being well dressed.[52]

Again, women—mothers—are to "watch" their children and be on the lookout for signs of pleasure or discomfort. The child's actions will give first indication of what to do and how to act.

Here, class-inflected anxieties about taste manifest in a child's presumed self-consciousness of dress and social placement. To mitigate the child's desire for the new and novel, and thereby likely un-tasteful, department-store clothing buyers themselves require proper training and discernment to assist mothers in molding children's character. Accomplishing such a balance requires attention to children themselves:

> But a [clothing department] buyer who is not interested in children outside of their clothes, and who knows nothing of their pursuits, education,

and desires is hardly eligible for this highly specialized job. In planning the children's department in former years, little thought was given to the important fact the child itself influences the ultimate merchandise selection of the parents. Children are susceptible to color from the time their eyes open to the daylight. Bright colors attract them. Dull colors repel them. Good taste as interpreted by older and wiser heads is, to the young child, a mystery. In order to promote good taste in a child, the buyer herself can be one of the greats aids to parents.[53]

The market actor, here in the form of a clothing buyer, is to serve as interlocutor, as broker, between the commercial world, the child, and the parent. She in effect stands in for, and at times supersedes, the mother in terms of knowledge and empathy, notably advocating for the acceptance of the child's native notion of taste.

By 1930, an advertiser was asking the readership in *Printers' Ink Monthly*, "Has enough attention been given to the appeal to children, the buyers of a few years hence; or is this a far-fetched idea?"[54] He was making a case for the importance of trademarks and brand or company recognition. Echoing what many "modern psychologists" contend, the author pointed out that "the majority of permanent impressions which influence our actions and desires are received before the age of six." Children's unique perspective has clear implications for package design. With a hunch that children favor "abstract"' over "concrete" design, the author conducted "some case studies" with a four-year-old child (clearly his daughter). He found that she could identify not only children's products by the images on the packaging but also adult products in a similar manner, sounding a by-now-familiar refrain: "Is it not the same with us adults? What packages stick out most clearly as we think back to childhood days?"[55] Another *Printers' Ink* writer asserted in 1931 that "manufacturers are awakening to the realization that even youngsters of two and three are a market whose tastes can be cultivated profitably."[56] If advertisers can get children to recognize and pay attention to their products, then these items may become part of one's "lasting impressions."

As disposition as well as "preference," taste remained largely something to be cultivated. Children could internalize the messages, meanings, and relations of commercial culture, just as they were thought to acquire taste or learn the Good Word. The child addressed as consumer in these discourses manifested no differently than working conceptions of the "generic" middle-class child,[57] as both share the dynamics of malleability, taste, and pleasure. The distinctive and striking turn, rather, can be located in a new kind of child-centeredness. It is a centeredness that steps beyond the simple recognition of children's views and into a radical centering of the child's perspective as privileged and authoritative accompanied by a decentering, though not outright disavowal, of the adult view. Never absolute or complete, the assertion of the child's perspective into the forefront—i.e., in the consideration of its wishes, desires and pleasures, however gleaned or presumed—staked an ideological-moral territory for commercial interest and actors. It was the child (in various forms and manifestations) into which increasing and increasingly specified forms of knowledge and energy were to be invested. Without the child's consent or assent at some level, efforts to cajole consumption would appear as little more than hokum, and promoters akin to carnival barkers.

Developmentalism as a Moral Undertaking

In certain ways, promoters and advice-givers of the 1920s and 1930s endeavored to secure such "assent" through developmental insights. A child consumer psychology germinated on the pages of trade and consumer publications, which strove to know children on their own terms. Psychological research of the time was undertaken to examine an array of issues: the color preferences (or reactions) of young children, the ages and stages when mastery of one's body and environment appeared to take hold, the function and instinct for the apparent penchant for "collecting" and organizing things and objects, and children's interest in reading and their knowledge of color, name, and form.[58] In addition, research on toys, play "equipment," and the "interests" of young children[59] found its way into pamphlets and onto the pages of mothers' and parents' magazines with increasing regularity to guide advice about "educational" toys, which were becoming solidified as cultural objects and a product category at this time.[60] As well, children's clothing grew both ideologically and commercially into a full-blown industry where scientifically informed notions of proper dress, hygiene, and "self-help" regularly became part of the marketing, manufacturing, and parent-advising mix.[61] The assembly of the "generic child" through scientific and scientific-like knowledge and practice, as detailed by culture theorist Nicholas Sammond, helped make the "child" a knowable and thus controllable entity to a significant degree.[62] Recall in the last chapter the strong linkage made by mothers and commentators that "fitting" the toy or object to the child involved a sensibility that was at once moral and developmental. Here, one can grasp the convergence of a morality of rights with a morality of developmentalism congealing in commercial goods and practices.

The understanding of the child in the lingua of a rising child developmentalism gave practical guidance to the manufacture, sale, and purchasing of toys. In the same breath, developmentalism as fitted to children's desires—especially through play—spoke also at a moral register, one that insinuated a universalistic stance, based in a scientific acumen, that espoused the essential "needs" of children pinned to particular ages. One writer in a 1928 article in Parents warned mothers that failing to secure the (developmentally) "appropriate" toys for a child is not only a "waste of money," but also "an insult to the child for whom they are purchased."[63] The author cautions against the tendency at Christmas-time to acquire the "best seller" and to buy as many (cheaply made) toys as possible, encouraging them instead to think of the child's "interest," which is dependent upon his age, sex, and individuality.[64] In the emergent view of developmentalism, to ignore the child's age-stage equates to an expression of a kind of indifference. An article interrogated the mother reading Parents in 1929 if she planned the family toy budget "with a view to satisfying the child's changing interests as they develop as well as to meet the seasonal requirements of play?" Rapidly developing children can hardly be expected to maintain the same interest all year. Hence, planning year-round toy purchasing responds to the child's changing experiences, a tactic which, if done correctly, introduces needed novelty when that of the Christmas deluge wears off.[65]

Child development—and what might be said to accompany it—encodes market turnover along an axis of child-centered pleasure, interest, and need. Ellen Seiter, writing of the early Parents magazine, argued that the notion that childhood was divided into "discrete, observable stages" and became both useful to advertisers and hegemonic to mothers.[66] "Parents encouraged mothers to see weekly and monthly changes in their children's development. If toys are so closely tied to a child's abilities, no parent would want to hold her son and daughter back by waiting for Christmas or a birthday before replacing old toys with new ones better suited to a child's developing abilities."[67] A children's commercial psychology arose initially as somewhat of an ad hoc admixture of popular child psychology, the enactment of commercial interest in a relatively new child-oriented marketplace, and the expression of hegemonic notions of maternal responsibility and liability.[68] It represents an effort to recognize the particularities and positionalities of the child over and above those of the adult/parent while at the same time construing children's motivations and desires as, at base, no different from those of adults.[69]

The endeavor to know what and how the child knows came under the purview of commercial practice in a systematic way in the 1930s with the application of the emergent field of child psychology to the emergent practices of children's marketeers in consumer contexts.[70] E. Evalyn Grumbine, an early and prominent proponent of the study of children's consumer behavior, offered a template that could connect gendered developmental stages of childhood with appropriate colors, toys, and activities (i.e., collecting, puzzles) as a way for manufacturers and designers to match their goods with what children might find desirable and pleasurable. For Grumbine, writing from the perspective of 1938, children's autonomy is rich with the potential for exchange value: "An important factor in the growth and development of the juvenile market is the trend toward stimulating greater self-expression in children themselves. Progressive mothers and educators not only allow children to make their own decisions during the early years of childhood, but urge them to choose their own clothes and work out plans for their own rooms."[71] As I previously noted about Grumbine's perspective, "Freedom of expression, the apex of freedoms in a liberal democratic society, here is coupled with perhaps the noblest form of selfless action—that of enhancing the child's ability to make choices."[72]

Acknowledging and accounting for the child's view—its pleasures and pains, its understandings and interests—acquired significant cultural and moral heft as it became entwined with the availability of increasingly differentiated goods, spaces, and meanings of an arising consumer society. Commercial actors endeavored to leverage the "child appeal" of images, popular culture, and literary characters and narrative forms as ways to put the authoritative and persuasive child to work as an ersatz domestic agent for their products. The persuasive child—the child who would advocate for products to parents—became the darling of the trade press, with writers extolling the wisdom of petitioning the child directly in a presumed youth "argot," in a visually "child-friendly" (as one would say today) manner or in narrative forms historically thought to entreat the attention of youngsters.[73] Here, as above, the impetus and effort directed copywriters and others to think and feel "like a child" and foster the ability to see as a child sees. To gain the child's attention is akin to gaining "his" goodwill, thereby forming a sort of alliance of interest and pleasure over and against parents.

In support of this alliance, as Lisa Jacobson illustrates, advertisers and promoters of the 1920s and 1930s took up the boy consumer as "hero of a new consumer age," as he was often depicted as being in a knowing and authoritative relationship to goods vis-à-vis adults.[74] Jacobson argues that the positioning of boys in this way provided something of an ideological counterweight to the historically feminized association of consumption with sumptuousness, especially for the middling and upper classes. For Jacobson, the performing figure of the boy consumer in these advertisements helped resolve tensions between the presumed hedonistic tendencies of women and the ideal of personal control thought exhibited best by menfolk.[75] In this boy—who both "craves" things (as the *Dry Goods Economist* above put it) and is knowledgeable about price and quality[76]—the "exuberance" of a masculinity felt to be under pressure in the new age could be expressed as excitement and knowledge about goods and in a felt sense of power as a persuader of others.[77] Both a conduit for and avatar of progress, the crafted persona of the boy consumer hero—as technically savvy, as entrepreneurial pitchman— enabled admen to externalize and materialize their own insecurities and aspirations in a rapidly commercializing world.

Sales-woman-ship, Convergence, and the Pleasure-able Child

The October 1926 issue of *Parents* magazine carried an article on "Salesmanship for Parents" offering suggestions about how to adapt business psychology to home problems.[78] Written by "Happy Goldsmith," this

If mothers used the methods of advertisers—

Figure 5.1. By the 1920s, the association of mothering with commercial persuasion was ripe for satire in the inaugural issue of *Parents* magazine. Source: *Parents* magazine, October, 1926, 19.

cheeky article reproved parents (i.e., mothers) for "underselling" their spinach to their youngsters in contrast to the successful efforts of businesses, which seem to be able to garner youth's excitement over candy, cereal, and soda pop (see figure 5.1). Chiding those who resort to bribes, pleading, or discipline, "Happy" advises mothers to "examine the product not the child" for eye appeal and taste. She should scrutinize the "salesforce: (read: parents) to see if they are attractive, popular and use their own product."[79] The writer continues: "How about the spinach you are trying to sell your customer? Is it highly endorsed by popular heroes? If it isn't, you aren't much of salesman. Try this out on your adolescent some time: 'One reason Red Grange [an American football star of the time] is always in the pink of condition is because he eats green vegetables.' I'll admit it isn't very clever, but it is better than what I once heard, which ran, 'For heaven's sake, eat your spinach.'"[80]

Goldsmith then asks, "How well do you know your child?" suggesting that it is parents' business to know and understand the interests of their children if they are to be effective persuaders. Using the example of the clerk at the corner establishment where the children seem to want to gather and take every opportunity to spend whatever pennies they have, Goldsmith drives his point home: "The clerk, although he never studied the subject, is probably a genius at child psychology. If anything he is no doubt inclined to be bit childlike himself. He knows the latest slang, the latest jokes. He knows the kind of people children like and so accordingly takes them as his friends, too. He knows baseball, basketball, football, hockey. And he *listens* to the children from morning until night. That's why the boys and girls trade there. . . . And so you, too, must adapt yourself to the life of your child, if you are ever to win his or her interest and confidence."[81] The manner of truth offered by this prism, this slice of light offered by Happy Goldsmith, bends analytic vision toward apprehending the extent to which children arise as social persons in the complex of commercial life. It is toward them—their interests, social circles, jokes, language, and foibles—which must be understood by the "clerk," who represents an aspirational model for unknowing, aloof parents and similarly positioned adults.

Moreover, the advice propounded to the maternal readership of *Parents* about how to enact motherhood differs almost imperceptibly from the bon mots doled out in trade journals to sales personnel and copywriters, discussed above, about how to consider, approach and treat children. Mother, salesclerk, and copywriter converge in transit to the "child." But the fact that it is the child that is being sold—i.e., being construed and configured as a consumer—is *not* the most significant point here; the key insight comes in the similar posture each takes or advocates in relation to this consumer-child. It is the posture toward the child—as subject and subjectivity, as worthy of personhood and deserving in and for commercial realms—which comprises the essential, constituent, indispensable ingredient for the making of a children's consumer culture, as it has come to be known.

Children's rights arise, firstly, in a register trained on enjoyment. Ruth Ashmore's statement in the *Ladies' Home Journal* from 1892, quoted in a previous chapter, is worth reiterating here: "You have no right to withhold from your child any innocent pleasure . . . A child has a right to its own belongings, to its own thoughts and to its own life."[82] Note that the pleasures, but not necessarily the child, can be innocent. The problem of "what children want" here speaks, as sociologist Erving Goffman advises, to that most secularly sacred thing—the self, the person.[83]

Integrity, the integrity of being recognized and acknowledged in the first place, marks the indispensable instance of personhood status. And the recognition of children in and through commercial contexts and practices marks both a culmination of a historical process and a pivot point of new trajectories.

Conclusion

Legacies of Value

> You said "Respect kids, how do I do that?" I would say it's
> to sort of honor the sort of perfection and totality of who
> they are—rather than to come to them with the presumption
> that you know better or that you're going to make something
> work that doesn't for them.
> —Janet H., Oct. 16, 2012

Janet, a 30-year veteran of the "kids' industry," iterates in my interview
with her a now rather commonplace urge to situate the child at the center of consideration—i.e., as an authority, as a non-derivative person.
Respecting "kids" involves approaching children as totalities, as per-
fections in the here-and-now, and not as incomplete beings in need of
fulfillment by adults and the adult world (excepting, of course, the products made by that adult world). Some readers will encounter no difficulty
recognizing the resonance of this view with the "new sociology of childhood" or childhood studies perspective which, since the early 1990s, has
arisen to become a strong stream of research and thought[1] in which
the child occupies a central position as a kind of fount of knowledge
and action. Children are similarly positioned in many recent parenting
philosophies and advice books[2] as well as in pedagogical tracts and in
treatises on the nature and value of play.[3]

Janet's posture toward the child evinces a philosophy that I found
commonplace throughout my work with kids' industry professionals—
namely, that children, except in some obvious developmental ways, are
no different from other people, and that this equality or egalitarianism
extends and should extend to that nexus of materials, values, and social
relationships known as the consumer marketplace. Take Robin G., another

New York–based, 30-year member of the industry, who responded to my question about the utility of market research with children:

> If you believe it makes sense to understand women and understand men, then why would you not want to understand kids in creating new products? We could just go out and develop any old razor, but you know they go out and talk to men about their feelings about masculinity and their feelings about being a man and how feelings about being a man change from when you are 16 to 46. So why not do it for kids? It is exactly the same. The more you know someone the more you can make a product for someone.
> —Robin G., March 21, 2013

When one conceives of children as authorities with their own knowledge about their own needs and wants, then gaining insight on this knowledge so as to be in a position to respond it it—to realize this knowledge and perspective in material form—constitutes something of a moral act and, additionally, implicates adults with moral obligation.

Like other children's market professionals, Robin and Janet voice a melded ideology that blends the age-old veridiction of markets with a recent, emergent veridiction of children and childhood. For Michel Foucault, neoliberalist thought conceptualized the marketplace as a site of justice and truth, a space of veridiction.[4] Markets, so understood, speak truths through their processes and outcomes, in the ways they sort the useful from the non-useful and the right from the wrong and thus operate in and as a moral register—a notion traceable at least to Adam Smith and the Scottish Enlightenment.[5] It is worth considering how this modern form of Anglo-American, bourgeois childhood that I have discussed has itself arisen as site of veridiction for a different set of truths that exist alongside and mix with the truths emitted from the marketplace, so conceived. Here, the first and primary source of child–market veridiction emerges from the "child" itself. The fundamental cultural pivot occurs as the child's perspective—in the form of likes, dislikes, wants, needs, and pleasures—moves, albeit unevenly over time, to the center of consideration to serve as a guide or template for action, be it for pedagogy, parenting, or commercial life. The shift, discussed throughout this text, begins to produce and contribute to the conditions for a child-centric social, cultural, and commercial order.

In the preceding pages, I have endeavored to name and give outline to some strands of the moral-epistemological provenance of the child consumer, to illustrate it as something continuous with the rise of a modern, bourgeois version of childhood, which itself stands as a rather dominant version of childhood writ large. A good deal of scholarship and everyday thinking on the matter often presumes or contends that the child consumer of the twentieth century represented a significant break from previous understandings, that it arose out of the sentimentalization of the domestic sphere and a newly arising child-centered home as a reflex against the ever-growing world of market calculus and commercial value (see the Introduction). In this understanding, the child consumer stands apart from childhood proper as an exception, as something requiring explanation of its departure from a normative childhood. Zelizer's notion of the "priceless child" gained significant analytic cachet in part because it explicated a historical transition.[6] As well, the priceless child as a concept also offered a measure of comfort and support to those positions that sought to maintain a resilient narrative about the distinction between economic and emotional worth.

Yet the priceless child thesis informs only one dimension of a dynamic. Neither it nor many of the deployments of the concept pursue the question of how a children's commercial culture ceaselessly expands in quantity and reach, all while the notion of a sacred, sentimental child—whose worth is supposed to transcend economic value—continues apace as a guiding trope and principle. The two appear irreconcilable. One response—perhaps the main one—has drawn on critical theory approaches that posit that the forces of capital have insinuated themselves into the fabric of emotional life to such an extent that most children and parents are duped into confusing consumption with authentic living, the "priceless child" mantra in a way serving as an ideological cover for commercial interests.[7] Underlying this general view operates the imagination of a pre-capitalist child—an essentialized figure that philosophically and ontogenetically precedes economic-social life and circumstances.

The historical turning point I offer here involves the instantiation of the white, middle-class child's standpoint as moral metric, whereby an accounting of how the child sees and knows the world arises as a necessity and as necessarily in conversation with commercial motives and practices as well as with parenting modes and understandings. All sides, all parties involved take part in this accounting—from mothers and pedagogues to advice-givers and salesclerks, from advertising copywriters to, ultimately, children themselves. It is an accounting in pursuit of calibrating value and different orders of value so as to render sentiment, market, and child compatible with one another, at least on an episodic, tentative basis—i.e., in the everyday lived worlds of food shopping, birthday parties, and the like.[8] Centering the child as authority, as we have seen, unfolds unevenly in a multiplicity of sites and along various registers as part and parcel of the making of a white, bourgeois culture centered on both things and children. Deferring to the authority of the child's view establishes a morality beyond consumer markets and commercial logics yet remains ever inextricable from them. It represents both a continuation and refined definition of a vein of practice and ideology as well as a new mode, a new platform, where the value of children and that of goods converge and differentiate.

For contemporary children's market researchers, the child's perspective operates at once as source of data and a portal to innovation and thus as a vital form of value in which to invest,[9] and as a site for moral calibration.[10] These firms and professionals draw on their expertise and techniques in gaining insight on children's understandings, practices, and preferences to wield as a competitive edge in securing clients.[11] The act of securing children's views and insights—of bringing children's voices into commercial practice—makes these voices and perspectives into commodities, exchangeable values, while all at once valorizing children as legitimate actors in the process. In this way, market research and other forms of commercial practice inflected toward the children's market participate in a historically embedded moral project of childhood, though many observers would not understand such actions as constituting a moral undertaking.

The most intensely addressed characteristic associated with the moral project of childhood considered here concentrates on and makes visible the structural-political position of mothers vis-à-vis the figuration of the child. In each case considered above, the cultural shape of appropriate motherhoods adjusted to ongoing concerns about the nature and trajectory of the childhoods in question. In the context of wealthy Global North cultural and economic arrangements, mothers historically and increasingly reside at a nexus where home, market, child, and commercial actors intermingle, and it is here where different, diverse kinds of values undergo sorting and negotiation. Structurally, politically, and ontologically, this nexus operates in a way strongly similar to the moral architecture encountered in the examinations of Evangelical and Victorian motherhoods of the nineteenth century, where issues of salvation and of taste, of reward, punishment, and desire inhabited the foreground of concern. At various historical points and in relation to different issues, mothers remained the primary liaisons, serving as gatekeepers, arbiters and, importantly, as disablers of children's engagements with the world. The "heathen" may no longer be invoked as an threat to present-day childhoods, but mothers remain duty bound to be ever vigilant against various moral poisons emanating from the world of media and commerce, and perhaps from other children. An often unkind liability stands as the price exacted for occupying this privileged nexus. Analytically and theoretically, the lesson must be reiterated that childhood and motherhood arise and exist in mutual relation, not in isolation from each other, as problematic as it is to conceptualize and articulate these relations.[12]

The Creative Child

In this light, the rise to prominence of the "creative child" over the twentieth century acquires profound cultural purchase. Design historian Amy Ogata insightfully details the robust intermingling of psychological theory, educational policy, parenting advice, toy industries, and design science that combined to produce a resolute, lasting connection between creativity, childhood, and play, particularly in US post–World War II middle-class social life.[13] For Ogata, "creative" toys or objects or sites[14] represented a transcendent ethos of personal liberation for the child that, in part, enabled middle-class families to remain remote from mass culture and social conformity while assuaging Cold War anxieties about America's geopolitical competitiveness.[15] Central in this period stands the image of the American child surrounded by toys and objects who, for play advocates and boosters alike, signified individuality and the potential of creativity.[16]

In many ways, it appears that "creativity" in the post–World War II context operated nearly the same as did "taste" in the later nineteenth century. Both enacted a cultural logic that enabled a simultaneous distancing from and engagement with the popular material worlds of their times, giving childhood a pathway through the commercial underbrush. Creativity, Ogata notes, works as a highly elastic category that nevertheless persists as working trope because it "promises hope" and "describes our longings rather than our certainties."[17] One may note that creativity also gives shape and direction to malleability—the persistent problematic configuring modern, middle-class childhoods and motherhoods for at least a century and a half. The hype around creativity also provides cultural-moral permission to psychologists, educators, parents, and others to accompany—indeed, to lead—children into commercial enterprise as a (market) solution to malleability, even as it was seen as an "antidote to modern consumer culture,"[18] as Ogata notes. The deep, underlying, class-inflected sense that "proper" goods will offer "correct" instruction—operative, as discussed, since the mid-nineteenth century—finds a new host, a suitable vehicle, in the open-ended toys and underdetermined objects and spaces designed to facilitate "imagination" at this time. Creativity, in this sense, maneuvers as a moral project of childhood in ways virtually identical to the questions of taste, the issues of punishment and reward, and the problems of simplicity, money, and property addressed herein.

Seen from this perspective, the rise of this version of the creative child represents not simply a longing—a parental/adult longing for a wondrous child[19]—it also inflects and embodies an existential uncertainty about the direction and trajectory of the life course. The reconstructed child that Ogata mines from the materials she examines necessarily implicates mothers and motherhoods even though her treatment, unfortunately, does not take into account the place of mothers and the politics of motherhood beyond noting some of the stated expectations in the parenting advice literature of the time. She thereby leaves no space to address how the domestic containment[20] efforts of the era may have been informed and supported by the figuration of this creative child. The expected, indeed demanded, creativity of the middle-class child would have to be extracted from the middle-class mother in whose hands rested the earthly salvation of her offspring—and the future of the nation and race—as an agentive, innovative being-in-the-world.

In 1955, anthropologist Martha Wolfenstein noted a change in attitude about fun and play in parenting advice literature from the US Children's Bureau since the 1910s. In her reading, publications at mid-century tended to see the child's "impulses" (crying, thumb sucking, mastur-bation) less as the threats they were portrayed to be in 1914 and more as benevolent guides to the child's interest. The difference in valence, Wolfenstein contends, relates to a larger change in ethos whereby the "good" and the "pleasant"—formerly opposite one another—were con-verging,[21] raising the question, "Is what the baby likes good for him?"[22] For Wolfenstein, the emerging centrality of the child's impulses as au-thority, as things to be followed rather than simply curtailed, carried a heavy imperative for mothers—a new "fun morality":

> When a mother is told that most mothers enjoy nursing, she may wonder what is wrong with her in case she does not. Her self-evaluation can no longer be based entirely on whether she is doing the right and necessary things but becomes involved with nuances of feeling which are not under voluntary control. Fun has become not only permissible but required, and this requirement has a special quality different from the obligations of the older morality.[23]

Wolfenstein enjoins the conception of the child with a felt obligation of mothers toward their mothering. The fun morality, along with the eli-sion of the good with the pleasant (see chapters 4 and 5), undergirds and feeds the creative child and its industries described by Ogata.

As a transform of gendered, maternal labor, the creative child also might be considered as an indispensable ingredient of Sharon Hays's no-tion of "intensive mothering."[24] Hays does not address creativity or the child consumer per se, although she does emphasize the point that in-tensive mothering involves financial expenditure.[25] Yet, if one takes the insights of Ogata and couples them with those of Wolfenstein, one is in a position to contemplate how ideologies of creativity and of the creative child positioned and repositioned mothers as arbiters of value *through* the child. Here, it is the recognition of the child's subject position, and the engagement with its interiority, that makes demands on mothers in order to frame their efforts in deference to the child's view, perspective, and voice—understood as legitimate and as legitimately primary—all

162 | CONCLUSION

the while absorbing the responsibility for "successful" creativity, for appropriate consumption. Hence, the effort and anxiety involved in finding the best schools and engaging children in the right kinds of activities—what Allison Pugh calls "pathway consumption"[26]—redound most often to mothers whose charge it is to take in hand a subject with an ever-present and worrisome malleability and give shape to it.

The Magic of Provisioning

Consumption, like creativity, requires provisioning. It is something never left to the child on its own, but rather involves acts of curation. Mothers, and adults generally, necessarily provide children with all kinds of goods and experiences—the typical "basic needs" trinity of food, clothing, and shelter. Indeed, part of what makes a child a child—or, for that matter, what makes anyone "childlike"—is arguably in part an inability to provide for oneself. Mothers do not simply deal with children in isolation, of course, but serve as interlocutors and liaisons with and to the commercial word, sometimes as gatekeepers, sometimes as enablers. Indeed, a significant aspect of everyday maternal labor entails handling the multifaceted tensions and counter-tensions arising between the offerings of the world of goods—the products, images, enticements, and associations—and the ever-present and ever-legitimate preferences, pleasures, and desires of children.[27] The promises of creativity can be found in old-school claims about "toys that teach,"[28] which parents endeavor to provide for their children. They also come in contemporary apps for digital games, lessons, and activities, which entail the interlocking practices of a multitude of actors—designers, engineers, retailers, marketers and market researchers, educators, and ultimately parents and mothers—which together put that tablet or device in front a preschool child in the first place so that it may become creative. Each takes part in a chain of provision.

For sociologist Marjorie DeVault, provisioning "supports the production of meaningful patterns of household life by negotiating connections between household and market."[29] In negotiating these connections, mothers and others also participate in the superintendence of meaning—what elsewhere I have referred to as semantic or interpretive provisioning.[30] The point of provisioning is usually to deliver things for others' use and perhaps for their pleasure, but the "things" provided are not self-evident in terms of their social meaning. Caregivers must make distinctions in the process of creating and assigning meaning, necessarily discerning right from wrong, good from bad, and appropriate from inappropriate goods, practices, and understandings. Importantly, this "meaning" does not exist on top of or apart from the things provided, but is embedded in the relationship being negotiated and enacted between provider and provided. Consumption and provision, understood along these lines, manifest inescapably as interpretive acts.

Marketers, advertisers, and retailers have long recognized the commercially strategic position occupied by mothers and, importantly, the emotional and moral significance of the mother as consumer.[31] In the 1980s, this relationship gained newfound significance in terms of several intersecting factors, including the increased participation of mothers in the workforce, a steadily high divorce rate, and a growing concern about the media presence in children's lives—in particular, programs designed to appeal to children that also offered licensed and branded character related toys, dolls, and figures.[32] Together, these sets of factors also helped chip away at lingering moral hesitations about the extent to which children should be addressed and targeted as direct consumers aside from the traditional Christmas season and gift-giving occasions such as birthdays. Many observers point to women's absence from the home to work in the labor force as a source of guilt for mothers who often "compensate" by acquiescing to children's requests for things more than she might have otherwise. Mothers' changing relationship to home food preparation also made for a market of convenience foods that can be easily prepared by the mother herself or by the children or father. Dining out or ordering food for take-out or delivery increased dramatically for similar reasons. Marketers began to realize that children were gaining a stronger voice in family purchasing decisions, not only in the area of their own food, toys, and clothes, as might be expected, but also in having a say in the choice of such big-ticket items as the family car, vacation destination, large appliances, and even the location of the new home.[33]

In this context, marketing firms and product manufacturers came to recognize and sought to exploit the dynamic of the growing centrality of the children's voice and perspective in household consumption, which thereby implicated mothers—their provisioning—in different ways.[34] Extensive research and commercial attention accrued to the child-mother consumer dynamic, with a growing consensus, philosophy, and ideology buttressing the idea of the child as a rightful participant in the economic process, and the concomitant expectation of "good" parenting as being responsive to children's desires and to the place and position of goods in their children's peer lives—what Pugh calls an "economy of dignity."[35] Here, attention and moral weight once again shift toward the child, whose expressions of preference arise as something worthy of attention, serious consideration, and as a gesture toward "respect"—as Janet H. noted in the quote at the beginning of this chapter.

The rise and instantiation of consumer industries since the early twentieth century, and related efforts to address children and mothers in a commercial vernacular, effectively accentuate and encourage the privileging of children's voices and perspectives while reinforcing anew the felt, and often enforced, maternal obligation to adjudicate value—in particular, to distinguish moral or emotional value from pecuniary worth and market calculus. Zelizer's priceless child returns not as a historical transformation from one kind of child to another, but as an everyday problematic of value creation and value cessation. The contemporary priceless child encounters price-value relations at every turn, in nearly every moment. Hence, mothers often exert labor (or are exhorted to do so) in the direction of making commercial things into sentimental ones—ones that imbue and symbolize care, in effect performing a kind of "transformational magic" (a reference to anthropologist James George Frazer's notion of magic) by endeavoring to turn commodities into gifts.[36] Rituals and events such as prenatal purchasing, baby showers, and children's birthday parties, as well as the everyday routines of food and clothing shopping, serve to mark and create the child as beholder of sentimental value through, and not despite, consumption.[37] The magic works (when it does) when mothers attempt to know, account for, and address children's desires and subjectivities, along with their "needs" (developmental or otherwise), and frame goods and experiences accordingly.

A Moral Metric

In the terms set out in this book, the historical-cultural novelty of the child consumer and children's consumer culture have as much to do with how the presence of the "child"—as figure, symbol, and person—fabricates and modifies economic value as it does with how capital shapes or overtakes childhood, understood as preexistently uncommodified. When one starts from the question and position of the child, as undertaken herein, it becomes evident that the problems posed by malleability—coupled with the reciprocal responsibilization of motherhood—help make for an emergent childhood that is engaged with, not turned away from, the materialities, values, and meanings of the world. This childhood side of the dynamic comes to gain a central, even hegemonic, position as the child's standpoint, subjectivity, perspective, interpretation, needs, wants, and pleasures procure the legitimacy of acknowledgment across numerous cultural fields like psychology, child study, education, child saving, and the commercial realm of goods and consumption.

Not simply a "First World problem," this child/child consumer—which has arisen out of particular racial, economic, religious, and historical circumstances—comes to stand institutionally as something of a deeply politically problematic normative ideal. Children in and of the Global South and those from economically challenged conditions and contexts are as implicated in consumer culture as are those from middle-class families in Cherry Hill, New Jersey, but of course in different ways. "Street kids" in Brazil have shown to possess finer-grained knowledge about brands and counterfeit products than researchers investigating their lives.[38] Subjective measures of children's understandings of their own well-being and poverty in Global South contexts often include reference to ideal standards of imagined childhoods beyond their immediate, lived contexts.[39] Likewise, children of color in low-income situations are shown to make and remake the materials and gadgets of consumer culture, like dolls, speak back to those who would look askance at them[40] as "flawed consumers."[41] "Flawed" consumption—i.e., not being able to aspire in appropriate ways—implies flawed parenting and flawed children.

The "child" that has been made and remade over time, across and between various contexts, on the pages of shared published texts and, to be sure, forged as an instrument of analysis and interpretation in this book—this child exists in no other way than as an amalgam of attributes that encode both concern and aspiration. It is a child differently real than the physical, biological beings who might sit at one's side and need to be taken to school and who grow up with and without one's efforts. The driving effort in this overall project has never been intended to enjoin the problem of detailing specific ties between discourse and practice, but rather to offer a glimpse of and a gesture at some possibilities about how an interlocking set of problems and questions might provide for a structured and structuring dynamic that is informative of something recognized as childhood.

In December 1999, the *Tallahassee Democrat* (Florida) newspaper, among others, ran a photograph of Elián González, a young Cuban refugee to the United States whose custody case became a highly charged political and international controversy. Elián's Florida-based family fought to keep him as a political refugee in the US while his Cuban resident father fought to bring him back home. The widely distributed photograph showed Elián kissing Barney, a dinosaur mascot of a popular US children's show, while visiting the Universal Studios theme park in Orlando.[42] "Free," American childhood—i.e., the kind of childhood Elián González might have and the kind he should have, as it is implied—can be found symbolized through a kind of commercial intimacy where virtually no space exists between the child and the consumer.

This childhood in question stands, clearly, as historically, racially, economically, and geographically specific; indeed, that is the point. The trick of childhood, and of the field of childhood studies more generally, turns on the problematic reconciliation between identifying particular childhoods in context and considering how the childhoods observed are made to speak to a generalized—perhaps even global—notion and construction. For, every depiction of a child—visual, written, or otherwise—connotes a specified version of childhood and, in so doing, wittingly or unwittingly positions itself in relation to an uneven universe of similar depictions. This tension becomes acute—even definitional—in the realm of international development work and in the wide-ranging discourses and debates over children's rights where the institutional need for a "global" or universalistic notion of the child regularly clashes with everyday, lived childhoods. Scholars and observers have long noted that the conception of the child invoked in the United Nations Convention on the Rights of the Child, ratified in 1989, embodies a Western, Global North, white-European, middle-class cultural ideal against which other childhoods are to be measured and, perhaps, toward which the many varied childhoods are converging. Many express disquiet that global capitalism, patriarchy, the rise and spread of scientific notions of child development, and a blind arrogance born of cultural domination fuel the ongoing, multifaceted globalization of childhood.[43]

My hope is that this work might open a door or reveal a pathway that will indicate an approach toward considering how the kind of "childhood" and notion of the "child" active in the worlds of legislation, international development, children's rights discourses, and marketing draw their ideological lineage from the dynamics addressed herein. That is, contemplating and analyzing this raced, classed, gendered, and religious complex—this architecture that I have named the moral project of childhood—will invite consideration of its ubiquity across domains rather than its exceptionality. In so doing, perhaps a different sort of challenge can be mounted against totalizing conceptions of good and right childhoods by demonstrating how the ideal is as something systemic, not remarkable. The kind of subject crafted out of an admixture of Christian conception, social class practice, and maternal accountability comprises the essential elements of a contemporary dominant, moral ideal. Here, the child does not simply exemplify Western, liberal individualism, but rather congeals as a desired and desirable aspirational subject, one melded from religion and capital, intimacy and voice, interiority and rights.

The moral project of childhood returns as the purview of those who seek to make or aid children to participate as consumers—something highly suspect and simultaneously complexly confluent with a long, deep, and substantive strand of ideology and belief. Over the extended arc of this process, the "child" does not simply accrue or represent value but, in a literal sense, becomes value. That is, the child of consumer culture, the progeny of a genealogy traced in these chapters, comes to stand not merely as this or that kind of value—neither wholly sentimental or unapologetically commercial—but rather as the instrument itself that draws, erases, and redraws these distinctions and these boundaries, again and again.

ACKNOWLEDGMENTS

Along the journey that is this manuscript, many have wittingly and unwittingly provided valuable assistance, both materially and spiritually.

Many thanks to Ilene Kalish, Executive Editor at NYU Press, who demonstrated remarkable faith in me and my work well before a word was ever written. The comments, critiques, and suggestions offered by the anonymous reviewers of this manuscript assisted me greatly in the revision process.

A generous mid-career grant from the Dean's Office of the Rutgers University–Camden College of Arts and Sciences allowed me to engage in the library and archival work that underlies much of this project.

I have always appreciated the gentle and patient assistance offered by those at libraries and archives during my visits. In particular, thanks goes to the staff members at the Rutgers University Libraries in Camden and in New Brunswick, NJ; the Free Library of Philadelphia; the Boston Public Library; the New York Public Library; the Radcliffe Library in Cambridge, MA; and the American Antiquarian Society in Worcester, MA.

I could not have put together this manuscript without the pleasing help of a number of graduate students over the years in the Department of Childhood Studies at Rutgers–Camden. I thank Jamie Dunaev, Matt Prickett, Brandi Venable, Eva Lupold, and Elisabeth Yang. You made all the annoying tasks easy and digestible.

I thank Lynne Vallone, an indispensable colleague, friend, and "partner in crime," as she puts it. My colleagues in Childhood Studies at Rutgers-Camden remain an inexhaustible fount of support and inspiration as we continue to work through that complex of problems called childhood studies—one that animates our mutual, collective, and collaborative endeavors.

To the baristas and staff at the OCF Fairmount coffee shop in Philadelphia—especially Josh, Coe, Eric, and Lauren. Your humor, antics, conversation, and overall good spirit helped make the "morning shift" an inviting, pleasurable time as my "third space," where I wrote much of this manuscript. Yes, this is what I have been doing all those mornings—crazy, right?

Finally, to Jessica Clark, my wife and life partner. Thank you for standing always beside me.

NOTES

INTRODUCTION

1   "The Infant. Essay No. II," *The Mother's Magazine.*
2   Calvert, *Children in the House.*
3   See Ryder, "The Cohort as a Concept."
4   On childhood and social structure, see Qvortrup, "Introduction"; Qvortrup, "Childhood as a Structural Form"; Honig, "How is the Child Constituted in Childhood Studies?"; and Alanen and Mayall, *Conceptualizing Child-Adult Relations.* See also Cook, *Symbolic Childhood.*
5   See, for instance, Heininger, "Children, Childhood, and Change."
6   Hays, *The Cultural Contradictions of Motherhood.*
7   Pugh, "Selling Compromise," 729; Goodwin and Huppatz, *The Good Mother.*
8   Zelizer, *Pricing the Priceless Child*; Kline, *Out of the Garden.*
9   Weber, *The Protestant Ethic.*
10 Cross, *Kids' Stuff*; Gary Cross, *The Cute and the Cool*; Cook, *The Commodification of Childhood*; Kline, *Out of the Garden*; Seiter, *Sold Separately.*
11 Denisoff, *The Nineteenth-Century Child*; Paul, *The Children's Book Business.*
12 Peter Gregg Slater, *Children in the New England Mind.*
13 Avery, *Behold the Child*; Paul, *The Children's Book Business.*
14 Van Horn, "Turning child readers into consumers"; Ringel, *Commercializing Childhood.*
15 Grant, *Raising Baby by the Book.*
16 Beecher, *Treatise on Domestic Economy*; Child, *The Frugal Housewife.*
17 Violas, *The Training of the Urban Working Class.*
18 Lears, *No Place of Grace*; Slater, *Children in the New England Mind*, 99; see also chapter 3.
19 Bernstein, *Racial Innocence.*
20 Heininger, "Children, Childhood, and Change."
21 Michals, "Experiments before Breakfast"; Kuhn, *The Mother's Role.*
22 Pleck, *Celebrating the Family*; Kooistra, "Home Thoughts and Home Scenes."
23 Cross, *The Cute and the Cool*; Ringel, *Commercializing Childhood.*
24 Kooistra, "Home Thoughts and Home Scenes"; Nissenbaum, *The Battle for Christmas*; Schmidt, *Consumer Rights.*
25 Pleck, *Celebrating the Family*; Cross, *The Cute and the Cool.*
26 Heininger, "Children, Childhood, and Change"; Michals, "Experiments before Breakfast"; Ringel, *Commercializing Childhood*; Leach, *Land of Desire*; Cross, *Kids' Stuff.*

27 Jacobson, *Raising Consumers*; Janet Golden, *Babies Made Us Modern*.

28 Ariès, *Centuries of Childhood*; James and Prout, "A New Paradigm for the Sociology of Childhood?"; Jenks, *Childhood*; Stearns, *Battleground of Desire*; Stearns, *Anxious Parents*; Fass, *The End of American Childhood*.

29 Cairns, Johnston, and MacKendrick, "Feeding the 'Organic Child.'"

30 Don Slater, *Consumer Culture and Modernity*.

31 Buckingham, *After the Death of Childhood*; see also Buckingham, *The Material Child* for reviews and critiques.

32 Cross, *Kids' Stuff*; Cross, *The Cute and the Cool*; Jacobson, *Raising Consumers*; Cook, "Children's Consumption in History."

33 Scott Ward, "Consumer Socialization"; John, "Consumer Socialization of Children."

34 Louv, *Last Child in the Woods*; Linn, *The Case for Make Believe*; Chudacoff, *Children at Play*; Riney-Kehrberg, *The Nature of Childhood*.

35 Hays, *The Cultural Contradictions of Motherhood*.

36 Ibid., 8.

37 Ibid., 97.

38 Ibid., 167.

39 Hochschild, *The Commercialization of Intimate Life*.

40 Ibid.

41 Hochschild, "'Rent a Mom' and other Services," 75.

42 Thorne, "Re-Visioning Women and Social Change," 85; Oakley, "Women and children first and last."

43 Zelizer, *Pricing the Priceless Child*.

44 Ibid., 11.

45 Coveney, *The Image of Childhood*.

46 Engels, *The Condition of the Working Class*.

47 Goldberg, *Lewis Hine*; see also Vallone, *Big and Small*, 197–201.

48 Cf. Campbell, *The Romantic Ethic*.

49 Sammond, *Babes in Tomorrowland*.

50 Shuttleworth, *The Mind of the Child*.

51 Henaghan, "Why judges need to know and understand childhood studies."

52 Nieuwenhuys, "Global childhood and the politics of contempt"; Burr, *Vietnam's Children in a Changing World*; Fattore, Mason, and Watson, "Locating the child centrally"; Tabak and Carvalho, "Responsibility to protect the future."

53 Lareau, *Unequal Childhoods*; Pugh, *Longing and Belonging*.

54 Abrams, *Historical Sociology*.

55 Abrams, *Historical Sociology*, xv.

56 Foucault, *The Archaeology of Knowledge*.

57 Smith and Green. *Key Thinkers in Childhood Studies*.

58 The main periodicals consulted include *The Mother's Magazine*, *Godey's Lady's Book*, *Ladies' Home Journal*, *Harper's Bazaar*, *Babyhood*, and *Parents*. See below and see Bibliography.

59 Anderson, *Imagined Communities*.
60 Ibid., 6.
61 Mechling, "Advice to Historians on Advice to Mothers."
62 Beetham, *A Magazine of Her Own?* 10–14.
63 Ibid., 12.
64 Ibid., 14.
65 Readers will note how few of the articles cited in periodicals used herein have specific, named authors.
66 Beetham, *A Magazine of Her Own?* 20.
67 Ibid., 20–21.
68 Steedman, *Strange Dislocations*.
69 Ibid., 96.

CHAPTER 1. A MORAL ARCHITECTURE

1 "Maternal Authority," *The Mother's Magazine*.
2 Greven, *The Protestant Temperament*; Slater, *Children in the New England Mind*; Wall, *Ethics in Light of Childhood*; Wishy, *The Child and the Republic*.
3 Peter Gregg Slater, *Children in the New England Mind*, 128–161; Greven, *The Protestant Temperament*, 14–16; see Wall, *Ethics in Light of Childhood*, 25–28; Locke, *Some Thoughts Concerning Education*.
4 Moran and Vinovskis, *Religion, Family and the Life Course*, 111.
5 Plumb, "The New World of Children in Eighteenth-Century England."
6 Marcus, *Minders of Make-Believe*.
7 Ringel, *Commercializing Childhood*.
8 Avery, *Behold the Child*; Marcus, *Minders of Make-Believe*; Paul, *The Children's Book Business*.
9 Violas, *The Training of the Urban Working Class*.
10 Shuttleworth, *The Mind of the Child*.
11 Moran and Vinovskis, *Religion, Family and the Life Course*; Slater, *Children in the New England Mind*.
12 Greven, *The Protestant Temperament*, 234–250; Tosh, *A Man's Place*.
13 Morgan, *Godly Learning*.
14 Ibid., 142–150.
15 Steedman, *Strange Dislocations*.
16 Bushnell, *Christian Nurture*.
17 Ann Douglas, *The Feminization of American Culture*.
18 Weber, *The Protestant Ethic*.
19 Ibid., 181.
20 Campbell, *The Romantic Ethic*.
21 Ibid., 133.
22 Ibid., 173–201.
23 Ibid., 220–227.

24 Slater, *Children in the New England Mind*, 111–13; see also Kuhn, *The Mother's Role in Childhood Education*; Ringel, *Commercializing Childhood*; see also chapter 3.

25 Douglas, *The Feminization of American Culture*.

26 Ibid., 50–93.

27 Ibid., 94–139.

28 Merish, *Sentimental Materialism*.

29 Ibid., 88–93.

30 Brewer, "Genesis of the Modern Toy"; Heininger, "Children, Childhood, and Change in America."

31 Weber, *The Protestant Ethic*.

32 Ibid., 99–110.

33 Ibid., 97.

34 Ibid., 110–112.

35 Meckel, "Educating a Ministry of Mothers"; Schertz, "The Mother's Magazine"; Morgan, *Godly Learning*; Moran and Vinovskis, *Religion, Family, and the Life Course*.

36 See Nissenbaum, *The Battle for Christmas*, 3–48.

37 As quoted in Stannard, "Death and the Puritan Child," 460–462.

38 Stannard, "Death and the Puritan Child," 461.

39 Slater, *Children in the New England Mind*, 30.

40 Ibid., 13; see Schertz, "The Mother's Magazine," 315.

41 Slater, *Children in the New England Mind*, 131–33; Meckel, "Educating a Ministry of Mothers"; Schertz, "The Mother's Magazine"; Morgan, *Godly Learning*; Moran and Vinovskis, *Religion, Family and the Life Course*.

42 Meckel, "Educating a Ministry of Mothers," 412–413.

43 Slater, *Children in the New England Mind*, 138.

44 Meckel, "Educating a Ministry of Mothers"; Schertz, "The Mother's Magazine."

45 Meckel, "Educating a Ministry of Mothers"; Schertz, "The Mother's Magazine."

46 Doyle, *Maternal Bodies*.

47 Morgan, *Godly Learning*.

48 Grant, *Raising Baby by the Book*, 24–29.

49 The magazine underwent numerous name changes over its more than thirty-year run, including *Mothers' Journal and Family Visitant*, *Mother's Magazine and Family Journal*, *The Mother's Magazine and Family Circle*, and *Mother's Magazine and Daughter's Friend*, among others. For the sake of simplicity, the publication will be referred to throughout as *The Mother's Magazine*.

50 Meckel, "Educating a Ministry of Mothers," 404.

51 See also Ryan, "A Women's Awakening"; Beetham, *A Magazine of Her Own?*

52 Schertz, "The Mother's Magazine," 312.

53 Meckel, "Educating a Ministry of Mothers," 416.

54 Schertz, "The Mother's Magazine."

55 Meckel, "Educating a Ministry of Mothers," 418.

56 Beetham, *A Magazine of Her Own?* 54.

57 "Character of Children Intrusted to Mothers," *The Mother's Magazine*, 79.

58 Calvert, *Children of the House*, 19, 38.

59 Ibid., 79.

60 Ibid., 79–80.

61 Greven, *The Protestant Temperament*, 25; Slater, *Children in the New England Mind*, 93–106; Ringel, *Commercializing Childhood*.

62 Sánchez-Eppler, "Raising Empires like Children."

63 Palimeri, "From Republican Motherhood to Race Suicide," 246.

64 See Shuttleworth, *The Mind of the Child*, 267–289.

65 "The Infant. Essay No. II," *The Mother's Magazine*.

66 Schertz, "The Mother's Magazine," 310.

67 I will not point out or correct all the uses of the masculine pronoun in quotations when it refers to children generally, but will do so in the text itself when relevant.

68 "What is the True Basis for Religious Beliefs?" *The Mother's Magazine*, 86.

69 Ibid.

70 "Parental Consistency," *The Mother's Magazine*, 22.

71 Ibid., 24.

72 Ibid., 24.

73 "Practical Hints," *The Mother's Magazine*, 162.

74 Ibid.

75 "Extracts from a Mother's Common Place Book," *The Mother's Magazine*, emphasis in original.

76 "Maternal Influence," *The Mother's Magazine*, 48.

77 "Report of the Maternal Association," *The Mother's Magazine*, 34–35.

78 "Children Early Taught Their Need of a Savior," *The Mother's Magazine*, 60, emphasis added.

79 "Children Taught to Exercise Their Judgment," *The Mother's Magazine*.

80 "Practical Hints," *The Mother's Magazine*, 165.

81 Ibid., 165–166.

82 Ibid., 166.

83 Slater, *Children in the New England Mind*, 120.

84 "Young Children Influenced by Family Prayer," *The Mother's Magazine*.

85 "Practical Hints," *The Mother's Magazine*; "Character of Children Intrusted to Mothers," *The Mother's Magazine*, 78; see also Slater, *Children in the New England Mind*, 117–121.

86 Greven, *The Protestant Temperament*, 178.

87 Douglas, *The Feminization of American Culture*, 178.

88 Doyle, *Maternal Bodies*, 184.

89 "Obedience is Better than Sacrifice," *The Mother's Magazine*.

90 Mrs. Phillips, "The Christian Mother," *The Mother's Magazine*.

91 Another writer, "Iota," put the matter this way when writing about "the infant" in the June 1833 issue, partially represented in the epigraph to the Introduction: "Before it can imitate an articulate sound, it can understand the looks, the tones,

and the actions of others, and according to the nature of these influences, will be the character of the impression produced. The first moral impression a child receives is it first lesson on religion; and this first idea is the foundation on which we are to base the superstructure of all future moral training. The habit of prayer, and a sense of dependence on God, maybe taught to a child before it can learn anything perceptively. Let then the pious mother, who feels that first impressions are the most durable, take the object of her solicitude with her when she goes to her heavenly Father, even before it can lisp His name. Let it kneel by her side while she commends if to His care, and asks those things which are needful for body and soul. The habit so early formed, will not be easily broken; and as soon as it can receive ideas form words let it be taught from the parental relation its dependence on God, who it cannot see, but who is its absent father." "The Infant. Essay No. II," *The Mother's Magazine.*
92 "Maternal Authority," *The Mother's Magazine.*
93 "Early Discipline," *The Mother's Magazine.*
94 Slater, *Children in the New England Mind*, 102–113.
95 Ibid., 104.
96 See Bloch, *Gender and Morality*, 57–77.
97 Bushnell, *Christian Nurture*, 23.
98 Ibid., 29.
99 Douglas, *The Feminization of American Culture.*
100 Bushnell, *Christian Nurture*, 21.
101 Ibid., 28.
102 Ibid., 21.
103 Ibid., 79.
104 Ibid., 22.
105 Ibid., 23.
106 But anticipated many decades before then; see Shuttleworth, *The Mind of the Child.*
107 Bushnell, *Christian Nurture*, 13.
108 Bushnell writes: "As little are young children to be taught that they are of course unregenerated. This, with many, is even a fixed point of orthodoxy, and of course they have no doubt of it. They put their children on the precise footing of heathens and take it for granted that they are to be converted in the same manner. But they ought not to be in the same condition as heathens. Brought up in their society, under their example, baptized into their faith and upon the ground of it, and bosomed in their prayers, there ought to be seeds of gracious character already planted in them; so that no conversion is necessary, but only the development of a new life already begun. Why should the parents cast away their privilege and count their child an alien still from God's mercies?" Bushnell, *Christian Nurture*, 372.
109 Cf. Heininger, "Children, Childhood, and Change in America."
110 Tosh, *A Man's Place*, 43.

111 Wall, *Ethics in Light of Childhood*.
112 Greven, *The Protestant Temperament*.
113 Even as Bushnell's salvo clearly caught the attention of a readership by plac-
    ing nurture at the center of Christian education (*Christian Nurture* would be
    reprinted in 1861 and again upon his death in 1876), it also inspired responses
    and clarifications from among other Protestant clergy. Notably, J.H.A. Bom-
    berger, pastor of the Race Street Evangelical Church in Philadelphia, in 1859
    published *Infant Salvation*, wherein he echoed many of Bushnell's basic themes
    and approaches, but with a decidedly stern emphasis on the inviolability of the
    twin doctrines of child depravity and predestination. On the idea that chil-
    dren naturally know right from wrong and need little instruction, for instance,
    Bomberger cites New Testament scripture to proclaim, "There is nothing said
    or implied which leads us to think that the Saviour intended to hold up these
    children as He did those in St. Matthew, xviii. 1–5, as specimens of moral fitness
    for His kingdom." J.H.A. Bomberger, *Infant Salvation*, 102.

CHAPTER 2. PRODUCTIVE MATERIALITIES

1 Higonnet, *Pictures of Innocence*.
2 Ibid.; Holland, *Picturing Childhood*; Heininger, "Children, Childhood, and
    Change in America."
3 As I have done elsewhere, I refer to the child as "it" when I seek to denote and
    emphasize that I am addressing a discursive figure with a history, rather than a
    sentient being with a biography; see Cook, *The Commodification of Childhood*,
    5–6.
4 Nazera Sadiq Wright. *Black Girlhood in the Nineteenth Century*.
5 Leora Auslander, "The Gendering of Consumer Practices."
6 McCracken, *Culture and Consumption*.
7 Kidwell and Christman, *Suiting Everyone*; See Leach, *Land of Desire*.
8 See Peter Gregg Slater, *Children in the New England Mind*.
9 Mintz, *Huck's Raft*; Heininger, "Children, Childhood, and Change."
10 Pleck, *Celebrating the Family*; Sutton-Smith, *Toys as Culture*, 15–22; Cross, *The
    Cute and the Cool*, 23–29.
11 Cross, *The Cute and the Cool*; Lasch, *Haven in a Heartless World*; Kooistra, "Home
    Thoughts and Home Scenes"; Ringel, *Commercializing Childhood*.
12 Cross, *The Cute and the Cool*, 29.
13 Nissenbaum, *The Battle for Christmas*, 140–155.
14 Ibid., 169–175.
15 Claudia Nelson, *Invisible Men*, 3.
16 Carrier, *Meanings of the Market*.
17 Auslander, "The Gendering of Consumer Practices," 82–85.
18 Nissenbaum, *The Battle for Christmas*; Davis, "Making Night Hideous."
19 Veblen, *The Theory of the Leisure Class*.

20 Douglas, *The Feminization of American Culture*; Leach, *Land of Desire*; Rosalind Williams, *Dream Worlds*; Tiersten, *Marianne in the Market*.

21 Auslander, *Taste and Power*; Hoganson, *The Consumer's Imperium*; deGrazia, *The Sex of Things*.

22 Merish, *Sentimental Materialism*.

23 Brown. *Domestic Individualism*.

24 deGrazia, *The Sex of Things*.

25 Auslander, "Taste and Power"; Auslander, "The Gendering of Consumer Practices."

26 Bernstein, *Racial Innocence*.

27 Elizabeth White Nelson, *Market Sentiments*.

28 Bourdieu, *Distinction*.

29 See Bourdieu, *Distinction*, 368–369; Cook, "The Missing Child."

30 Bourdieu, *Distinction*, 6.

31 Ibid.

32 Campbell, "Early Influences," *The Mother's Magazine*, 49.

33 Ibid., 51.

34 Ibid., 52.

35 Ibid., 52

36 "Woman—At Home," *Godey's Lady's Book*.

37 Knox, *The Works of Vicesimus Knox*, 641.

38 "Woman—At Home," *Godey's Lady's Book*.

39 Vallone, *Disciplines of Virtue*.

40 Featherstone, *Consumer Culture and Postmodernism*; Goldman and Papson, *Sign Wars*; Haug, *Commodity Aesthetics, Ideology, and Culture*.

41 Latour, *Reassembling the Social*; Miller, *Materiality*.

42 Merish, *Sentimental Materialism*; Brown, *Domestic Individualism*.

43 Auslander, "The Gendering of Consumer Practices."

44 "Woman—At Home," *Godey's Lady's Book*.

45 Ibid.

46 Ibid.

47 Auslander, *Taste and Power*.

48 Sigourney, "Taste," *Godey's Lady's Book*, 88.

49 Ibid.

50 Arnold, *Culture and Anarchy*.

51 Sigourney, "Taste," *Godey's Lady's Book*, 88.

52 Ibid.

53 Cook, "Moral Order."

54 Miller, *Materiality*.

55 Embury, "The Rights of Children," *Godey's Lady's Book*, 82.

56 For example, "Dressing Children," *Godey's Lady's Book*; see also chapter 3.

57 "Our Little Children," *Godey's Lady's Book*.

58 In an 1837 piece in *The Mother's Magazine*, an unnamed writer makes a strikingly similar case for the provenance of bad behavior in adulthood. See "Young Children Influenced by Family Prayer," *The Mother's Magazine*.

59 "Our Little Children," *Godey's Lady's Book*.

60 Ibid.

61 Ibid.

62 "The Mother," *Godey's Lady's Book*.

63 For example, Harriet Elliot, "Our Childhood's Home," *Babyhood*.

64 See Crowley, "Biting the Hand that Feeds Us."

65 See Lears, *No Place of Grace*, 22.

66 As quoted in Lears, *No Place of Grace*, 22.

67 Child, *The Frugal Housewife*, 6–7.

68 Beecher, *Treatise on Domestic Economy*, 255.

69 Ibid.

70 Ibid., 255–56.

71 "Dressing Children," *Godey's Lady's Book*.

72 Foucault, "Truth and Power."

73 "Report of the Maternal Association," *The Mother's Magazine*, 36.

74 Mintz, *Huck's Raft*.

75 "Moral Poisons: The Antidote," *The Mother's Magazine*, 184–188.

76 Ibid., 185.

77 Ibid., 185.

78 "The Rights of Children," *Godey's Lady's Book*, 82.

79 "Parental Indulgence," *Godey's Lady's Book*.

80 "Domestic Education," *Godey's Lady's Book*, 56.

81 Cross, *The Cute and the Cool*.

82 Portions of this section appear in a similar form in Cook, "Moral Order."

83 "The Rights of Children," *Godey's Lady's Book*, 82.

84 "The Boy's Room," *Ohio Farmer*.

85 Ibid.

86 "My Boys' Room," *Ladies' Home Journal*; "A Boy's Room," *Arthur's Home Magazine*; "The Boy's Room," *Southern Planter*; "Room for the Boys," *Babyhood*.

87 "Fix up the Boys' Room," *Ohio Farmer*.

88 Ibid.

89 "The Expression of Rooms," *St. Nicholas*, 486.

90 Ibid.

91 Ibid.

92 "A Young Girl's Room," *Harper's Bazaar*.

93 "A Young Girl's Room," *Arthur's Home Magazine*.

94 Ibid.

95 Durkheim, *The Elementary Forms of the Religious Life*, 55.

96 Carolyn Steedman, *Strange Dislocations*.

97 See Pugh's discussion of "symbolic indulgence" among middle-class families as a contemporary expression of this dynamic. Pugh, *Longing and Belonging*.

98 Or the domestic work of men, for that matter; see Tosh, *A Man's Place*, 11–52.

99 Weber, *The Protestant Ethic*, 21–24.

100 Ibid., 104.

CHAPTER 3. FROM DISCIPLINE TO REWARD

1 Hubert, "The Punishment Ledger," *Babyhood*, 50.

2 Lears, *No Place of Grace*, 43–45; see also Santayana, "The Poetry of Christian Dogma," and Bierbower, "On the Drift in the New Theology," as cited in Lears, *No Place of Grace*, 331.

3 Nevertheless, invocations of child depravity continued throughout the century, often in relation to a young child's "temperament," which can be corrected or corralled, as opposed to serving as an overarching, intractable essence of a child. See Bulkley, *A word to parents*.

4 Shuttleworth, *The Mind of the Child*; Cunningham, *Children of the Poor*.

5 See "Health Department," *Godey's Lady's Book*; "Children's Food," *Godey's Lady's Book*; "Play with Children," *Godey's Lady's Book*.

6 See Campbell, *The Romantic Ethic*, 138–160.

7 "An Ungovernable Temper," *Babyhood*, 117.

8 "Tact in Management," *Babyhood*, 309.

9 Ibid., 310.

10 "What Really Happened," *Babyhood*.

11 Ibid., 181, emphasis in original.

12 "What John Senior Might Have Done," *Babyhood*, 211.

13 Ibid., 211–212.

14 Ibid., 212.

15 Ibid.

16 "What Ought He Have Done? Mark Twain's Opinion," *Babyhood*, 276.

17 Ibid., 276.

18 Ibid., 277.

19 Ibid., 276.

20 "Comments on a Crisis?" *Babyhood*.

21 "Untruthful Children," *Babyhood*, 304.

22 Ibid., 305.

23 Ibid., 305.

24 Ibid., 305.

25 Editorial, *Babyhood*, November 1890.

26 "A Mother's Notebook," *Babyhood*.

27 "A Need for Sympathy," *Babyhood*, 310.

28 "A Protest against Whipping," *Babyhood*.

29 Ibid., 253.
30 Palmer, "Justice in the Home," *Babyhood*, 217.
31 See also the response of "L.P." to the John, Sr. incident above: "What John Sr. Ought to Have Done?" *Babyhood*; see article by Johnson, "Mistakes," *Babyhood*.
32 "Current Issues in Our Nursery," *Babyhood*.
33 "Frightening Children," *Babyhood*.
34 "When and How Do We Educate," *Babyhood*.
35 See Sánchez-Eppler, *Dependent States*; Bernstein, *Racial Innocence*.
36 Steedman, *Strange Dislocations*, 12.
37 Ibid., 73.
38 Anderson, *Imagined Communities*.
39 Sánchez-Eppler, "Raising Empires like Children."
40 "Thoughts on Home Training," *Babyhood*.
41 "Anxiety About that Baby," *Babyhood*.
42 "Misdirected Selections of Toys," *Babyhood*.
43 See Shuttleworth, *The Mind of the Child*.
44 Hubert, "The Punishment Ledger," *Babyhood*, 48–49.
45 See "Delayed Punishments," *Babyhood*; "Few Children are Conscienceless," *Babyhood*.
46 See "Correct Methods in the Nursery," *Babyhood*.
47 Le Row, "The Decline of Sentiment in Children," *Babyhood*.
48 "Wise and Unwise Punishment," *Babyhood*.
49 Holt, *The Care and Feeding of Children*.
50 Glenn, *Campaigns Against Corporal Punishment*.
51 "A Phase of Governing," *Babyhood*.
52 "Self-Control," *Babyhood*.
53 Mangasarian, "The Punishment of Children."
54 "The Punishment of Children," *Babyhood*, 90.
55 Ibid.
56 Ibid., 91.
57 Ibid.
58 "Self-control," *Babyhood*, 381.
59 Hays, *The Cultural Contradictions of Motherhood*.
60 "Another Hint to 'An Ohio Farmer,'" *Babyhood*.
61 "The Credit System as Incentive to Good Behavior," *Babyhood*.
62 "Unusually Good Children," *Babyhood*.
63 "A Chapter on Prizes," *Babyhood*.
64 "Amusements which Do Not Amuse," *Babyhood* 248.
65 Ibid.
66 "The Rewarding of Children," *Ladies' Home Journal*.
67 "The Education of Children," *Babyhood*.

68 Ibid.
69 Editorial, *Babyhood*, November 1885.
70 "High-flying at Fashion," *Babyhood*.
71 "A Happy Childhood," *Babyhood*.
72 "A Renewed Plea," *Babyhood*; "Children's Use of Money," *Babyhood*.
73 "Fastidious Children," *Babyhood*.
74 Franklin, "Self-consciousness in Children," *Babyhood*.
75 "Sharp and Forward Children," *Babyhood*.
76 "Baby's Wardrobe," *Babyhood*; "High-flying at Fashion," *Babyhood*.
77 Editorial, *Babyhood*, October 1888.
78 Greven, *The Protestant Temperament*, 74.
79 "The Spirit of Christmas Giving," *Babyhood*.
80 "Amusements which Do Not Amuse," *Babyhood*.
81 Editorial, *Babyhood*, April 1890.
82 "Games and Prizes," *Babyhood*.
83 "The Appetite of Children," *Babyhood*.
84 "A Chat with the Indigent," *Babyhood*, 328–332.
85 Ibid., 327–329.
86 "Punishment and Rewards for Children," *Babyhood*, 133.
87 "The Decline of Sentiment in Children," *Babyhood*.
88 Cross, *The Cute and the Cool*, 15.
89 See Norman Rockwell Museum, "Norman Rockwell's 323 'Saturday Evening Post' Covers."
90 Cross, *The Cute and the Cool*; Kooistra, "Home Thoughts and Home Scenes."
91 Pleck, *Celebrating the Family*.
92 Nissenbaum, *The Battle for Christmas*, 169–175.
93 "The Faults of Children," *Babyhood*.
94 "The Spoiling of Children," *Babyhood*.
95 Cook, "Spatial Biographies of Children's Consumption"; Cook, *The Commodification of Childhood*.
96 "The Faults of Children," *Babyhood*, 127.
97 Ibid., 128, emphasis added.

CHAPTER 4. SIMPLICITY, MONEY, AND PROPERTY
1 See, for instance, Wolfenstein, "Fun Morality"; Seiter, *Sold Separately*; Rutherford, *Adult Supervision Required*.
2 Simmel, "Objective Culture."
3 Kline, *Out of the Garden*.
4 Cross, *Kids' Stuff*.
5 Cook, *The Commodification of Childhood*.
6 Forty, *Objects of Desire*.
7 See Cross, *Kids' Stuff*; Jacobson, *Raising Consumers*.

8 Leach, *Land of Desire*; Lears, *Fables of Abundance*; Marchand, *Advertising and the American Dream*.
9 Schlereth, *Victorian America*.
10 See Wolfenstein, "Fun Morality"; Stearns, *Battleground of Desire*.
11 "A Plea for Fewer Playthings," *Babyhood*.
12 "A Renewed Plea for Fewer Playthings," *Babyhood*.
13 Ibid.
14 See for instance, "Amusements for Children," *Babyhood*, 380.
15 "Misdirected Selections of Toys," *Babyhood*.
16 See Ogata, *Designing the Creative Child*, and see Conclusion below.
17 "Pleas for the Home-Made Toy," *Babyhood*, 87–88.
18 Ibid., 89.
19 "Cultivating Contentment," *Ladies' Home Journal*.
20 "Good Taste in Clothes for Girls," *Ladies' Home Journal*.
21 "How Can I Make Simple Clothes for my Children," *Ladies' Home Journal*.
22 Cook, *The Commodification of Childhood*, 78–85.
23 See discussion of children's room in chapter 2; See also Cook, "Moral Order."
24 "Peasant Arts in the Children's Room," *New York Times*.
25 Bederman, *Manliness and Civilization*; Lears, "From Salvation to Self-Realization."
26 "Complicating Christmas" *Ladies' Home Journal*.
27 "The Rush of American Women," *Ladies' Home Journal*.
28 "The Secrets of a Happy Life," *Ladies' Home Journal*.
29 Lears, *No Place of Grace*, 146.
30 Ibid.
31 Ibid., 47.
32 Ibid.
33 See Bederman, *Manliness and Civilization*, esp. 77–120.
34 "Pocket Money," *Godey's Lady's Book*.
35 Ibid.
36 Ibid.
37 Twain and Warner, *The Gilded Age*.
38 "Children's Use of Money," *Babyhood*, 281; Abbott, *Gentle Measures*, 268.
39 "Children's Use of Money," *Babyhood*, 281; Abbott, *Gentle Measures*, 268.
40 "Children's Use of Money," *Babyhood*, 282; Abbott, *Gentle Measures*, 268.
41 "Children's Use of Money," *Babyhood*, 285; Abbott, *Gentle Measures*, 279.
42 "Children's Use of Money," *Babyhood*, 284; Abbott, *Gentle Measures*, 274–75.
43 "Under My Study Lamp," *Ladies' Home Journal*.
44 "The Money Problem in Education," *Babyhood*.
45 Ibid., 250.
46 See Jacobson, *Raising Consumers*, 57–58; Cross, *The Cute and the Cool*, 3–18; Zelizer, *Pricing the Priceless Child*, 73–112.
47 And perhaps extending to working class children as well; see Golden, *Babies Made Us Modern*.

48 "The Money Problem in Education," *Babyhood*, 250.

49 See also Jacobson, *Raising Consumers*, 57.

50 "The Child and Money," *Harper's Bazaar*.

51 Ibid.

52 Jacobson, *Raising Consumers*, 58–70.

53 Ibid., 81–85.

54 Zelizer, *Pricing the Priceless Child*, 97–98.

55 Zelizer, *Pricing the Priceless Child*; Zelizer, *The Social Meaning of Money*.

56 Zelizer, *The Social Meaning of Money*.

57 See, for instance Igor Kopytoff, "The Cultural Biography of Things"; Douglas and Isherwood, *The World of Goods*.

58 Nasaw, *Children of the City*.

59 See Nasaw, *Children of the City*, 130–137; Peiss, *Cheap Amusements*; see also Ewen, *Immigrant Women*.

60 "The Child and Money," *Harper's Bazaar*.

61 Ibid.

62 See "Pocket Money," *Godey's Lady's Book*; Abbott, *Gentle Measures*; Eliot, "The Money Problem in Education," *Babyhood*.

63 Zelizer, *Pricing the Priceless Child*, 225–228.

64 "The Child and Money," *Harper's Bazaar*.

65 "Obstinate Children," *Babyhood*; "Amusing the Baby," *Babyhood*.

66 "Respect Due the Young," *Ladies' Home Journal*; "Kissing by Force," *Babyhood*; see also "Compulsory Kissing," *Babyhood*.

67 Embury, "The Rights of Children," *Godey's Lady's Book*, 80.

68 "The Sensitiveness of Little Children," *Babyhood*; "The Needle in the Nursery," *Babyhood*.

69 Or not over- or unhealthily dressed; see "Hints About Health: Exercise for Girls" *Godey's Lady's Book*; see also Cook, *The Commodification of Childhood*.

70 "The Rights of Babyhood," *Babyhood*.

71 "The Rights of Children," *Godey's Lady's Book*, 80.

72 Ibid.

73 Ashmore, "Side Talks with Girls," *Ladies' Home Journal*.

74 Ibid.

75 "How Missing Children can be Found," *Babyhood*, 279; "Compulsory Kissing," *Babyhood*.

76 "A Hint to Toy-Makers," *Babyhood*; "Prompt and Absolute Obedience," *Babyhood*; "Current Issues in our Nursery," *Babyhood*; "Some Notes as to Christmas Toys," *Babyhood*.

77 "The Property Rights of Children," *Babyhood*, 53.

78 Ibid., 53.

79 Ibid., 55.

80 Ibid., 55.

81 "Too Tenacious of Her Rights," *Babyhood*, 153.

82 See "The Relation of Growth to Education," *Babyhood*; "Helping Baby Respect Property Rights," *Babyhood*; "A Mother's Convocation," *Babyhood*.

83 "Nursery Furniture," *Babyhood*; "Baby at the Table," *Babyhood*.

84 "The Needle in the Nursery," *Babyhood*.

85 Eliot, "The Money Problem in Education," *Babyhood*, 249.

86 "Development versus Repression," *Babyhood*.

87 "Acquisitiveness and Its Cures," *Babyhood*.

88 Eliot, "The Problem of Property Rights," *Babyhood*, 214.

89 Ibid., 215.

90 Ibid.

CHAPTER 5. THINK AND FEEL LIKE A CHILD

1 Wiggin and Smith, *Children's Rights*, 130.

2 Scott, *The Psychology of Advertising*, 77.

3 Smith, *Wealth of Nations*.

4 Bentham, *Principles of Morals*.

5 "The Value of an Orderly Nursery," *Outlook*.

6 Scott, *The Psychology of Advertising*, 24.

7 Ibid., 25.

8 Ibid., 80–92.

9 Wiggin and Smith, *Children's Rights*, 33.

10 As quoted by Wiggin and Smith, *Children's Rights*, 43.

11 Wiggin and Smith, *Children's Rights*, 45–46.

12 Ibid., 46.

13 Ibid., 10.

14 Ibid., 11.

15 See Cook, *The Commodification of Childhood*, 49–54.

16 Seiter, *Sold Separately*.

17 Scott, *The Psychology of Advertising*, 77–78.

18 Garvey, *The Adman in the Parlor*.

19 Ibid., 27–49.

20 Ibid., 43.

21 May, *Homeward Bound*.

22 Beard and Beard, *The American Girl's Handy Book*.

23 Garvey, *The Adman in the Parlor*, 34–35.

24 Beard and Beard, *The American Girl's Handy Book*, 396.

25 Garvey, *The Adman in the Parlor*, 34–35.

26 Garvey, "Advertising Competitions," 158–170.

27 Ibid., 160.

28 Ibid., 164.

29 Ibid., 167.

30 Portions of this section have appeared in similar form in Cook, *The Commodification of Childhood*.

31 Leach, "Child-world in the Promised Land"; Benson, *Counter Cultures*.

32 Leach, *Land of Desire*; Leach, "Child-World in the Promised Land."

33 Cook, *The Commodification of Childhood*, 96–121.

34 On children's consumer culture, see Kline, *Out of the Garden*; Seiter, *Sold Separately*; Jacobson, *Raising Consumers*; Cross, *The Cute and the Cool*; Sammond, *Babies in Tomorrowland*. On clubs and contests, see Grumbine, *Reaching Juvenile Markets*.

35 Gridley, "Ideas That are Making Sales to and Through Children," *Printers' Ink Monthly*.

36 Gridley, "Ideas That are Making Sales to and Through Children," *Printers' Ink Monthly*.

37 See Cook, "The Other 'Child Study'"; Jacobson, *Raising Consumers*.

38 "Put Yourself in the Child's Place," *Dry Goods Economist*.

39 Ibid., emphasis in original.

40 Ibid.

41 Most women working in urban department stores in the 1920s were single women who often lived with other single women to afford rent on pitifully low salaries; see Benson, *Counter Cultures*.

42 "Put Yourself in the Child's Place," *Dry Goods Economist*.

43 Ibid.

44 Wade, "What Kind of Advertisements Do Boys Like?" *Printers' Ink Monthly*.

45 Ibid.

46 "Buying the Gift to Fit the Child," *Parents*.

47 As quoted in Cook, *The Commodification of Childhood*, 114; see also "Selling to the Young Girls," *Dry Goods Economist*.

48 Ibid.

49 "Selling to the Young Girls," *Dry Goods Economist*.

50 Ibid.

51 See Cook, *The Commodification of Childhood* for a detailed description of *Earnshaw's* and its key place in the making of the child consumer in the 1910s to 1960s.

52 "Molding Character with Clothes," *Earnshaw's*, 692.

53 Ibid.

54 Howell, "With Designs upon the Next Generation," *Printers' Ink Monthly*.

55 Ibid.

56 "Cutouts for Children," *Printers' Ink*.

57 Sammond, *Babes in Tomorrowland*.

58 See, for instance Imada, "Color Preference of School Children"; Jordan, *Children's Interests in Reading*; Florence Williams, "An Investigation of Children's Preferences for Pictures," 119.

59 Stolz and Taylor, *Interests of Young Children*; Taylor, "The Right Toy for the Young Child"; Hunt, *A Catalogue of Play Equipment*; Mitchell, *Play and Play Materials for the Preschool Child*; Wolf and Boehm, *Play and Playthings*; Boyd, *Play Equipment for the Nursery*.

60 Seiter, *Sold Separately*; Cross, *Kids' Stuff*.

61 Cook, *The Commodification of Childhood*.

62 Sammond, *Babes in Tomorrowland*.

63 Leonard, "Choose the Toy to Fit the Child," *Parents*.

64 Ibid.

65 "Toys the Year Round," *Parents*.

66 Seiter, *Sold Separately*, 65.

67 Ibid.

68 See also Golden, *Babies Made Us Modern*.

69 See Cook, "Knowing the Child Consumer."

70 See Cook, "Exchange Value as Pedagogy"; Cook, *The Commodification of Childhood*; Cook, "Knowing the Child Consumer"; Golden, *Babies Made Us Modern*.

71 Grumbine, *Reaching Juvenile Markets*, 11.

72 Cook, *The Commodification of Childhood*, 77.

73 See Kline, *Out of the Garden*; Cross, *Kids' Stuff*.

74 Jacobson, *Raising Consumers*, 93–126.

75 Ibid., 93–96.

76 As Jacobson shows in the advertisements of the time; see ibid., 97–109.

77 Ibid., 109–126.

78 Goldsmith, "Salesmanship for Parents," *Parents*, 19–21.

79 Ibid., 19.

80 Ibid., 20.

81 Ibid., 21, emphasis in original.

82 "Side Talks with Girls," *Ladies' Home Journal*.

83 Goffman, *The Presentation of Self in Everyday Life*.

CONCLUSION

1 James and Prout, "A New Paradigm for the Sociology of Childhood?"; Jenks, *Childhood*; James, Jenks, and Prout, *Theorizing Childhood*.

2 For example, Carlsson-Paige, *Taking Back Childhood*; Guldberg, *Reclaiming Childhood*.

3 Linn, *The Case for Make Believe*; Chudacoff, *Children at Play*; see Cook, "Panaceas of Play."

4 Foucault, *The Birth of Biopolitics*.

5 Smith, *Wealth of Nations*.

6 Zelizer, *Pricing the Priceless Child*.

7 Kline, *Out of the Garden*; Cross, *The Cute and the Cool*; Schor, *Born to Buy*; see also Buckingham, *The Material Child*, for a review and critique of this perspective.

8 See Buckingham and Tingstad *Childhood and Consumer Culture*; Sparrman, Sandin, and Sjöberg, *Situating Child Consumption*; Buckingham, *The Material Child*.
9 Cook, "Children's Market Researchers as Moral Brokers."
10 Cook, "Semantic Provisioning of Children's Food"; Cook, "Leveraging the Child's Perspective."
11 Schor, *Born to Buy*.
12 See Thorne, "Re-visioning Women and Social Change"; Oakley, "Women and Children First and Last"; Burman and Stacey, "The Child and Childhood in Feminist Theory."
13 Ogata, *Designing the Creative Child*.
14 Like newly designed playgrounds or the child's playroom of many middle-class homes; see also Jacobson, *Raising Consumers*.
15 Ogata, *Designing the Creative Child*, 70.
16 Ibid., 64.
17 Ibid., 193.
18 Ibid., 6.
19 Although this must be so at some level, as Cross (*The Cute and the Cool*) would concur.
20 May, *Homeward Bound*.
21 Wolfenstein, "Fun Morality," 201–204.
22 Ibid., 201.
23 Ibid., 204.
24 Hays, *The Cultural Contradictions of Motherhood*.
25 Ibid., 8.
26 Pugh, *Longing and Belonging*.
27 Seiter, *Sold Separately*.
28 Cross, *Kids' Stuff*.
29 DeVault, *Feeding the Family*, 59.
30 Cook, "Semantic Provisioning of Children's Food."
31 Cook, "The Mother as Consumer"; Allison J. Pugh, "Selling Compromise," 729.
32 Englehardt, "The Shortcake Strategy"; Kinder, *Kids' Media Culture*; Hendershot, *Nickelodeon Nation*.
33 Guber and Berry, *Marketing To and Through Kids*; McNeal, *Kids as Consumers*; McNeal, *The Kids' Market*.
34 See Cook, "The Missing Child in Consumption Theory"; Cook, "Knowing the Child Consumer."
35 Pugh, *Longing and Belonging*; see also Power, "The Unfreedom of Being Other"; Elizabeth Chin, *Purchasing Power*.
36 Frazer, *The Golden Bough*.
37 Theodorou and Spyrou, "Motherhood in utero"; Clarke, "Maternity and Materiality"; Cairns, Johnston, and MacKendrick, "Feeding the 'Organic Child.'"
38 Marcelo Diversi, "Street Kids in Nikes."

39 Fattore, Mason, and Watson, "Locating the Child Centrally"; Camfield, "'Stew Without Bread or Bread Without Stew.'"
40 Chin, *Purchasing Power*.
41 Bauman, *Work, Consumerism and the New Poor*.
42 Stevenson, "Elian's father contends son will return to Cuba."
43 See Stephens, "Children and the Politics of 'Late Capitalism'"; Burr, *Vietnam's Children*; Burman, "Local, Global or Globalized?"; Olga Nieuwenhuys, "Global Childhood and the Politics of Contempt."

BIBLIOGRAPHY

SECONDARY SOURCES: BOOKS/JOURNAL ARTICLES

Abbott, Jacob. *Gentle Measures in the Management and Training of the Young*. Teddington, UK: Echo Library, 1872.

Abrams, Philip. *Historical Sociology*. Ithaca, NY: Cornell University Press, 1982.

Alanen, Leena, and Berry Mayall *Conceptualizing Child-Adult Relations*. New York: Routledge, 2001.

Anderson, Benedict. *Imagined Communities: Reflections on the Origin and Spread of Nationalism*. London: Verso, 1983.

Ariès, Philippe. *Centuries of Childhood: A Social History of Family Life*. New York: Vintage, 1962.

Arnold, Matthew. *Culture and Anarchy*. Oxford: Oxford University Press, 2009.

Auslander, Leora. *Taste and Power: Furnishing Modern France*. Berkeley: University of California Press, 1996.

———. "The Gendering of Consumer Practices." In *The Sex of Things: Gender and Consumption on Historical Perspective*, edited by Victoria deGrazia, 79–112. Berkeley: University of California Press, 1996.

Avery, Gillian. *Behold the Child: American Children and their Books, 1621–1922*. Baltimore: Johns Hopkins University Press, 1994.

Bailey, Maria, and Bonnie Ulman. *Trillion-Dollar Moms: Marketing to a New Generation of Mothers*. Chicago: Dearborn Trade Publishing, 2005.

Barnett, James H. *The American Christmas: A Study in National Culture*. Salem, NH: Ayer, 1984.

Bauman, Zygmunt. *Work, Consumerism and the New Poor*. Buckingham: Open University Press, 1998.

Beard, Lina, and Adelia B. Beard. *The American Girl's Handy Book: How to Amuse Yourself and Others*. Boston: Nonpareil Books, 1887.

Bederman, Gail. *Manliness and Civilization: A Cultural History of Gender and Race in the United States, 1880–1917*. Chicago: University of Chicago Press, 1995.

Beecher, Catherine. *Treatise on Domestic Economy for the Use of Young Ladies at Home and at School*. Boston: Marsh, Capeen, Lyon and Webb, 1841.

Beetham, Margaret. *A Magazine of Her Own? Domesticity and Desire in the Woman's Magazine, 1800–1914*. London: Routledge, 1996.

Belk, Russell W. "A Child's Christmas in America: Santa Claus as Deity, Consumption as Religion." *Journal of American Culture* 10, no. 1 (Spring 1987): 87–100.

Benson, Susan Porter. *Counter Cultures: Saleswomen, Managers, and Customers in American Department Stores, 1890–1940*. Champaign: University of Illinois Press, 1986.

Bentham, Jeremy. *An Introduction to the Principles of Morals and Legislation*. Edited by J. H. Burns and H. L. A. Hart. The Athlone Press, 1970.

Bernstein, Robin. *Racial Innocence: Performing American Childhood and Race from Slavery to Civil Rights*. New York: New York University Press, 2011.

Bierbower, Austin. "On the Drift in the New Theology." *Christian Union* 27, no. 4 (1883), 428–429.

Bloch, Ruth H. *Gender and Morality in Anglo-American Culture, 1650–1800*. Berkeley: University of California Press, 2003.

Bomberger, J. H. A. *Infant Salvation in its Relation to Infant Depravity, Infant Regeneration, and Infant Baptism*. Philadelphia: Lindsay & Blakiston, 1859.

Boorstin, Daniel J. *The Americans: The Democratic Experience*. London: Vintage, 1973.

Bourdieu, Pierre. *Distinction: A Social Critique of the Judgement of Taste*. Cambridge, MA: Harvard University Press, 1984.

Boyd, Neval L. *Play Equipment for the Nursery*. Chicago: Chicago Association of Day Nurseries, n.d.

Brewer, John. "Genesis of the Modern Toy." *History Today* 30 (1980): 32–39.

Brown, Gillian. *Domestic Individualism: Imagining Self in Nineteenth-Century America*. Los Angeles: University of California Press, 1990.

Burr, Rachel. *Vietnam's Children in a Changing World*. New Brunswick, NJ: Rutgers University Press, 2006.

Buckingham, David. *After the Death of Childhood: Growing Up in the Age of Electronic Media*. Cambridge: Polity Press, 2000.

———. *The Material Child*. Cambridge: Polity Press, 2011

Buckingham, David, and Vebjørg Tingstad (eds.) *Childhood and Consumer Culture*. Basingstoke, UK: Palgrave, 2011.

Bulkley, Hiram Worthington. *A word to parents, or, The obligations and limitations of parental authority*. Philadelphia: Presbyterian Board of Publication, 1858.

Burman, Erica. "Local, Global or Globalized? Child Development and International Child Rights Legislation." *Childhood* 3, no. 1 (February 1996): 45–66.

Burman, Erica, and Jackie Stacey. "The Child and Childhood in Feminist Theory." *Feminist Theory* 11, no. 3 (2010): 227–240.

Burr, Rachel. *Vietnam's Children in a Changing World*. New Brunswick, NJ: Rutgers University Press, 2006.

Bushnell, Horace. *Christian Nature*. 1847. Reprint, Grand Rapids: Baker Book House, 1979.

Cairns, Kate, Josée Johnston, and Norah MacKendrick. "Feeding the 'Organic Child': Mothering Through Ethical Consumption." *Journal of Consumer Culture* 13, no. 2 (2013): 97–118.

Calvert, Karin. *Children in the House: The Material Culture of Early Childhood, 1600–1900*. Boston: Northeastern University Press, 1992.

Camfield, Laura. "'Stew Without Bread or Bread Without Stew': Children's Understanding of Poverty in Ethiopia." *Children and Society* 24 (2010): 271–281.

Campbell, Colin. *The Romantic Ethic and the Spirit of Modern Consumerism*. Oxford: Basil Blackwell, 1987.

Carlsson-Paige, Nancy. *Taking Back Childhood: A Proven Roadmap for Raising Confident, Creative, Compassionate Kids*. New York: Penguin, 2008.

Carrier, James G. *Meanings of the Market: The Free Market in Western Culture*. Oxford: Berg, 1997.

Child, Lydia. *The Frugal Housewife: Dedicated to Those Who Are Not Ashamed of Economy, a Book of Kitchen, Economy and Directions*. Boston: Carter, Hendee, and Co., 1832.

Chin, Elizabeth. *Purchasing Power*. Minneapolis: University of Minnesota Press, 2001.

Chudacoff, Howard. *Children at Play: An American History*. New York: New York University Press, 2007.

Clarke, Alison J. "Maternity and Materiality: Becoming a Mother in Consumer Culture." In *Consuming Motherhood*, edited by Janelle S. Taylor, Linda L. Layne, and Danielle F. Wozniak, 55–71. New Brunswick, NJ: Rutgers University Press, 2004.

Clement, Priscilla Ferguson. *Growing Pains: Children in the Industrial Age, 1850–1890*. New York: Twayne Publishers, 1997.

Coffey, Tim, David Siegel, and Gregory Livingston. *Marketing to the New Super Consumer: Mom & Kid*. Ithaca, NY: Paramount Market Publishers, 2006.

Cook, Daniel Thomas. "The Mother as Consumer: Insights from the Children's Wear Industry, 1917–1929." *The Sociological Quarterly* 36, no. 3 (1995): 505–522.

———. "Exchange Value as Pedagogy in Children's Leisure: Moral Panics in Children's Culture at Century's End." *Leisure Studies* 32, no. 2 (2000): 81–98.

———, ed. *Symbolic Childhood*. New York: Peter Lang, 2002.

———. "Spatial Biographies of Children's Consumption." *Journal of Consumer Culture* 3, no. 2 (July 2003): 147–169.

———. *The Commodification of Childhood: The Children's Clothing Industry and the Rise of the Child Consumer*. Durham, NC: Duke University Press, 2004.

———. "The Missing Child in Consumption Theory." *Journal of Consumer Culture* 8, no. 2 (2008): 219–243.

———. "The Other 'Child Study': Figuring Children as Consumers in Market Research, 1910s–1990s." *The Sociological Quarterly* 41, no. 3 (Summer 2000): 487–507.

———. "Semantic Provisioning of Children's Food: Commerce, Care and Maternal Practice." *Childhood* 16, no. 3 (2009), 317–334.

———. "Knowing the Child Consumer: Historical and Conceptual Insights on Qualitative Children's Consumer Research." *Young Consumers* 10, no. 4 (2009), 269–282.

———. "Children's Subjectivities and Commercial Meaning: The Delicate Battle Mothers Wage when Feeding their Children." In *Childhood, Food and Identity in Everyday Life*, edited by Allison James, Anne Trine Kjørholt, and Vebjørg Tingstad, 112–130. Basingstoke, UK: Palgrave, 2009.

———. "Commercial Enculturation: Moving Beyond Consumer Socialization." In *Childhood and Consumer Culture*, edited by David Buckingham and Vebjørg Tingstad, 63–79. Basingstoke, UK: Palgrave, 2010.

———. "Leveraging the Child's Perspective: Commercial Epistemologies of Children's Consumption." In *Inside Marketing*, edited by Detlev Zwick and Julian Kayla, 257–268. Oxford: Oxford University Press, 2011.

———. "Children's Consumption in History." In *Oxford History Handbook: Consumption in History*, edited by Frank Trentmann, 585–600. Oxford: Oxford University Pres, 2012.

———. "Moral Order and Moral Ordering in Public Advice about American Children's Rooms, 1876–1909." *Strenæ: Recherches sur les livres et objects culturels de l'enfance* 7 (2014).

———. "Panaceas of Play: Stepping Past the Creative Child." In *Reimagining Childhood Studies*, edited by Spyros Spyrou, Rachel Rosen, and Daniel Thomas Cook, 123–136. London: Bloomsbury, 2019.

———. "Children's Market Researchers as Moral Brokers." *Journal of Cultural Economy* 12, no. 1 (2019): 17–82.

Coveney, Peter. *The Image of Childhood: The Individual and Society: A Study of the Theme in English Literature*. Baltimore: Penguin Books, 1957.

Cross, Gary. *Kids' Stuff: Toys and the Changing World of American Childhood*. Cambridge, MA: Harvard University Press, 1997.

———. *The Cute and the Cool: Wondrous Innocence and Modern America's Children's Culture*. Oxford: Oxford University Press, 2004.

Crowley, Sharon. "Biting the Hand that Feeds Us: Nineteenth-Century Uses of a Pedagogy of Taste." In *Rhetoric, Cultural Studies and Literacy*, edited by Jay Frederick Reynolds, 11–20. Hillsdale, NJ: Lawrence Erlbaum Associates, 1995.

Cunningham, Hugh. *Children of the Poor: Representations of Childhood Since the Seventeenth Century*. Oxford: Oxford University Press, 1991.

———. *Children and Childhood in Western Society since 1500*. Harlow, UK: Pearson Longman, 2005.

Davis, Susan B. "Making Night Hideous: Christmas Revelry and Public Order in Nineteenth-Century Philadelphia." *American Quarterly* 34, no. 2 (Summer, 1982): 185–199.

deGrazia, Victoria, ed. *The Sex of Things: Gender and Consumption on Historical Perspective*. Berkeley: University of California Press, 1996.

Denisoff, Dennis, ed. *The Nineteenth-Century Child and Consumer Culture*. Burlington, VT: Ashgate Publishing, 2008.

DeVault, Marjorie. *Feeding the Family*. Chicago: University of Chicago Press, 1991.

Diversi, Marcelo. "Street Kids in Nikes: In Search of Humanization Through the Culture of Consumption." *Cultural Studies ↔ Critical Methodologies* 6, no. 3 (2006): 370–390.

Douglas, Ann. *The Feminization of American Culture*. New York: Farrar, Straus, and Giroux, 1977.

Douglas, Mary, and Baron Isherwood. *The World of Goods: Towards an Anthropology of Consumption*. New York: Basic Books, 1979.

Doyle, Nora. *Maternal Bodies: Redefining Motherhood in Early America*. Chapel Hill: University of North Carolina Press, 2018.

Durkheim, Émile. *The Elementary Forms of the Religious Life*. 1915. Reprint, New York: Free Press, 1965.

Englehardt, Tom. "The Shortcake Strategy." In *Watching Television*, edited by Todd Gitlin, 68–110. New York: Pantheon, 1986.

Engels, Friedrich. *The Condition of the Working Class in England*. Oxford: Blackwell, 1958.

Ewen, Elizabeth. *Immigrant Women in the Land of Dollars*. New York: Monthly Review Press, 1985.

Fattore, Tobia, Jan Mason, and Elizabeth Watson. "Locating the child centrally as subject in research: towards a child interpretation of well-being." *Child Indicators Research* 5, no. 3 (2012), 423–435.

Fass, Paula. *The End of American Childhood: A History of Parenting from Life on the Frontier to the Managed Child*. Princeton: Princeton University Press, 2016.

Featherstone, Mike. *Consumer Culture and Postmodernism*. London: Sage Publications, 1991.

Flusser, Marilise. *Party Shoes to School and Baseball Caps to Bed: The Parents' Guide to Kids, Clothes and Independence*. New York: Simon and Schuster, 1992.

Forty, Adrian. *Objects of Desire: Design and Society Since 1750*. London: Thames and Hudson, 1986.

Foucault, Michel. *The Archaeology of Knowledge*. New York: Pantheon Books, 1972.

———. "Truth and Power." In *Power/Knowledge: Selected Interviews and Other Writings*, edited by C. Gordon, 109–133. New York: Prentice Hall, 1980.

———. *The Birth of Biopolitics*. New York: Picador, 2004.

Frazer, James George. *The Golden Bough*. New York: McMillan and Company, 1890.

Garvey, Ellen Gruber. *The Adman in the Parlor: Magazines and the Gendering of Consumer Culture, 1880s to 1910s*. Oxford: Oxford University Press, 1996.

———. "Advertising Competitions in St. Nicholas Magazine: Training the Magazine Reader." In *St. Nicholas and Mary Mapes Dodge: The Legacy of a Children's Magazine Editor*, edited by Susan R. Gannon, Suzanne Rahn, and Ruth Anne Thompson, 158–170. Jefferson, NC: McFarland, 2004.

Glenn, Myra. *Campaigns Against Corporal Punishment: Prisoners, Sailors, Women, and Children in Antebellum America*. Albany, NY: SUNY Press, 1984.

Goffman, Erving. *The Presentation of Self in Everyday Life*. New York: Anchor, 1959.

Goldberg, Vicki. *Lewis Hine: Children at Work*. Munich: Prestal, 1999.

Golden, Janet. *Babies Made Us Modern: How Infants Brought America into the Twentieth Century*. Cambridge: Cambridge University Press, 2018.

Goldman, Robert, and Stephen Papson. *Sign Wars: The Cluttered Landscape of Advertising*. New York: Guilford Press, 1996.

Goodwin, Susan, and Kate Huppatz, eds. *The Good Mother: Contemporary Motherhoods in Australia*. Sydney, Australia: Sydney University Press, 2010.

Grant, Julia. *Raising Baby by the Book: The Education of American Mothers.* New Haven: Yale University Press, 1998.

Greven, Philip. *The Protestant Temperament: Patterns of Child-Rearing, Religious Experience, and the Self in Early America.* New York: Alfred A. Knopf, 1977.

———. *Spare the Child: The Religious Roots of Punishment and the Psychological Impact of Physical Abuse.* New York: Alfred A. Knopf, 1990.

Grumbine, E. Evalyn. *Reaching Juvenile Markets: How to Advertise, Sell, and Merchandise through Boys and Girls.* New York: McGraw-Hill, 1938.

Guber, Selina S., and Jon Berry. *Marketing to and Through Kids.* New York: McGraw-Hill, 2003.

Guldberg, Helene. *Reclaiming Childhood: Freedom and Play in an Age of Fear.* London: Routledge, 2009.

Halttunen, Karen. *Confidence Men and Painted Women: A Study of Middle-Class Culture in America, 1830–1870.* New Haven: Yale University Press, 1983.

Haug, Wolfgang Fritz. *Commodity Aesthetics, Ideology, and Culture.* New York: International General, 1987.

Hays, Sharon. *The Cultural Contradictions of Motherhood.* New Haven: Yale University Press, 1996.

Heininger, Mary Lynn Stevens. "Children, Childhood, and Change in America, 1820–1920." In *A Century of Childhood, 1820–1920,* edited by Mary Lynn Stevens Heininger, Karin Calvert, Barbara Finkelstein, Kathy Vandell, Anne Scott MacLeod, and Harvey Green, 1–32. Rochester, NY: Margaret Woodbury Strong Museum, 1984.

Henaghan, Mark. "Why judges need to know and understand childhood studies." *Law and Childhood Studies: Current Legal Issues* 14 (2012): 39–55.

Hendershot, Heather, ed. *Nickelodeon Nation: The History, Politics, and Economics of America's Only TV Channel for Kids.* New York: New York University Press, 2004.

Higonnet, Anne. *Pictures of Innocence: The History and Crisis of Ideal Childhood.* London: Thames and Hudson, 1998.

Hiram Worthington Bulkley. *A word to parents, or, The obligations and limitations of parental authority.* Philadelphia: Presbyterian Board of Publication, 1858.

Hochschild, Arlie Russell. *The Commercialization of Intimate Life: Notes From Home and Work.* Berkeley, CA: University of California Press, 2003.

———. "'Rent a Mom' and Other Services: Markets, Meanings and Emotions." *International Journal of Work Organization and Emotion* 1, no. 1 (2005): 74–86.

———. "Emotional Life on the Market Frontier." *Annual Review of Sociology* 37, no. 1 (2011): 21–33.

Hoganson, Kristin. *The Consumer's Imperium: The Global Production of American Domesticity, 1865–1920.* Chapel Hill: University of California Press, 2007.

Holland, Patricia. *Picturing Childhood: The Myth of the Child in Popular Imagery.* London: I. B. Tauris, 2004.

Holt, L. Emmett. *The Care and Feeding of Children: A Catechism for the Use of Mothers and Children's Nurses.* New York: D. Appleton and Company, 1907.

Honig, Michael-Sebastian. "How is the Child Constituted in Childhood Studies?" In *The Palgrave Handbook of Childhood Studies*, edited by Jens Qvortrup, William A. Corsaro, and Michael-Sebastian Honig, 62–77. Houndsmills, UK: Palgrave, 2009.

Hunt, Jean Lee. *A Catalogue of Play Equipment*. New York: Bureau of Educational Experiments, 1918.

Hutchison, William R. *The Modernist Impulse in American Protestantism*. Cambridge, MA: Harvard University Press, 1976.

Imada, M. "Color Preference of School Children." *Japanese Journal of Psychology* 1 (1926): 1–21.

Jacobson, Lisa. *Raising Consumers: Children and the American Mass Market in the Early Twentieth Century*. New York: Columbia University Press, 2004.

James, Allison, and Alan Prout. "A New Paradigm for the Sociology of Childhood?" In *Constructing and Reconstructing Childhood*, edited by Alan Prout and Allison James, 7–33. London: Falmer, 1991.

James, Allison, Chris Jenks, and Alan Prout. *Theorizing Childhood*. Cambridge: Polity Press, 1998.

Jenks, Christopher. *Childhood*. London: Routledge, 1996.

John, Deborah R. "Consumer Socialization of Children: A Retrospective Look at Twenty-five Years of Research." *Journal of Consumer Research* 26, no. 3 (1999): 183–213.

Jordan, Arthur Melville. *Children's Interests in Reading*. New York: Teachers College, Columbia University, 1921.

Kidwell, Claudia B., and Margaret C. Christman. *Suiting Everyone: The Democratization of Clothing in America*. Washington DC: Smithsonian Institution Press, 1974.

Kinder, Marsha, ed. *Kids' Media Culture*. Durham, NC: Duke University Press, 1998.

Kline, Stephen. *Out of the Garden: Toys and Children's Culture in the Age of TV Marketing*. London: Verso, 1993.

Knox, Vicesimus. *The Works of Vicesimus Knox, D.D.: With a Biographical Preface*. London: J. Mawman, 1824.

Kooistra, Lorraine Janzen. "Home Thoughts and Home Scenes: Packaging Middle-Class Childhood for Christmas Consumption." In *The Nineteenth-Century Child and Consumer Culture*, edited by Dennis Denisoff, 151–172. Aldershot: Ashgate, 2009.

Kopytoff, Igor. "The Cultural Biography of Things: Commoditization as a Process." In *The Social Life of Things: Commodities in Cultural Perspective*, edited by Arjun Appadurai, 65–91. Cambridge: Cambridge University Press, 1986.

Kuhn, Anne L. *The Mother's Role in Childhood Education: New England Concepts, 1830–1860*. New Haven: Yale University Press, 1947.

Lasch, Christopher. *Haven in a Heartless World*. New York: Norton, 1977.

Lareau, Annette. *Unequal Childhoods*. Berkeley: University of California Press, 2003.

Latour, Bruno. *Reassembling the Social: An Introduction to Actor-Network-Theory*. Oxford: Oxford University Press, 2005.

Layne, Linda. "'He was a Real Baby with Baby Things': A Material Culture Analysis of Personhood, Parenthood and Pregnancy Loss." *Journal of Material Culture* 5, no. 3 (2000): 321–345.

Leach, William R. *Land of Desire: Merchants, Power, and the Rise of a New American Culture.* New York: Vintage, 1993.

———. "Child-World in the Promised Land." In *The Mythmaking Frame of Mind: Social Imagination and American Culture,* edited by James Gilbert, Amy Gilman, Donald Scott, and Joan Scott. Belmont, CA: Wadsworth Publishing, 1993.

Lears, T. J. Jackson. *No Place of Grace: Antimodernism and the Transformation of American Culture, 1880–1920.* Chicago: University of Chicago Press, 1981.

———. "From Salvation to Self-Realization." In *The Culture of Consumption,* edited by T.J. Jackson Lears and Richard Wightman Fox, 3–38. New York: Pantheon, 1983.

———. *Fables of Abundance: Cultural History of Advertising in America.* New York: Basic, 1994.

Levison, Deborah. "Children as Economic Agents." *Feminist Economics* 6 (2000): 125–134.

Linn, Susan. *Consuming Kids: The Hostile Takeover of Childhood.* New York: New Press, 2004.

———. *The Case for Make Believe: Saving Play in a Commercialized World.* New York: New Press, 2008.

Locke, John. *Some Thoughts Concerning Education.* 1693. Reprint, Indianapolis: Hackett Publishing, 1996.

Louv, Richard. *Last Child in the Woods: Saving Our Children from Nature-Deficit Disorder.* Chapel Hill: Algonquin Press, 2005.

Malleson, Mrs. Frank. *Notes on the Early Training of Children.* London: W. Swan Sonnenschein, 1885.

Mangasarian, M. M. "The Punishment of Children." *International Journal of Ethics* 4, no. 4 (July 1894): 493–498.

Marchand, Roland. *Advertising and the American Dream: Making Way for Modernity, 1920–1940.* Berkeley: University of California Press, 1985.

Marcus, Leonard S. *Minders of Make-Believe: Idealists, Entrepreneurs, and the Shaping of American Children's Literature.* Boston: Houghton Mifflin Company, 2008.

Martens, Lydia, Sue Scott, and David Southerton. "Bringing Children (and Parents) into the Sociology of Consumption." *Journal of Consumer Culture* 4, no. 2 (2004): 155–182.

Marx, Karl. "Commodities." *The Marx-Engels Reader,* 2nd ed., edited by Robert C. Tucker, 302–329. New York: Norton, 1978.

May, Elaine Tyler. *Homeward Bound: American Families in the Cold War Era.* New York: Basic, 1988.

McCracken, Grant David. *Culture and Consumption: New Approaches to the Symbolic Character of Consumer Goods and Activities.* Bloomington, IN: Indiana University Press, 1990.

McDannell, Colleen. *The Christian Home in Victorian America, 1840–1900.* Bloomington: Indiana University Press, 1994.

McKendrick, John Brewer, and John Plumb, eds. *The Birth of a Consumer Society*. Bloomington: Indiana University Press, 1982.

McLoughlin, William G. *The Meaning of Henry Ward Beecher: An Essay on the Shifting Values of Mid-Victorian America, 1840–1870*. New York: Alfred A. Knopf, 1970.

McNeal, James U. *Kids as Consumers: A Handbook of Marketing to Children*. New York: Lexington Books, 1992.

———. *The Kids' Market: Myths and Realities*. New York: Paramount, 1999.

Mechling, Jay. "Advice to Historians on Advice to Mothers." *Journal of Social History* 9, no. 1 (1975): 44–63.

Meckel, Richard A. "Educating a Ministry of Mothers: Evangelical Maternal Associations, 1815–1860." *Journal of the Early Republic* 2, no. 4 (1982): 403–423.

Merish, Lori. *Sentimental Materialism: Gender, Commodity Culture, and Nineteenth-Century American Literature*. Durham: Duke University Press, 2000.

Michals, Teresa. "Experiments before Breakfast: Toys, Education and Middle-Class Childhood." In *The Nineteenth-Century Child and Consumer Culture*, edited by Dennis Denisoff, 29–42. Aldershot, UK: Ashgate, 2008.

Miller, Daniel. *Materiality*. Durham: Duke University Press, 2005.

Mintz, Steven. *Moralists and Modernizers: America's Pre-Civil War Reformers*. Baltimore: Johns Hopkins University Press, 1995.

———. *Huck's Raft: A History of American Childhood*. Cambridge, MA: The Belknap Press of Harvard University Press, 2004.

Mitchell, Harriet. *Play and Play Materials for the Preschool Child*. Ottawa: Canadian Council on Child Welfare, 1923.

Moran, Gerald F., and Maris A. Vinovskis. *Religion, Family and the Life Course: Explorations in the Social History of Early America*. Ann Arbor: University of Michigan Press, 1992.

Morgan, John. *Godly Learning: Puritan Attitudes Towards Reason, Learning and Education, 1560–1640*. Cambridge: Cambridge University Press, 1986.

Morgan, Lady (Sydney). *Lady Morgan's Memoirs: Autobiography, Diaries, and Correspondence*. London: Wm. H. Allen & Co., 1829.

Nasaw, David. *Children of the City: At Work and at Play*. New York: Anchor Press/Doubleday, 1985.

Nelson, Claudia. *Invisible Men: Fatherhood in Victorian Periodicals, 1850–1910*. Athens: The University of Georgia Press, 1995.

Nelson, Elizabeth White. *Market Sentiments: Middle-Class Market Culture in Nineteenth-Century America*. Washington, DC: Smithsonian, 2004.

Nieuwenhuys, Olga. "Global Childhood and the Politics of Contempt." *Alternatives: Global, Local, Political* 23, no. 3 (July–September 1998), 267–289.

———. "Can the Teddy Bear Speak?" *Childhood* 18, no. 4 (2001): 411–418.

Nissenbaum, Stephen. *The Battle for Christmas: A Social and Cultural History of Our Most Cherished Holiday*. New York: Vintage Books, 1997.

Norman Rockwell Museum. "Norman Rockwell's 323 'Saturday Evening Post' Covers." www.nrm.org, March 2010.

Oakley, Ann. "Women and children first and last: Parallels and differences between women's and children's studies." In *Childhood As a Social Phenomenon*, edited by Jens Qvortrup, 51–69. Vienna: European Centre, 1993.

Ogata, Amy Fumiko. *Designing the Creative Child: Playthings and Places in Midcentury America.* Minneapolis: University of Minnesota Press, 2013.

Palmieri, Patricia A. "From Republican Motherhood to Race Suicide; Arguments on the Higher Education of Women in the United States, 1820–1920." In *Educating Men and Women Together: Coeducation in a Changing World*, edited by Carol Lasser, 49–64. Urbana, IL: University of Illinois Press with Oberlin Colleges, 1987.

Paul, Lissa. *The Children's Book Business: Lessons from the Long Eighteenth Century.* New York: Routledge, 2011.

Peiss, Kathy. *Cheap Amusements: Working Women and Leisure in Turn-of-the-Century New York.* Philadelphia: Temple University Press, 1986.

Pellegrini, A. D., ed. *Psychological Bases for Early Education.* New York: John Wiley & Sons, 1988.

Pleck, Elizabeth H. *Celebrating the Family: Ethnicity, Consumer Culture, and Family Rituals.* Cambridge, MA: Harvard University Press, 2000.

Plumb, John. H. "The New World of Children in Eighteenth-Century England." In *The Birth of a Consumer Society*, edited by Neil McKendrick, John Brewer, and John Plumb. Bloomington: Indiana University Press, 1982.

Power, Elaine "The unfreedom of being other: Canadian lone mothers' experiences of poverty and 'life on the cheque.'" *Sociology* 39, no. 4 (2005): 643–660.

Pugh, Allison J. *Longing and Belonging: Parents, Children, and Consumer Culture.* Berkeley: University of California Press, 2009.

———. "Selling Compromise: Toys, Motherhood, and the Cultural Deal." *Gender and Society* 19, no. 6 (December 2005): 729–749.

Qvortrup. Jens. "Introduction." *International Journal of Sociology* 17, no. 3 (1987): 3–30.

———. "Childhood as a Structural Form." In *The Palgrave Handbook of Childhood Studies*, edited by Jens Qvortrup, William A. Corsaro, and Michael-Sebastian Honig, 21–33. Houndsmills, UK: Palgrave, 2009.

Ratner, Lorman A., Paula T. Kaufman, and Dwight L. Teeter Jr. *Paradoxes of Prosperity: Wealth-Seeking Versus Christian Values in Pre-Civil War America.* Chicago: University of Illinois Press, 2009.

Reid, Jason. *Get Out of My Room! A History of Teen Bedrooms in America.* Chicago: University of Chicago Press, 2017.

Reinier, Jacqueline S. *From Virtue to Character: American Childhood, 1775–1850.* New York: Twayne Publishers, 1996.

Riney-Kehrberg, Pamela. *The Nature of Childhood: An Environmental History of Growing Up in America Since 1865.* Lawrence: University of Kansas Press, 2014.

Ringel, Paul B. *Commercializing Childhood: Children's Magazines, Urban Gentility, and the Ideal of the Child Consumer in the United States, 1823–1918.* Amherst: University of Massachusetts Press, 2015.

Rutherford, Markella B. *Adult Supervision Required: Private Freedom and Public Constraints for Parents and Children.* New Brunswick: Rutgers University Press, 2011.

Ryan, Mary P. "A Women's Awakening: Evangelical Religion and the Families of Utica, New York, 1800–1840." *American Quarterly* 30, no. 5 (1978): 602–623.

Ryder, Norman B. "The Cohort as a Concept in the Study of Social Change." *American Sociological Review* 30, no. 6 (December 1965): 843–861.

Sammond, Nicholas. *Babes in Tomorrowland: Walt Disney and the Making of the American Child, 1930–1960.* Raleigh, NC: Duke University Press, 2008.

Sánchez-Eppler, Karen. "Raising Empires like Children: Race, Nation, and Religious Education," *American Literary History* 8, no. 3 (Autumn 1996): 399–425.

———. *Dependent States: The Child's Part in Nineteenth-Century American Culture.* Chicago: University of Chicago Press, 2005.

Santayana, George. "The Poetry of Christian Dogma." In *Interpretations of Poetry and Religion,* 76–117. New York: Charles Scribner's Sons, 1900.

Schertz, Matthew Victor. "The Mother's Magazine: Moral Media for an Emergent Domestic Pedagogy, 1833–1848." *Gender and Education* 21, no. 3 (2009): 309–320.

Schlereth, Thomas J. *Victorian America: Transformations in Everyday Life, 1876–1915.* New York: HarperPerennial, 1991.

Schmidt, Leigh Eric. *Consumer Rites: The Buying and Selling of American Holidays.* Princeton: Princeton University Press, 2007.

Schor, Juliet. *Born to Buy: The Commercialized Child and the New Consumer Culture.* New York: Scribner, 2004.

Scott, Walter Dill. *The Psychology of Advertising: A Simple Exposition of the Principles of Psychology in their Relation to Successful Advertising.* Boston: Small, Maynard, and Co., 1908.

Seiter, Ellen. *Sold Separately: Mothers and Children in Consumer Culture.* Bloomington: Indiana University Press, 1993.

Shuttleworth, Sally. *The Mind of the Child: Child Development, Science, and Medicine, 1840–1900.* Oxford: Oxford University Press, 2010.

Simmel, Georg. "Objective Culture." In *Georg Simmel on Individuality and Social Forms,* edited by Donald N. Levine, 227–235. Chicago: University of Chicago Press, 1971.

Slater, Don. *Consumer Culture and Modernity.* London: Polity Press, 1997

Slater, Peter Gregg. *Children in the New England Mind: In Death and in Life.* Hamden: Archon Books, 1977.

Smith, Adam. *An Inquiry into the Nature and Causes of the Wealth of Nations.* 1776. Reprint, Chicago: University of Chicago Press, 1976.

Smith, Carmel, and Sheila Green. *Key Thinkers in Childhood Studies.* Basingstoke, UK: Palgrave, 2014.

Sparrman, Anna, Bengt Sandin, and Johanna Sjöberg, eds. *Situating Child Consumption: Rethinking Values and Notions of Children, Childhood and Consumption.* Lund, Sweden: Nordic Academic Press, 2012.

Stannard, David E. "Death and the Puritan Child." *American Quarterly* 26 (December 1974): 456–476.

Stearns, Peter. *Battleground of Desire: The Struggle for Self-Control in Modern America*. New York: New York University Press, 1999.

———. *Anxious Parents: A History of Modern Childrearing in America*. New York: New York University Press, 2003.

Steedman, Carolyn. *Strange Dislocations: Childhood and the Idea of Human Interiority, 1780–1930*. Cambridge, MA: Harvard University Press, 1995.

Stephens, Sharon. "Children and the Politics of 'Late Capitalism.'" In *Children and the Politics of Culture*, edited by Sharon Stephens, 3–49. Princeton: Princeton University Press, 1995.

Stevenson, Mark. "Elian's father contends son will return to Cuba." *Tallahassee Democrat*, December 14, 1999, 1A.

Stolz, Lois Meek, and Nell Boyd Taylor. *Interests of Young Children, Guidance Materials for Study Groups*. Washington, DC: American Association of University Women, 1930.

Sussman, Warren I. "'Personality' and the Making of Twentieth-Century Culture." In *New Directions in American Intellectual History*, edited by John Hingham and Paul Conklin, 212–226. Baltimore: Johns Hopkins University Press, 1989.

Sutherland, Anne, and Beth Thompson. *Kidfluence: Why Kids Today Mean Business*. Toronto: McGraw-Hill, 2001.

Sutton-Smith, Brian. *Toys as Culture*. White Plains, NY: Gardner Press, 1986.

Tabak, Jana, and Leticia Carvalho. "Responsibility to Protect the Future: Children on the Move and the Politics of Becoming." *Global Responsibility to Protect* 10, no. 1–2 (2018): 121–144.

Taylor, Nell Boyd. "The Right Toy for the Young Child." *Journal of the American Association of University Women* 22 (October 1928): 29–33.

Tosh, John. *A Man's Place: Masculinity and the Middle-Class Home in Victorian England*. New Haven: Yale University Press, 1999.

Theodorou, Eleni, and Spyros Spyrou. "Motherhood In Utero: Consuming Away Anxiety." *Journal of Consumer Culture* 13, no. 2 (2004): 79–96.

Thompson, C. "Caring Consumers: Gendered Consumption Meanings and the Juggling Lifestyle." *Journal of Consumer Research* 22 (March 1996): 388–407.

Thomsen, Thyra Uth, and Elin Brand Sørensen. "The First Four-Wheeled Status Symbol: Pram Consumption as a Vehicle for the Construction of Motherhood Identity." *Journal of Marketing Management* 22, no. 9 (2006): 907–927.

Thorne, Barrie. "Re-Visioning Women and Social Change: Where are the Children?" *Gender and Society* 1, no. 1 (1987): 85–109.

Tiersten, Lisa. *Marianne in the Market: Envisioning Consumer Society in Fin-de-Siècle France*. Berkeley: University of California Press, 2001.

Tosh, John. *A Man's Place: Masculinity and the Middle-Class Home in Victorian England*. New Haven: Yale University Press, 1999.

Twain, Mark, and Charles Dudley Warner. *The Gilded Age: A Tale of Today*. Hartford: American Publishing Company, 1873.

Vallone, Lynne. *Disciplines of Virtue: Girls' Culture in the Eighteenth and Nineteenth Centuries*. New Haven: Yale University Press, 1995.

———. *Big and Small: A Cultural History of Extraordinary Bodies*. New Haven: Yale University Press, 2018.

Van Horn, Catherine. "Turning Child Readers into Consumers: Children's Magazines and Advertising, 1900–1920." In *Defining Print Youth Culture: The Cultural Work of Children's Literature*, edited by Anne Lundin and Wayne A. Wiegand, 121–138. Westport, CT: Libraries Unlimited, 2003.

Veblen, Thorstein. *The Theory of the Leisure Class*. New York: Penguin, 1976.

Violas, Paul. *The Training of the Urban Working Class: A History of Twentieth Century American Education*. Rand McNally College Publishing, 1978.

Wall, John. *Ethics in Light of Childhood*. Washington, DC: Georgetown Press, 2010.

Ward, Scott. "Consumer Socialization." *Journal of Consumer Research* 1, no. 2 (1974): 1–14.

Weber, Max. *The Protestant Ethic and the Spirit of Capitalism*. New York: Charles Scribner's Sons, 1958.

Wiggin, Kate Douglas, and Nora Archibald Smith. *Children's Rights: A Book of Nursery Logic*. New York: Houghton Mifflin, 1892.

Williams, Florence. "An Investigation of Children's Preferences for Pictures." *Elementary School Journal* 25, no. 2 (October 1924): 119–126.

Williams, Rosalind. *Dream Worlds: Mass Consumption in the Late Ninetieth-Century France*. Berkeley: University of California Press, 1982.

Wishy, Bernard. *The Child and the Republic*. Philadelphia: University of Pennsylvania Press, 1968.

Wolf, Anna W. M., and E. L. Boehm. *Play and Playthings*. New York: Child Study Association of America, 1930.

Wolfenstein, Martha. "Fun Morality: An Analysis of Recent American Child-Training Literature." In *Childhood in Contemporary Cultures*, edited by Margaret Mead and Martha Wolfenstein, 168–178. Chicago: University of Chicago Press, 1955.

Wright, Nazera Sadiq. *Black Girlhood in the Nineteenth Century*. Urbana, IL: University of Illinois Press, 2016.

Zelizer, Viviana A. *Pricing the Priceless Child: The Changing Social Value of Children*. Princeton: Princeton University Press, 1985.

———. *The Social Meaning of Money: Pin Money, Paychecks, Poor Relief, and Other Currencies*. Princeton: Princeton University Press, 1994.

PRIMARY SOURCES: PERIODICALS

Babyhood

"Acquisitiveness and Its Cures," *Babyhood*, December 1897, 28.

"Amusements for Children," *Babyhood*, November 1885, 380–381.

"Amusements which Do Not Amuse," Mary E. Albright, *Babyhood*, July 1888, 248–249.

"Amusing the Baby," *Babyhood*, January 1885, 57.

"Another Hint to 'An Ohio Farmer,'" *Babyhood,* November 1888, 382.

"Anxiety about That Baby," *Babyhood*, March 1887, 140.

"The Appetite of Children," *Babyhood*, March 1888, 118.

"Baby at the Table," *Babyhood*, October 1889, 348–350.

"Baby's Wardrobe," *Babyhood*, March 1885, 123.

"A Chapter on Prizes," *Babyhood*, March 1891, 126.

"A Chat with the Indigent," *Babyhood*, September 1887, 327–332.

"Children's Use of Money," *Babyhood*, August 1888, 281–284.

"Comments on a Crisis?" *Babyhood*, October 1885, 319–320.

"Compulsory Kissing," *Babyhood*, September 1885, 311.

"Correct Methods in the Nursery," *Babyhood*, April 1890, 161–162.

"The Credit System as Incentive to Good Behavior," *Babyhood*, February 1889, 94.

"Current Issues in our Nursery," Mrs. J. H. Grove, *Babyhood*, June 1893, 204–207.

"The Decline of Sentiment in Children," Caroline Le Row, *Babyhood*, August 1891, 274–275.

"Delayed Punishments," *Babyhood*, August 1891, 151–152.

"Development versus Repression," *Babyhood*, December 1901, 20.

Editorial, *Babyhood*, November 1885, 332.

Editorial, *Babyhood*, April 1890, 133.

Editorial, *Babyhood*, October 1888, 332.

Editorial, *Babyhood*, November 1890, 357.

"The Education of Children," *Babyhood*, July 1891, 260–262.

"Exaggerating Children's Faults," *Babyhood*, June 1893, 211.

"Exaggerating Children's Faults," *Babyhood*, June 1893, 210–211.

"Fastidious Children," *Babyhood*, February 1885, 89.

"The Faults of Children and How to Deal with Them," *Babyhood*, April 1901, 126–128.

"Few Children are Conscienceless," *Babyhood*, November 1890, 358.

"Frightening Children," *Babyhood*, December 1884, 162.

"Games and Prizes," *Babyhood*, May 1891, 180.

"A Happy Childhood," *Babyhood*, May 1891, 79.

"Helping Baby Respect Property Rights," *Babyhood*, December 1896, 19.

"Heredity in Moral Traits and How to Meet Them in Training Children," *Babyhood*, August 1891, 268–271.

"High-flying at Fashion," *Babyhood*, October 1885, 341–343.

"A Hint to Toy-Makers," *Babyhood*, October 1889, 348–349.

"How Missing Children Can Be Found," *Babyhood*, August 1885, 278–279.

"Justice in the Home," Lucy White Palmer, *Babyhood*, June, 1888, 217–218."Kissing by Force," *Babyhood*, September 1901, 279–280.

"Misdirected Selections of Toys," Julia E. Peck, *Babyhood*, August 1893, 280–281.

"Mistakes," Mary Johnson, *Babyhood*, July 1887, 257–258.

"The Money Problem in Education," Grace Eliot, *Babyhood*, September 1898, 249–250.

"A Mother's Convocation," *Babyhood*, January 1897, 46–48.

"A Mother's Notebook," Emma W. Babcock, *Babyhood*, April 1885, 150–151.

"A Need for Sympathy," *Babyhood*, August 1887, 310.

"The Needle in the Nursery," Lavina S. Goodwin, *Babyhood*, November 1893, 381–382.

"Nursery Furniture," *Babyhood*, October 1896, 317–318.

"Obstinate Children," *Babyhood*, June 1885, 223–224.

"Our Childhood's Home," Harriet Elliot, *Babyhood*, August 1897, 230–231.

"Parental Responsibility for Infant Morality," *Babyhood*, July 1888, 263–264.

"A Phase of Governing," *Babyhood*, October 1891, 406.

"A Plea for Fewer Playthings," *Babyhood*, June 1888, 223–224.

"Pleas for the Home-Made Toy," Helen Townsend, *Babyhood*, December 1894, 87–89.

"The Problem of Property Rights," Grace Eliot, *Babyhood*, July 1901, 214–215.

"Prompt and Absolute Obedience," C. S. V., *Babyhood*, August 1893, 276–277.

"The Property Rights of Children," Lavina Goodwin, *Babyhood*, January 1895, 53–55.

"A Protest against Whipping," *Babyhood*, July 1891, 252–253.

"Punishment and Rewards for Children," *Babyhood*, April 1901, 133.

"The Punishment Ledger," Philip Hubert, *Babyhood*, January 1887, 48–50.

"Punishment of Children," *Babyhood*, February 1895, 90.

"The Relation of Growth to Education," *Babyhood*, June 1896, 201–204.

"A Renewed Plea for Fewer Playthings (and More Substantial Ones)," *Babyhood*, December, 1888 24–25.

"The Rights of Babyhood," *Babyhood*, May 1901, 153.

"Self-Consciousness in Children," Christine Ladd Franklin, *Babyhood*, March 1887, 115.

"Self-control," Mrs. W. A. Kellerman, *Babyhood*, November 1893, 381–382.

"The Sensitiveness of Little Children," *Babyhood*, September 1893, 322.

"Sharp and Forward Children," *Babyhood*, November 1888, 374–375.

"Some Notes as to Christmas Toys," *Babyhood*, December 1893, 13.

"The Spirit of Christmas Giving," *Babyhood*, December 1897, 24.

"The Spoiling of Children," *Babyhood*, December 1885, 6–9.

"Tact in Management," *Babyhood*, August 1887, 309.

"Textbooks for Disciplinarians," *Babyhood*, October 1893, 379.

"Thoughts on Home Training," *Babyhood*, October 1885, 344.

"Too Tenacious of Her Rights," *Babyhood*, April 1901, 153.

"An Ungovernable Temper, *Babyhood*, February 1885, 117–118.

"Untruthful Children," *Babyhood*, September 1888, 304–305.

"Unusually Good Children," *Babyhood*, March 1889, 129–130.

"What John Senior Might Have Done," *Babyhood*, June 1885, 211–212.

"What John Sr. Ought to Have Done?" L.P., *Babyhood*, August 1885, 276–277.

"What Ought He Have Done? Mark Twain's Opinion," *Babyhood*, August 1885, 275–276.

"What Really Happened," *Babyhood*, May 1885, 180–181.

"When and How Do We Educate," *Babyhood*, October 1890, 344.

"Wise and Unwise Punishment," *Babyhood*, February 1894, 85–86.

Godey's Lady's Book

"Children's Food," *Godey's Lady's Book*, July 1863, 97.

"Domestic Education," Mrs. Francis, *Godey's Lady's Book*, July 1866, 56–57.

"Dressing Children," *Godey's Lady's Book*, August 1858, 189.

"Health Department," *Godey's Lady's Book*, June 1862, 608.

"Hints about Health," *Godey's Lady's Book*, August 1865, 175.

"Hints About Health: Exercise for Girls," *Godey's Lady's Book*, August 1867, 80.

"Mothers, as Christian Teachers," *Godey's Lady's Book*, January 1839, 1–4.

"Mirror of the Graces," *Godey's Lady's Book*, August 1831, 12.

"The Mother," *Godey's Lady's Book,* June 1860, 529–530.

"Our Little Children," *Godey's Lady's Book*, September 1859, 272.

"Parental Indulgence," *Godey's Lady's Book*, June 1862, 578.

"Play with the Children," *Godey's Lady's Book*, August 1878, 175.

"Pocket Money," *Godey's Lady's Book*, April 1879, 357.

"The Rights of Children," Emma C. Embury, *Godey's Lady's Book,* February 1844, 80–83.

"Taste," Lydia Sigourney, *Godey's Lady's Book,* February 1840, 88.

"Woman—At Home," *Godey's Lady's Book*, February 1831, 97.

"Maternal Instruction," *Godey's Lady's Book*, March 1845, 108.

Harper's Bazaar

"The Child and Its World: VIII.—The Child and Money," *Harper's Bazaar*, November 3, 1900, 1721–1722.

"A Young Girl's Room," *Harper's Bazaar*, October 1891, 826.

Ladies' Home Journal

"Complicating Christmas," *Ladies' Home Journal*, December 1899, 16.

"Cultivating Contentment," *Ladies' Home Journal*, May 1891, 16.

"Good Taste in Clothes for Girls," *Ladies' Home Journal*, May 1910, 93.

"How Can I Make Simple Clothes for My Children," *Ladies' Home Journal*, April 1913, 56.

"My Boys' Room: A True Story," Clara Potter, *Ladies' Home Journal*, April 1886, 7.

"Respect Due the Young," *Ladies' Home Journal*, September 1895, 14.

"The Rewarding of Children," *Ladies' Home Journal*, October 1893, 20.

"The Rush of American Women," *Ladies' Home Journal*, January 1899, 14.

"The Secrets of a Happy Life," *Ladies' Home Journal*, May 1899, 8–9.

"Side Talks with Girls," Ruth Ashmore, *Ladies' Home Journal*, November 1892, 20.

"Under My Study Lamp," *Ladies' Home Journal*, October 1890, 11.

The Mother's Magazine

"Character of Children Entrusted to Mothers," *The Mother's Magazine*, March 1844, 33–34.

"Children Early Taught Their Need of a Savior," *The Mother's Magazine*, April 1837, 60–61.

"Children Taught to Exercise Their Judgement," *The Mother's Magazine*, October 1836, 153.

"The Christian Mother—No. VI," Mrs. Phillips, *The Mother's Magazine*, June 1837, 130.
"Early Discipline," Addis, *The Mother's Magazine*, June 1937, 127–130.
"Early Influences," Mrs. Sarah Campbell, *The Mother's Magazine*, September 1845, 49–53.
"Extracts from a Mother's Common Place Book," *The Mother's Magazine*, July 1833, 10.
"The Infant. Essay No. II," Iota, *The Mother's Magazine*, June 1833, 86–87.
"Moral Poisons: The Antidote," FCW, *The Mother's Magazine*, June 1845, 184–188.
"Maternal Authority," *The Mother's Magazine*, March 1844, 73–74.
"Maternal Influence," *The Mother's Magazine*, February 1833, 48.
"Obedience is Better than Sacrifice," *The Mother's Magazine*, December 1836, 36–37.
"Parental Consistency," *The Mother's Magazine*, February 1833, 22–24.
"Practical Hints to Members of Maternal Associations by a Mother," *The Mother's Magazine*, November 1836, 161–168.
"Report of the Maternal Association, Connected with the Calvinistic Church in Worcester, (Mass)," *The Mother's Magazine*, December 1836, 33–38.
"What is the True Basis for Religious Beliefs?" *The Mother's Magazine*, June 1836, 81–87.
"Young Children Influenced by Family Prayer," *The Mother's Magazine*, January 1837, 20.

Parents
"Buying the Gift to Fit the Child," Minetta Sammis Leonard, *Parents*, November 1926, 32.
"Choose the Toy to Fit the Child," Minetta Sammis Leonard, *Parents*, November 1928, 18.
"Salesmanship for Parents," Happy Goldsmith, *Parents*, October 1926, 19–21.
"Toys the Year Round," A. M. and Marguerite A. Snyder, *Parents*, June 1929, 29.
"Unspoiling the Spoiled Child," Alfred Adler, *Parents*, May 1929, 19.

Printers' Ink
"Advertising to the Child to Reach the Parent," *Printers' Ink*, October 12, 1933, 70–72.
"Building a Business on Children's Good Will," S. C. Lambert, *Printers' Ink*, July 29, 1920, 89–91.
"Children Are Joiners," *Printers' Ink*, August 18, 1932, 68–69.
"Children's Club as Sales Aid," *Printers' Ink*, May 2, 1935, 85–90.
"Cutouts for Children," *Printers' Ink*, May 21, 1931, 56–57.

Printers' Ink Monthly
"Advertising to Children," E. Evalyn Grumbine, *Printers' Ink*, June 1937, 49.
"Ideas That Are Making Sales to and Through Children," Don Gridley, *Printers' Ink Monthly*, November 1923, 23.
"Juvenile Clubs and Contests," *Printers' Ink Monthly*, E. Evalyn Grumbine, June 1936, 26–28.
"Pictures and Colors Children Like," E. Evalyn Grumbine, *Printers' Ink Monthly*, March 1938, 39–40.

"Psychology Offers New Approach to Marketing Problems," S. W. Stevens, *Printers' Ink Monthly,* October 1933, 53–54.

"Specially Designed Packages for Children," *Printers' Ink Monthly*, April 1932, 65.

"What Kind of Advertisements Do Boys Like?" Horace A. Wade, *Printers' Ink Monthly*, February 1920, 32.

"With Designs upon the Next Generation," Wilbur F. Howell, *Printers' Ink Monthly*, October 1930, 118.

Other

"A Young Girl's Room: Design for Darning on Net," *Arthur's Home Magazine*, May 1895, 470.

"A Boy's Room," Rena Reynolds, *Arthur's Home Magazine*, May 1890, 443.

"The Boy's Room," *Ohio Farmer*, October 1875, 283.

"The Boys' Room," Mary Early, *Southern Planter*, June 1899, 304.

"The Expression of Rooms," H.H., *St. Nicholas*, June 1876, 486–488.

"Fix up the Boys' Room," in *Ohio Farmer*, October 1881, 210.

"The Home: Money Matters with Young People," Helen B. Seymour, *Outlook*, September 1893, 553.

"How Grouping Goods Reduces Sales Resistance," *Dry Goods Economist*, November 19, 1921, 231.

"Molding Character with Clothes," Alice Mason Johnson, *Earnshaw's*, May 1930, 692.

"Peasant Arts in the Children's Room," Walter Rendell Storey, *New York Times*, November 23, 1930, 81.

"Put Yourself in the Child's Place to Learn the Toy He Craves," *Dry Goods Economist*, February 1920, 321.

"Selling to the Young Girls," *Dry Goods Economist*, August 1919, 45.

"The Value of an Orderly Nursery," Mary R. Chappell, *Outlook*, December, 1895, 1021.

INDEX

Abbot, Jacob, 117–19
Abrams, Philip, 14
abundance, 5, 103, 106, 110
actor-network theory, 62
The Adman in the Parlor (Garvey), 138
advertising, 109, 137; child's view in, 144–45, 150–51; for clothing, 146–47; memory and, 143; play and, 140; pleasure of, 138–40; in stores, 141–42; taste and, 147; trade cards, 139. *See also* marketing
age of reason, 24; Locke on, 40; *The Mother's Magazine* on, 41
Alcott, Louisa May, 27
allowances, 121–22
The American Girl's Handy Book (Beard A., and Beard L.), 139
American Revolution, 32
Anderson, Benedict, 15–16, 93
appetite, 67–68, 72, 102, 109
Arnold, Matthew, 64
Arthur's Home Magazine, 76
Ashmore, Ruth, 126–27, 153
assent, children's, 148
Atlantic Monthly, 99–100
Auslander, Leora, 54, 57, 63
authentic self, 21
authority: maternal authority, 42; punishment and, 98; subjectivity as, 141–48

Babyhood: advertisements in, 109; on appetite, 102; on child governance, 94–95; on clothing of child, 101; de-

bates in, 94; on delayed punishment, 96; on discipline, 82, 84–98; editorials, 83; on empathy, 91–94; forums in, 85, 86–88; on good and happy children, 105; on lying, 90–91; on money, 117–21; on property, 129; on rewards, 99, 100, 101–2; on savage child, 129; on sympathy, 91; on toys, 111–13; on truthfulness, 89
Baxter, Richard, 27, 30, 47
Beard, Adelia, 139
Beard, Lina, 139
beatings, 84–85, 92
beauty: instruction in, 64; propensity for, 134; of taste, 63
Beecher, Catherine, 68
Beetham, Margaret, 16–17, 33
Bentham, Jeremy, 134
Bernstein, Robin, 6
black girlhood, 54
Bourdieu, Pierre, 59, 70
bourgeois child/childhood, 6, 67, 156; configuration of, 9; innocence of, 19; production of, 96; prominence of, 25; simplicity and, 115
boys' rooms, 74
The Boys' World, 110
bribery, 72, 100
Brown, Gillian, 57
Bushnell, Horace, 25, 72, 82, 94; role in moral architecture, 46–51

Calvert, Karin, 33–34
Calvin, John, 24, 29–30, 47

ABOUT THE AUTHOR

Daniel Thomas Cook is Professor of Childhood Studies at Rutgers University–Camden, New Jersey, USA. His work explores the various ways in which tensions between the "child" and the "market" intermingle along various sites of cultural-commercial life, such as play, food, ritual, material, and digital cultures.